I0816191

BY DAISY HERNÁNDEZ

Citizenship: Notes on an American Myth

The Kissing Bug: A True Story of a Family, an Insect, and a Nation's Neglect of a Deadly Disease

A Cup of Water Under My Bed: A Memoir

Colonize This! Young Women of Color on Today's Feminism (co-editor)

CITIZENSHIP

CITIZENSHIP

NOTES ON AN AMERICAN MYTH

Daisy Hernández

HOGARTH

London / New York

Hogarth
An imprint of Random House
A division of Penguin Random House LLC
1745 Broadway, New York, NY 10019
randomhousebooks.com
penguinrandomhouse.com

Library of Congress Cataloging-in-Publication Data
Names: Hernández, Daisy author
Title: Citizenship / by Daisy Hernández.
Description: First edition. | New York, NY: Hogarth, 2026. |
Includes bibliographical references.
Identifiers: LCCN 2025032662 (print) | LCCN 2025032663 (ebook) |
ISBN 9780593730171 hardcover | ISBN 9780593730195 ebook
Subjects: LCSH: Hernández, Daisy—Family | Citizenship—United States |
Hispanic Americans—Social conditions | Americanization—Social aspects |
Emigration and immigration law—United States
Classification: LCC JK1759 .H427 2026 (print) | LCC JK1759 (ebook)
LC record available at lccn.loc.gov/2025032662
LC ebook record available at lccn.loc.gov/2025032663

Printed in the United States of America

1st Printing

First Edition

BOOK TEAM: Production editor: Evan Camfield •
Managing editor: Rebecca Berlant • Production manager: Kevin Garcia •
Copy editor: Amy Schroeder • Proofreaders: Emily Cutler, Jolanta Benal,
Liz Carbonell

Book design by Fritz Metsch

The authorized representative in the EU for product safety and compliance is Penguin Random House Ireland, Morrison Chambers, 32 Nassau Street, Dublin D02 YH68, Ireland. https://eu-contact.penguin.ie

For Yoel Enrique Sanchez Hernandez,

Natalia Tapia Moreno,

and all those writing the next story

In all lands alien, nowhere citizen.

—GLORIA ANZALDÚA

CONTENTS

CITIZENSHIP

INVITATIONS

THE YEAR I turned forty, my mother, sister, and I flew north to Toronto, and together, almost giddy, we marched to the United States consulate. We squinted in the morning sun, and I took selfies with the consulate's glass door in the background until a security guard jogged over and said, You can't take photos here. You have to erase them.

My mother's eyes narrowed at me. She did not understand the man's English, but she knew from his tone that I was the guilty party.

It's a selfie, I stammered.

Doesn't matter, the guard said. It's a security issue. You can't take pictures.

I tried, but failed, to find the words to tell the guard that once upon a time my mother had needed to exist beyond the borders of the United States to receive a fiancée visa, and she had come here to Toronto, to this building. She had been pregnant with me. I wanted to tell the man that my Colombian mother was an extremely shy woman, but once when I asked her how she had convinced immigration officials that she was not marrying my Cuban father for a green card, that she actually did love the man, Mami had puffed her chest and exclaimed, I was pregnant! What more proof is there?

The sun dazzled overhead, and I wanted to tell the security guard: There's a story here about citizenship and language, about the policies of the state and the bodies of women. There's a story here about defiance. A story about the narratives we, as a nation, tell about who we are. For my mother and me, it started at this gray building with the hard glass and an American flag sagging in the morning light. But I glimpsed my mother's face: her dark, worried eyes, her lips a firm line insisting that I follow the rules, as if the uniformed man were my father. I bit my lip and deleted the photographs, erasing Mami's smile, my sister's curls, the gloss of my red lipstick, and the doors to the consulate.

Satisfied, the guard turned away, and I tucked the phone into my pocketbook. I had managed to keep twenty-one photographs.

In northern New Jersey, in the early 1970s, my mother looked like a young Cher. She had thick black hair and a face that could be interpreted as Italian or Greek, Armenian or Jewish. When she wasn't cleaning offices or working at a clothing factory, she sauntered through Jersey City in bell-bottoms and fitted tops. Those who didn't understand Spanish probably mistook her for one of the most recent arrivals in that part of the state: the women fleeing Fidel Castro's new Cuba.

A decade later, in 1981, at the age of six, I began silently recording my mother's stories about citizenship. She did not use the terminology of those years: resident aliens, nonresident aliens, illegal aliens. She did not even tell me about visas or green cards. She spoke only of invitations.

Her stories were told at night, in the bedroom she shared with Papi, when he was working at the factory until dawn and it was only her, me, and my sister. All the lights off, we huddled under the comforter, my toddler sister on one side of Mami and my six-year-old body on the other, in that bedroom at the end of our railroad apartment in Union City. I must have said, Tell me a story, and she started with the first invitation.

My mother was in her twenties in this story. At the factory in Bogotá, during the late 1960s, she and a friend bent their heads over men's blazers, day after day, the tailor's chalk in their hands. They marked the fabric so the seamstresses would know where to stitch the pockets, so the men would have a place for their secrets. My mother and her friend lunched together with their co-workers, sometimes feasting on sopas brimming with potatoes and carne, and other times delighting in freshly baked buñuelos and pandebono. One day, her friend announced that she was joining her son in Jersey City. In the dark, my mother whispered, She said to me, When I get to the United States, I'll send for you.

The woman kept her promise. She mailed a letter, and here the story took a difficult turn. My mother did not want to go north, but everyone told her not to be stupid. There was money to be made in the United States, more than she could imagine. She could work and come back. No one spoke about the recession in the United States, because the worst moments inside the empire were better than those at the edges, and besides, over there, the factories paid in dollars. Mami hesitated. An older sister urged her to go, and before Mami could decide, her sister bought the airline ticket with her own savings. What could I do? my mother asked in the dark. I left, she said with a sigh.

Cocooned under blankets, her sad voice in my black hair,

I made a note to not trust the invitations of women, not even the ones I liked.

My mother did not tell me that she had to apply for a visa to the United States. She did not mention that procuring such a visa was not easy. People were routinely turned away. She did not tell me about the papers she submitted and the man at the United States consulate in Bogotá who approved her request. She did not speculate, at least not to me, on what that man thought when he looked at her: twenty-eight, childless, unmarried, living at home with her parents, a woman who would return or a woman the country did not need. She arrived in New York City, at John F. Kennedy International Airport, in the winter of 1970.

My mother never spoke of colonialism. She said nothing of fear or la migra. I was a child, and she was my mother, and so even though she had never read a novel set in Victorian London about wealthy women, she crafted a story where women extended invitations.

In northern New Jersey, she found work and two, maybe three years later, a local woman invited her to coffee. Someone had nicknamed the woman La Coca-Cola. I interrupted Mami to ask, Why did they call her that?

She was as popular as Coca-Cola, my mother replied, matter-of-fact.

La Coca-Cola brewed coffee on her kitchen stove. Maybe the woman served the café both ways: a tiny cup overloaded with sugar for the white Cuban man she had invited and ceramic mugs brimming with milk, sugar, and coffee for my mother and her sister Rosa.

By then my auntie had also become the recipient of invitations. In Colombia, Tía Rosa had taught elementary school in the campo, but once my mother settled in Jersey, she sent her a letter asking her to visit, and a man at the consulate approved Tía Rosa for a visa. My auntie boarded an airplane bound for New York City, then rented an apartment with Mami. By then, Tía Rosa was forty years old, more than a decade older than my mother, and with short curls, she had the confidence of a zealous talent manager, a woman who saw opportunity in every conversation. She had no patience for the factories with their demanding hours and their sewing machines squealing like small animals. Tía Rosa started cleaning the homes of the well-to-do.

La Coca-Cola invited my mother and Tía Rosa to meet a handsome man, a Cubano. In his mid-thirties and thin, Ygnacio turned up with his shirt tucked into his jeans, his black hair cropped short. He smiled easily and wore a stylish flimsy jacket that ended high on his waist and made him look even taller and more flaco than he was. He said very little but smiled.

Another invitation arrived for Mami. Ygnacio wanted to take her out. He showed up with pastries and sent more invitations. She said yes. He bought a red Chevy so he could drive her down the shore. He proposed marriage on a park bench, the trees flush with summer leaves and house sparrows. Let's get married, he said, and there it was: another invitation.

My mother did not tell me stories of the Cold War. Neither did my father. He grew up in the mountains in Cuba, on the outskirts of Fomento, in a one-room home without running water or a toilet. He had a third-grade education. He was the kind of man the Communists intended to save from the clutches of capitalism, but Papi had his own ideas. He planned to be rich, and when the war began, he had already joined the army of the dictator Fulgencio Batista. In the late 1950s, that's where the money was. A poor man could work his way up the ranks of the military, or at least have a uniform and a paycheck.

The revolution swept the island. The revolution won. Along with other soldiers, Papi, hours from Havana, surrendered his pistol to the new government. A year later, friends told him to flee. They whispered that the new government had begun its revenge by disappearing enemies of the state. In the first days of 1961, John F. Kennedy's administration broke off diplomatic relations with Fidel Castro's government, and the same week Papi boarded an airplane for South Florida with five pesos from a cousin in his pocket.

My mother could have said it this way: Citizenship is a game of tic-tac-toe. Your father was *X* and I was *O*. Here, on the sidewalk, the United States and the Soviet Union chalked three squares across, then up and down, until nine openings appeared. Your father was *X* and I was *O*. The Soviets supported Castro's Communist government, and the Americans began offering green cards in 1966 to the Cuban exiles who reached the United States. Your father was born in Cuba. Your father had a Cuban passport. Your father landed on American soil. Your father won.

My mother did not reveal that La Coca-Cola knew this intricate game of citizenship, but the woman named after the empire's most popular drink surely saw the situation. Here stood a woman who needed papers, and over there, a man who had papers, who had permanent legal residency. Neither was married. Neither had a child. They needed only an invitation.

My mother could have made her courtship sound romantic: Your father relinquished his country to be with me. Yes, he had a green card when we met, but he had no intention of becoming a citizen of the United States until he fell in love with me. She could have said: To keep my love, your papi had to renounce his allegiance to the land where he first saw the sun rise and where he first learned to say the word mamá. My mother could have said: He loved me so much that he threw himself into the fire and vowed to defend this country with his life.

My mother said none of this. Instead, in the dark of her bedroom, she shared with me the blunt, almost crude, memory. When she spoke to my father about her citizenship, her status, he replied, Let's talk to the man who does my taxes.

The tax man had an office in the basement of his house in Union City. My parents gingerly walked down the few steps into the waiting room, which was dimly lit, with a low ceiling. Padded folding chairs had been arranged along the perimeter of the room so clients could sit in a circle. At intervals, the door to the tax man's office swung open, and an enormous shower of light poured over everyone. The tax man's wife called out for a client, noted my father's name on her pad, and then closed the door.

Everyone had come here to sit in a circle of dim light because of papers. They had a W-2 for the first time. They had received a letter from the government. They had a new dependent to claim. They had a new negocio and a stack of receipts and canceled checks. They loved someone with an expired tourist visa.

When their turn arrived, my parents stepped into an office engulfed by fluorescent light and with just enough room for two big wooden desks covered with stacks of folders and reams of paper. The tax man was a Cuban with a large waistline, and my father was right about him. He did know what to do to make marriage possible for my parents. To my father, he said, The best way is for you to get citizenship, and then you can petition for her.

The tax man knew another Cuban who worked in a law office, and between the tax man and the law man, my father began the paperwork to become a citizen of the United States, and that was the start of their marriage: piles of government-issued forms, the clacking of a typewriter, and the flourish of my father's signature learned in the hills of Fomento. But in the 1970s, my father could only petition to marry a foreign woman who existed beyond the borders of the United States. The tax man shrugged. Go to Canada, he suggested. You can drive there.

I learned as a child that citizenship was a private story, one women told in the dark, where faces could not be seen. Sometimes the story was never told. Decades later I can still only suspect that Tía Rosa secured her green card because she attended a music concert in New York City. In between salsa numbers, she met her husband, a Puerto Rican whose own citizenship was the result of his having been born in a colony of the United States.

It strikes me now that although my mother and her sister were born in South America, at the foot of the Andes

Mountains, in a place once thought of as a remote region, they became citizens of the United States because of the Caribbean. Or to be more exact, they became citizens of the United States because this country's empire extended into the Caribbean.

My father drove. They arrived in Toronto, my mother pregnant with me. They spoke almost no English but managed to find a modest hotel and the U.S. consulate. They brought their paperwork in a manila envelope. They looked like every other immigrant couple from the so-called Third World, with their dark eyebrows and their thin faces, both dressed politely, he in a turtleneck and she in a white maternity blouse. They took pictures of each other. She smiled from ear to ear. She had wanted so badly to become a mother, and now here she was, expecting. For my mother, the story had always careened toward this moment. After leaving home and her own mother, after marrying a man her mother had never met, after working so many hours, after all of that, here she finally was: her first baby on the way. Motherhood, for her, was the true citizenship.

Mami married into a very specific political community. By 1975, Union City already boasted the second-largest population of Cubans in the country after Miami. My mother hauled me in a stroller to the local bakeries, where she bought fresh Cuban bread and guava pastries. A Cuban neighbor taught her to slice onions for the bistec. A Cuban neighbor instructed her on the necessity of routine for newborns: the feeding time, the burping time, the napping time. A Cuban at the bank was surely the one who approved the mortgage for my parents to buy a three-story apartment building where we lived on the first floor.

My mother became a citizen of the United States, and she also became a citizen of a white Cuban community in the United States.

In the 1980s, during those years when my mother was telling me stories in the dark, the Library of Congress, the world's largest library, acquired a total of 170 books in English with the word citizenship in the title or subtitle. The following decade, in the 1990s, the number of such books jumped to more than 500. The increase was curious because the Library of Congress had held fewer than 2,000 books on the subject of citizenship for the entire twentieth century. The change proved to be neither temporary nor an anomaly. Since 2000, the library has purchased more than 8,000 books about citizenship.

Citizenship itself has migrated beyond its historical confines in international law and electoral politics. There are now books and articles on sexual citizenship, ecological citizenship, literary citizenship, biomedical citizenship, digital citizenship, fetal citizenship, post-pandemic citizenship, homemade citizenship, and, yes, garbage citizenship. This obsession with citizenship has been described by scholars as both a "renaissance" and a "vengeance." At times, citizenship is a proxy for belonging, identity, or community. Other times, it refers to engaging government officials around a specific issue, such as the collection of trash. Sometimes, as with the citizen scientist, it indicates a person who can contribute regardless of their technical training. Citizenship serves too as shorthand for a situation in which a person has a duty to a particular community, as in the time I heard an author inform an audience that a literary citizen has an obligation to subscribe to journals with small circulations and high fees.

Writing about my mother's journey, I began to wonder why the obsession with citizenship began at the close of the twentieth century. Even terminology that sounds as if it belongs to a post-Covid world originated then. The phrase *biological citizenship* might evoke the image of a world where people brave a deadly virus by sewing face masks from old T-shirts, but the term was coined in the 1990s by a scholar describing the political mobilization of people in Ukraine over the impacts of the 1986 Chernobyl disaster.

What had driven academics to start writing about citizenship?

Maybe it was the factories. Companies in the 1990s shuttered more of their factories in Jersey and across the United States. They closed completely or opened operations across the border in Mexico. They began buying from companies in China. Borders collapsed for corporate America, and scholars studying the advent of globalization noted that a company based in one country could be responsible for an ecological disaster in another, and how exactly would that afflicted community seek justice? What citizenship could those communities call upon?

Something else changed at the close of the twentieth century: More citizens sprang up.

When the United Nations was established in 1945, it counted a total of fifty-one members. By the 1990s, that number had more than tripled as people around the globe revolted against imperial powers and proclaimed their independence. With this ongoing decolonization and the collapse of the Soviet Union, the U.N. added thirty more nations to its roster during the 1990s.

I reached out to Professor Dimitry Kochenov, a legal scholar at Central European University in Vienna and Budapest, and the author of an introductory book on the subject of citizenship for MIT Press. He told me the issue was *who* had become a citizen. "Before citizenship gains prominence, it was not actually important for the distribution of rights in the world, because race was the most important thing," he told me on a video call. The imperial powers, he explained, used race as a way to stop people at their borders. "Once decolonization is a success, you don't need to be racist anymore, because the majority of those whom you didn't want to see because of their race acquire a different citizenship," Kochenov said. "So what you do is simply compile a list of all those passports and say the guys with these passports will not be able to enter. So then citizenship plays fundamentally the racist function which used to be reserved for special race-based exceptions in U.S. law."

For more than a century, the United States used race to decide who could become a citizen. Starting in 1790, only free white people could apply for U.S. citizenship. This led to more than fifty court cases in which presumably white judges had to decide if Mexicans, Indians, Japanese, and Syrians could be considered white for the purposes of naturalization. Black people were barred altogether from citizenship until the 1868 ratification of the Fourteenth Amendment, which said that anyone born in this country was automatically a citizen, except for Native people, who, until 1924, were required to leave their tribes and live among white people or find other ways of accessing U.S. citizenship. In 1882, the government outright banned migration from China with the Chinese Exclusion Act, a law that stood until the middle of the twentieth century and came to encompass almost everyone from Asia. In 1924, Congress placed racial quotas on migration to favor white people from Britain and western Europe. That law, the Johnson-Reed Act, made it so no one could technically be permitted into the country if they were not eligible for citizenship. As the historian Mae M. Ngai notes, "By one account, the provision barred half of the world's population from entering the United States."

But not people from Latin America.

The 1924 law kept the door open to people migrating to the United States from Mexico and Central America and Venezuela and anywhere else in Latin America. The men who ran the agriculture industry here still needed other men to work farmlands in Texas, California, and the Southwest, men whose movements could be monitored, men who could be sent home when their labor was no longer required. Instead of outright exclusion, the federal government instituted new regulations. Starting in 1919, Mexicans had to pass a literacy test and pay a head tax to enter the United States at designated ports on the southern border, though exemptions were made for the agriculture industry. The federal government created the Border Patrol in 1924, and the number of Mexicans deported rose from 1,751 in 1925 to more than 15,000 four years later. When the Great Depression hit, cities, counties, and the U.S. attorney general created a shadow deportation program that removed more than a million Mexicans and Mexican Americans from the country during the 1930s. Around 60 percent of those deported were U.S. citizens, usually the children of Mexican immigrants. In 1931, the Los Angeles city manager commented on the motivation for the deportations: "It is a question of pigment, not a question of citizenship or right."

The United States stopped using race to control its borders in 1965, at least on paper. It had, by then, done away with the Chinese Exclusion Act in order to form a closer alliance with China during World War II, but it still limited the number of people who could migrate from Asia. When Congress passed the Hart-Celler Act in 1965, it formally ended the racial quotas favoring white Europeans. While the legislation is celebrated for that reason, and for its emphasis on family reunifications, it limited for the first time the number of people migrating from Latin America. It capped arrivals from the entire Western Hemisphere at 120,000 people each year, which might have worked except that in 1964 alone, around 240,000 Mexicans had come to the United States.

The documents Mexicans and other Latinx carried began to matter in a new way. Within two years of the passage of the 1965 immigration law, the Border Patrol apprehended twice as many immigrants. On paper, it looked like a spike in the number of the undocumented. But that was not true. The people had not changed. The policies had.

In 1965, Congress also amended immigration law to clarify that the United States did not permit the entry of any immigrant who was gay or lesbian or nonhetero. For years, the exclusion of queers had been based on whether the immigrant was diagnosed as a "psychopathic personality." That wording proved to be vague in the courts and for immigration officials. Congress members clarified that no immigrant could enter this country if they were found to be "afflicted with . . . sexual deviation."

There was another possible reason scholars and politicians and pundits became obsessed with citizenship in the 1990s. The United States spent the 1970s and '80s fighting a series of wars Americans did not watch on television. These were the wars the United States lost, the wars in Central America, the wars that could be called the Other Vietnam.

In Nicaragua, during the 1970s, the United States supported the dictator Anastasio Somoza, whose regime murdered thousands of people. After the left-leaning group the Sandinistas came to power in 1979, the Reagan administration, intent on keeping communism out of Latin America, infamously bypassed Congress to fund the Contras, a guerrilla group, in their attacks on the Sandinista government. More than thirty thousand people lost their lives during that conflict.

In Honduras, the CIA trained the country's military on torture tactics during the 1980s, while the Reagan administration used the country as a base for the Contras, at one point funneling $70 million in military aid to the group with approval from Congress. More than 150 people were murdered or disappeared by the death squads in Honduras.

In Guatemala, the CIA overthrew the country's president in 1954 in favor of one willing to yield to the demands of the United Fruit Company, a U.S. corporation that had been an economic force in the country since the 1800s. A thirty-six-year civil war began in the 1960s, with the United States training and equipping Guatemalan military forces, including the officers responsible for murdering or disappearing more than two hundred thousand people, most of them Mayans.

In El Salvador, the United States supported the country's leaders during the 1970s and '80s with $6 billion in economic and military aid, even as soldiers and death squads there tortured and murdered more than seventy-five thousand people, including killing Archbishop Óscar Romero while he celebrated Mass. An outspoken critic of the violence, Romero had sent a letter to President Jimmy Carter pleading with him to stop funding the death squads, and in his last sermon, he asked the military to stop the massacres.

During the 1970s and '80s, about a third of a million people lost their lives in El Salvador, Honduras, Nicaragua, and Guatemala—approximately five times the number of American soldiers who died in Vietnam. The survivors of these wars, the survivors of U.S. imperialism in these countries, sought refuge in Mexico, then farther north in California and Colorado and New Jersey. I watched them arrive in my hometown year after year. The brothers from Guatemala. The husbands from Nicaragua. The primos from El Salvador and Honduras. Sometimes they were not men but boys, lanky and baby-faced, hands shoved in their jeans pockets for warmth in the first days of autumn. They joined my mother and me at the bus stop. Later the wives turned up and the sisters and the younger children and the abuelas. They crossed multiple borders because of the crimes committed by the elites of their countries and also by the U.S. military and private corporations that had crossed many fronteras into their lives. "Colonialism and immigration are part of the same continuum—we are here because you were there," observed the novelist and activist Ambalavaner Sivanandan.

In 1960, two-thirds of immigrants to the United States hailed from Europe. By 1990, that number had flipped. Latin Americans and Asian Americans accounted for about 71 percent of the new arrivals.

A legal scholar and recipient of a MacArthur "genius grant," E. Tendayi Achiume has argued that immigrants are in a colonial relationship with the United States, which wields so much power over their homelands, so immigrants have a political claim to this country. They are not outsiders, not strangers, not foreigners. They are a part of our political community. Looked at this way, political membership is defined not by geographic borders but rather by the political relationships colonialism has created.

Scholars were not the only ones obsessed with citizenship in the 1990s. *Time* magazine wondered at the start of that decade what the "browning of America" would mean for the "national psyche." In 1993, a few weeks before I started college, *Newsweek* editors paid an artist for a cover illustrating the Statue of Liberty drowning in the harbor, surrounded by boats filled with people who had dark faces. Above the statue ran the words "Immigration Backlash." The absence of a question mark or an exclamation mark indicated that the magazine was simply describing a newsworthy event. If I had picked up the international edition, I would have seen a headline screaming, "Keep Out! Now Americans Are Joining the Backlash Against Immigration."

The *Newsweek* cover, along with the headline, portrayed the United States as the Statue of Liberty, as an innocent woman, a woman who had never left home, a woman who was coveted, and now here were all these Black and Brown people in boats flooding the famous harbor, flooding the country itself. The magazine cover did not whisper about the Other Vietnam, about the U.S. government and military and businesses in Latin America and many other countries. The United States was not an empire, the magazine implied; it was only a woman overwhelmed by the needs of immigrants.

Often when speaking of migration, regardless of the decade, the creative class turns to water. Not fire. Not wind. But water. Authors, editors, and journalists speak of immigrants as a flood, a tidal wave, a surge of water that cannot be controlled. The insistence on water, this fear of being drowned by the Other, says nothing, of course, about immigrants, but a great deal about the political anxieties of the creative class in the United States.

In late 2024, more than three decades after *Newsweek* and *Time* ran their stories, *The New York Times* declared an "immigration surge." Its analysis showed that the largest migration in United States history had started in 2021 and averaged 2.4 million people over a two-year period. Under causes, the reporter primarily cited President Joe Biden's decision to accept immigrants seeking asylum.

While it will be for historians to debate the reasons so many immigrants arrived in the United States during these years, it remains surprising what the reporter and his editors did not chronicle: More than half of the 412,000 asylum applications filed between October 2022 and August 2023 came from people fleeing three countries under a one-party political system cracking down on its opponents: Venezuela, Cuba, and Nicaragua. The United States has intervened in the internal political life of all three countries for decades. In 2021, one million people in Honduras and Guatemala lived on the brink of famine caused by the climate crisis. The *Times* reporter mentioned Ukraine but not the details. Between 2022 and 2024, almost half a million Ukrainians arrived in the United States with temporary visas or as part of a program that let them skip the visa line if they had a sponsor here. In short, the Ukrainians became the new Cubans—immigrants showered with visas and exemptions the way my father and his generation from Cuba had been.

Jerome Powell, the chair of the Federal Reserve, did not need the analysis of *The New York Times*. In May 2024, after the central bank's policy meeting, he remarked, "We've had what amounts to a significant increase in the potential output of the economy that's not about productivity. It was about having more labor . . . in 2022, both through participation and immigration."

The Johnson-Reed Act of 1924, which established the racist immigration quotas that were in place for decades, has been viewed as a backlash to the twelve million immigrants who arrived at the turn of the twentieth century. Because it is 2024, not 1924, the federal government no longer uses explicitly racist quotas. It relies instead on citizenship. The citizens of unwanted countries are stopped at the border. The citizens of unwanted countries are detained and deported. The citizens of unwanted countries are called criminals. The construct of citizenship does the work of race. In the 2024 election, eight states changed their constitutions to underscore that without U.S. citizenship people could not vote in local elections. Where the state constitutions of Iowa, Missouri, and North Carolina, among others, once proclaimed that "every citizen" or "all citizens" could vote, now the documents will read that "only citizens" can vote.

I have no reason to think that the white girls at my Catholic high school in the suburbs of New Jersey were reading newsmagazines in the 1990s, but they were reading something. Or listening. Maybe to their parents. Maybe to the English-language news. Maybe to a teacher. They knew my friends and I lived more than forty minutes away, in the small towns at the southern end of the county, and when my friends and I, a tiny cluster of Latinas, bounced off the school bus one day, a white girl, her hair sprayed high into the air, barked: Go back where you came from!

My mother never heard about that girl from high school. I never told her. I also never told her that once we left the Cuban world of Union City and moved into southern Bergen County, to a predominantly white neighborhood, the bus driver and the shopkeepers and the receptionists, all of them openly mocked us for not speaking English. I never asked her if she understood the blunt edges of their voices or how she made sense of their sneers. I wanted to protect her, so I said nothing. Or perhaps I wanted to protect myself.

My mother never spoke to me about her citizenship status when I was a child. Neither did my father or my aunties or my auntie-husbands. Papers were never discussed in front of children, and so I paid attention from the corners of their lives, latching on to snippets of conversations when my mother's murmurs thickened with anxiety. Someone's husband had been detained. Someone bought a fake Social. Someone could only work under the table because they didn't have papeles.

A new citizen emerged in the United States at the end of the twentieth century. The social justice movements of the 1960s and '70s made it possible for women and people of color and LGBTQ folks who had been born within the borders of this country to make new demands of citizenship. They wanted more than the vote. They wanted to live in neighborhoods from which they had been historically barred. They wanted the jobs, the mortgages, the doctors. They wanted to walk down the street past the police station without fearing for their lives. They wanted to live. To write books and teach and speak the language of their mothers. To decide where the new bus stops should be erected and what the healthcare system should look like. In 1994, the anthropologist Renato Rosaldo remarked, "In effect, new citizens have come into being as new categories of persons who make claims on both their fellow citizens and the state."

This new citizen was a darker, bolder, more feminine citizen, and not everyone was pleased. White male scholars had always imagined citizenship as a political membership untouched by race and religion and class and gender and sexuality. The idea that a queer or a Latina or a queer Latina might have an experience of citizenship different from that of a straight white man was, according to two white male philosophy professors writing in the 1990s, "a radical development in citizenship theory." But it was more than theory. It is always more than theory.

When people began asking more of the citizenship they had on paper, a conservative backlash began that peaked in the 1980s with Ronald Reagan, Margaret Thatcher, and their political parties attacking the welfare systems of the United States and Britain. These politicians invoked the idea of "good citizens," who took care of themselves and required nothing of their government. To invent such a citizen, it was first necessary to create the anti-citizen. It helped that one of Reagan's staffers read the *Chicago Tribune.* In the mid-1970s, the newspaper began running stories about Linda Taylor, a biracial woman who used a number of aliases to collect food stamps, welfare checks, and veterans' benefits. She was doing the work of consuming that all good citizens were expected to do in a free-market economy, but she carried it out with other people's money. For Reagan, that was the offense. The outrage. The failures of her citizenship. He began telling the story of the "welfare queen," of the bad citizen, who made $150,000 a year from cheating government assistance programs. The truth, it turned out, was that Taylor stole about $40,000 over many years and was convicted of welfare fraud amounting to $9,000. But the facts did not matter. The story did.

Unemployment hit 11 percent in the early 1980s, and Reagan, along with other Republicans, blamed poor women and insisted that the welfare system had become too costly. They believed the government should stop providing apartments and cereal and money for diapers to teenage mothers and their children. The girls should be good citizens.

The girls should marry. In this scenario, the welfare system needed to be dismantled, and Medicaid cut back, and young women—"both black and white," Reagan said—encouraged to marry men with jobs. When the president shared these ideas with the country over the radio on February 15, 1986, he did not explain where exactly the teenage girls would find these men, these good men with good jobs, nor what should be done with the teenage mother who fell in love with a woman.

It was all talk, but talk is the origin of public policy. Almost a decade later, in 1994, Republicans won control of Congress for the first time in forty years with an agenda called the Contract with America, which proposed, among other things, that the federal government stop providing cash assistance to teenage mothers. By 1996, Bill Clinton and the Democratic Party thought they could only hold on to the White House by agreeing with the Republicans, and so Clinton signed the end-welfare-as-we-know-it bill into law. The federal government would now send a chunk of welfare money to each state, which could, to a large degree, set its own rules. A state could demand that women with young children take low-wage jobs or that they get job training rather than pursue college degrees. It could deny women with children welfare checks after a few years.

A new citizenship emerged in those years: a state-based citizenship. At first, it was limited to those who needed the government the most: the poor, the disabled, single moms, HIV-positive men. Now, thirty years later, state-based citizenship applies to more Americans, albeit still the most vulnerable ones: poor women, transgender folks, the undocumented. It meant that at the end of 2024, women and pregnant people could have an abortion in Ohio during the first twenty-two weeks of a pregnancy, but not in Texas, Oklahoma, or Kentucky. It meant a person could change the gender designation on their driver's license in Minnesota and New Hampshire but not in Tennessee or Kansas. It meant people without papeles could arrive in Illinois or California and be welcomed at homeless shelters, but in Iowa and Texas they had to monitor the local news for updates on whether the police would turn them over to Immigration and Customs Enforcement.

This state-based citizenship reminds me of when I was a twenty-year-old college student living in England for a few months and sharing a house with students mostly from across the United States. The father of one of my housemates came to visit from Nebraska. In the kitchen, he heard me speaking in Spanish to the one other bilingual student, and he turned to me and asked, What exotic country are you from?

I was leaning against the sink, washing a dish, thinking about all the dishes my mother had washed and how she never let me wash my own dishes. I was busy with my contemplations, and I was used to the question: Where are you from?

New Jersey, I replied in a flat voice, and was startled when the man's wife and son burst into laughter.

Many people complain these days about the divisiveness of political life in the United States, as if it were only a matter of disagreeing over policies and values, when it could be said that we are at odds with one another because we do not live in the same country. We do not have the same citizenship.

In 1986, Congress granted amnesty to 2.7 million undocumented immigrants, mostly from Mexico, living in the United States. Ten years later, it passed the Latino Exclusion Act. No, the law was not called that, but the sociologists Néstor P. Rodríguez and Cecilia Menjívar have suggested it as another name for the Illegal Immigration Reform and Immigrant Responsibility Act of 1996, given that Latinx people make up a large share of those who have been deported under this law and the majority of them were not deported for committing a crime.

The Latino Exclusion Act created the policy of expedited removal. If Border Patrol agents stopped you at the border and you could not prove that you had been in the United States for two years with papeles, you were immediately expelled from the country and barred from coming back for at least three years. Later this immediate deportation process was expanded to include people arriving by sea and those stopped within a hundred miles of any border. The state of Florida, which has become home to almost six million Latinx, is entirely within a hundred miles of a border.

The new law created the 287(g) program, allowing local police officers to collaborate with Immigration and Customs Enforcement, the federal agency responsible for deportations. In September 2022, ICE reported that, through this program, officers had detained more than eight thousand people in the previous fiscal year. A third of them had been charged with traffic violations.

Immigration judges lost the power to consider the details of immigration cases because of the Latino Exclusion Act. Doris Meissner, who led the Immigration and Naturalization Service through most of the 1990s, told *Vox:* "Discretion was taken away from district directors and immigration judges almost entirely." It used to be that if you faced a deportation order, you would get a chance to tell an immigration judge that you had children, and your sister lived down the block from you, and you had a job here. You would tell the judge that you waited for the bus at the same stop every day, and you knew the cold wind that whipped down Fairview Avenue and the price of coffee at the Greek deli. You had built a life in this country, a life worth considering when the judge looked at the deportation order, and the judge had the option to say: Yes, you can stay. The Latino Exclusion Act did away with this possibility. A judge could no longer permit you to continue living in the United States unless you could prove that you feared persecution in your home country.

The Latino Exclusion Act created more mixed-status families—families whose members have different relationships to citizenship. If you married a U.S. citizen but didn't have papers, not even an expired tourist visa, you generally had to leave the country to adjust your status, and the law barred you from coming back for years. People, being reasonable, did the reasonable thing: They stayed, without papeles, but with their families.

People who had papers were not spared by the Latino Exclusion Act.

The legislation worked hand in hand with an antiterrorism law, also passed in 1996, that turned certain misdemeanors into felonies for the purposes of immigration. If you had a green card and you did something stupid like steal a ten-dollar video game, you were no longer treated as if you were a U.S. citizen who had broken the law. It did not matter that you had grown up in this country and that you'd had legal residency since you were a child. Your shoplifting now made you subject to deportation, and the new law applied retroactively, so suddenly people with green cards who had been here for decades could be deported for having stolen that video game years earlier. Or for having had an extra beer and driving home. Yes, there were people without citizenship who committed awful crimes, ones that made the nightly news, but the new legislation made no distinction between those crimes and the stolen video game or the DUI.

Two years after the passage of the Latino Exclusion Act, the number of people detained and deported jumped by 70 percent. It also dramatically changed how Americans talked about citizenship. Immigration advocates strained to remind them that not having papers did not make someone a criminal, but politicians and journalists told stories linking those without citizenship to criminal activity until many people forgot it was only that—a story.

Americans, historically speaking, often turn to the story of criminality. Freed from slavery, Black families found white America preoccupied with crime and legislation. The rise of Black codes and Jim Crow laws meant you could be arrested for being Black and going out after dark with friends, riding in a train car reserved for whites, or marrying a white person. When the Civil Rights Movement led to those policies being abolished, President Richard Nixon's War on Drugs created sentencing guidelines targeting Black people, shoving millions into prison and creating a system of mass incarceration that the legal scholar Michelle Alexander has called the New Jim Crow. Politicians could maintain, then and now, that they were not racist. This was not about race. They were talking only of criminals. If you were a good citizen, you had no reason to worry.

In 2024, the second-largest policing agency in the United States, after the New York City Police Department, was the Border Patrol, with more than nineteen thousand agents.

The police came looking for me one day in the mid-1990s. I was working at the public library in town, scanning children's picture books, and the police had a man in their jail cell with whom they could not speak. One of the officers thought of me. I was the nineteen-year-old working next door at the library. I was the nineteen-year-old who spoke Spanish, the one at the counter when the police and their children checked out video games and new picture books. The blue uniform stood at the library's narrow counter and asked, Could you come over and help us talk to this guy? He doesn't speak any English.

He presented it to me like an invitation, but it was not, because I did not feel that I could decline. I panicked. My heart rate spiked. My throat narrowed. My vision blurred. But I forced a smile and said yes, and I followed the white man with the gun in his holster next door to the police station, where I stood at the door of a very tiny concrete cell and waved apologetically at a young Brown man in jeans and a T-shirt sitting on a bench, a man who could have been my brother or cousin. I don't remember anything I said or what he said, because I was not in my body, which stood between a white man with a gun and a Brown man with nothing in his hands. It all happened very quickly, and then it was over, and I was back in the library behind the counter checking out children's books on caterpillars. I don't know when I came back to my body, when the panic subsided, or whether the man was released.

I did not tell my mother about the man in the jail cell. I told her instead that the police had come for me, as if I had been the guilty party. The police took me to jail today! I called from the doorway to the kitchen.

Mami stood at the stove. The onions sizzled in the pan. Her face froze, then frowned. She knew I was a goody two-shoes. I never drank. I never smoked anything. I had a full college scholarship and two part-time jobs. Quietly she asked, Cómo que te llevaron?

I explained that the police had needed an interpreter. I made it sound like I had done something important, something official, like I had been fearless. I told her about the things I hoped she would never see: the L-shaped desk behind the bulletproof glass, the switchboard with all its dials, and the jail cell smaller than the shed we had once used for her sewing machines. Mami listened, then sighed.

This obsession with citizenship, which began in the 1990s, surged after the terrorist attacks on September 11, 2001, and the subsequent War on Terror. Politicians charged that there were now citizens and terrorists, good and evil. The border had to be patrolled for Muslim men who would kill us. The Muslim men were never us and had to register with the federal government if they were older than sixteen and came from one of twenty-five Muslim-majority countries, or else face deportation. In early 2003, the journalist Maria Hinojosa reported for CNN from the border, the one with Canada. Pakistani families were fleeing the United States, asking Canada for asylum because some of the men registering with the federal government were being detained for weeks or months and were even being thrown out of the country. The only way to stay together as a family was to leave together.

At the Library of Congress, meanwhile, the staff bought almost three thousand books in English on the subject of citizenship in the first decade after 9/11. The authors of these texts examined citizenship in the Arab world and in modern China and in the global cities of the Western world. They analyzed citizenship in public health and in American literature and in ecological philosophy. They looked at how citizenship had once been imagined and considered how it was being reimagined. Among the titles were *Becoming a Citizen, Americans in Waiting,* and *Composing the Citizen,* all of which suggested that citizenship was a red-tailed hawk, a feathered beast in motion, not a fixed entity but one that moved and changed and flitted out of reach.

A few weeks after 9/11, I traveled to an artists' community in New Hampshire. I was to live there for a month with composers, mixed-media artists, and other writers, all of us working on creative projects while the United States began dropping bombs on Muslim families in Afghanistan and then in Iraq. On the television in a nook of the shared house, we watched the news from New York City, where workers moved slowly among the ruins where the towers had stood. A white artist, a woman in her sixties, turned to me to complain about a story she'd read. In Chinatown, people were posting the American flag upside down on the windows of their apartments. The woman was furious. They don't even know how to hang the flag! she growled.

I had already seen the upside-down flags. At the time, I still lived with my parents and an auntie in New Jersey, and I had come home one day to find that my tiá had taped a tiny American flag to our front door upside down. It was a paper flag. It didn't move. Tía had affixed it to the door with layers of transparent tape.

It was, as far as I knew, the first flag of any country ever displayed at our home. I don't know if my auntie wanted the neighbors to know that we were not terrorists. We were not criminals. We were Americans. We were citizens. On paper, we were citizens. Or maybe this was not it at all. Everywhere we went, the flag had popped up: on lawns, on trees, on supermarket windows. The stores on Bergenline Avenue were selling U.S. flags perhaps for the first time. Maybe Tía understood the surveillance of her citizenship and mine by our neighbors, or maybe she only wanted to signal that we shared in the grief of those days.

I never thought it strange that as a child I was acutely aware of my papers. I figured every child knew this fact about themselves. Every child born in the United States was surely told over and over again by their mothers: Nacistes aquí—eres Americana. It is what I imagined millions of mothers in many languages had whispered to their children for years: You were born here—you're American.

In today's legal world, citizenship springs from one of two sources: the soil or your blood—the land on which you were born or the citizenship of your parents. Birthright citizenship is based on the principle of jus soli, Latin for "right of the soil." Years before the Civil War, Black Americans claimed this citizenship at political conventions and in Black newspapers. "Birthright citizenship was a fully formed idea by the early 1850s," writes the historian Martha S. Jones in her book *Birthright Citizens: A History of Race and Rights in Antebellum America,* in which she chronicles how Black people in Baltimore engaged in the practices of citizenship by traveling between states, suing in court, and gathering in public to discuss politics and religion. After the Civil War, in 1868, the Fourteenth Amendment made jus soli the law of the land in the United States.

The other kind of citizenship comes from the principle of jus sanguinis, or "right of blood," meaning that your nationality is based on that of your parents. It has nothing to do with biology but with the papers your parents have. It is a practice unfamiliar to most Americans since the United States, Canada, and every country in Latin America except for the Dominican Republic and Colombia offer birthright citizenship.

At least two professors have warned that the Dominican Republic serves as a harbinger of what could happen in the United States. In 2010, the Caribbean country began denying birthright citizenship to the children of undocumented immigrants, and then the country's Constitutional Court made the law retroactive to 1929, stripping birthright citizenship from several generations of children whose parents didn't have papeles, the vast majority of them Haitian.

Colombia, my mother's homeland, recognizes only a blood-bound citizenship. In other words, being born in the country does not automatically grant you citizenship, and this offers another type of caution. In 2019, Colombia found itself home to twenty-four thousand stateless babies, all of them the children of Venezuelan immigrants. They had no constitutional right to the soil of Colombia until a law was passed making a temporary exception for them.

In the United States, Republicans tried to eliminate jus soli citizenship in 1995, a year before Congress passed the Latino Exclusion Act. They proposed changing immigration law to deny birthright citizenship to anyone whose parents were not citizens or legal residents. Hearings were held, and the Justice Department's top constitutional scholar testified that aside from the legislation being "unconstitutional on its face," such a move would create "a permanent caste of aliens, generation after generation after generation born in America but never to be among its citizens." The bill failed to pass, but the Republican Party included the idea of eliminating birthright citizenship in its platform for the 1996 election.

More than a decade later, in 2011, Representative Lamar Smith, a Republican from Texas, took charge of the argument. In an op-ed for *Roll Call,* he explained that the great men who drafted the Fourteenth Amendment had not intended to include the children of undocumented parents. He knew this because one of those men, a senator, had said in the 1800s that birthright citizens did not include "persons born in the United States who are foreigners." If this wording sounds incomplete, it's because Smith omitted the rest of the sentence, which clarifies that the senator was talking about children born on this soil to foreigners "who belong to the families of ambassadors." In other words, an ambassador's wife could give birth here but not necessarily to a U.S. citizen.

Representative Steve King of Iowa introduced a bill in 2011 that would have changed the Constitution so a person born in the United States could only be a citizen if one of their parents was a citizen, had a green card, or was serving in the military. He introduced the bill every year until he left Congress in 2020, having lost his seat to a fellow Republican after he told a reporter that he didn't know why the term *white supremacist* was offensive.

The reasons for dismantling the Fourteenth Amendment have grown more elaborate in recent years. Yes, "all persons born or naturalized in the United States, and subject to the jurisdiction thereof, are citizens of the United States," but according to former vice president Mike Pence, the Supreme Court never ruled on the phrase "subject to the jurisdiction thereof." The court actually did rule on this in 1898 in *United States v. Wong Kim Ark,* declaring that a child born in this country to Chinese immigrant parents was a citizen. However, Michael Anton, the director of policy planning in the State Department for Donald Trump's second term, pointed out in a 2018 op-ed for *The Washington Post* that the parents in the 1898 court case had papers. They were legal residents. Surely, the Supreme Court did not mean to extend the right of this soil to the newborns of people without papers.

After the 2024 election, Judge James Ho of the U.S. Court of Appeals for the Fifth Circuit proposed that children born in the United States might not be citizens if their parents were trying to take over the country. "Birthright citizenship obviously doesn't apply in case of war or invasion," he told the libertarian magazine *Reason*. "No one to my knowledge has ever argued that the children of invading aliens are entitled to birthright citizenship."

Ho was born in Taiwan. His first citizenship came to him by blood; Taiwan does not recognize citizenship bound to the land. Brought to the United States as a child, he grew up in the wealthy suburbs of Los Angeles and became a naturalized citizen of this country. He is now on a short list of nominees for the Supreme Court if Trump has the chance to appoint another justice. By several accounts, he hopes to be the first Asian American on the court.

The reasons to eliminate jus soli citizenship run on a loop in my mind: You cannot have a right to this land because you are not subject to the laws of the United States, because your parents don't have papers, because your parents are invading the country, because your parents were not slaves. Yes, Republicans have contended that Congress only intended to grant birthright citizenship to Black Americans. The Fourteenth Amendment, Amy Swearer, a legal policy analyst at the Heritage Foundation, told *Politico* in 2018, "was intended primarily to guarantee citizenship rights for newly freed slaves, not to create a universal right for anyone temporarily or illegally in the country, and therefore not subject to the complete jurisdiction of the United States."

The white men who drafted and debated and approved the Fourteenth Amendment were quite aware that its impact would extend beyond Black Americans. In 1866, one of Pennsylvania's senators pointed this out, complaining that the amendment would grant birthright citizenship to the children of "Gypsies" and the Chinese.

Perhaps the concern over birthright citizenship in the last thirty years springs from the numbers. There are now close to sixty-four million Latinx in the United States. If we constituted our own country, we would rank among the twenty-five most populated, with more residents than Spain, Italy, or Canada.

It is worth pausing to consider that the only reason we have a constitutional amendment on birthright citizenship is that we went to war over citizenship for Black Americans. The amendment was not the result of civil discourse, of compromise, of long negotiations into the night. The Supreme Court's decision in *Dred Scott* declared that Black people could not be citizens of the United States, not even if they were free, and this accelerated the start of the Civil War, which led to the creation of the Fourteenth Amendment, since that was the only way to undo the *Dred Scott* decision. We did not reason our way toward birthright citizenship. We killed one another over the course of about 1,343 days. We killed one another over the origins of citizenship, and more than 150 years later, we are fighting about it again.

I spent my childhood falling asleep, night after night, not to tales of wizards and dragons but to stories about borders and citizenships. I learned that citizenship was a fiction. I could not grab it with my hands like my mother's sewing needles or the chalk she used to mark fabric. Citizenship was a story, an invention, a social construct. In the United States, white men created this fiction of citizenship and used it to organize our lives, to determine when and how and under what circumstances my mother and I could live on this land. The white men issued papers: birth certificates, alien numbers, deportation orders. The white men insisted the fiction was a fact rather than a political and legal and social system they had devised. My mother told me the truth: Citizenship was a story the white men wrote so they could have what they wanted.

Historians told me the rest: The white men, free of the British Empire, created a citizenship to produce a country and a political institution that belonged exclusively to them. They massacred noncitizens. They enslaved noncitizens. They declared in 1790 that citizenship was only for white immigrants. When the story began to fall apart in the 1800s, when the Civil War barreled into kitchens and town squares, the white men revised the story. Citizenship would be a prize bestowed on Black people in 1868, on Indigenous people in 1924, and on everyone else when the white men deemed fit. Citizenship became a marker of how free this country was, of how far it had come, of how much it had grown—even as Black and Indigenous and Mexican and queer activists battled on the streets and in the courts during the twentieth century for the most basic of human rights.

Citizenship is now a proxy for race. Politicians and political commentators—and aunties and co-workers and the guy at the city council meeting—can profess to not be racists. They don't care about the color of anyone's skin. It's just that too many noncitizens have arrived at the southern border, at the edge of town, and in the local schools. They want these people to go back home to their own countries, to the places where they were born, where they have papeles. When protests erupted in 2017 over the U.S. ban on the entry of Muslims from seven countries, Trump's White House circumvented the courts by asserting that the policy had nothing to do with discrimination based on race or religion. It was a matter of national security, which is another way of saying, We don't want people with *that* citizenship. In the arguments for eliminating birthright citizenship, no one has to mention the disproportionate racial impact on Brown and Black children from Latin America, Haiti, and China. It's not about their race, the argument goes. It's about what papers their parents have.

All of this means that citizenship is a social construct in much the same way that race and gender are, and the value of pulling back the curtain, of saying, This is a social construct, is that we can better see the facts. We can see that the social construct of citizenship, like race and gender, governs the contours of our days. It dictates whether or not we call the police, whether or not we drive alone after dark, whether or not we worry about our mothers when they board the public bus. It is easy to forget that race is a social construct when the story favors you, and you do not expect the security guard to follow you around the store. Likewise, when you have citizenship, when that story favors you, you do not worry about your parents driving from Los Angeles to Iowa to visit you at college. You do not think of border checkpoints. You do not pay attention when a woman says the public library issues cards to residents regardless of where they were born.

Social construct—the term feels awkward in my mouth. It is nothing I could say to my mother without a dictionary. So I prefer to say that citizenship is a story, a fiction, a cuento, and I find it useful to turn to the conventions of narrative: Once upon a time, the white men offered citizenship to Cubans but not Colombians or Peruvians, not Pakistanis or Palestinians. Once upon a time, the white men could make deportation orders vanish. Once upon a time, the white men granted amnesty and everyone scrambled to find their pay stubs, their apartment leases, their old tourist visa, any document to show how long they had been on this land. Once upon a time, the white men did not care if you spoke English. They helped you when you took the citizenship test. Once upon a time, the white men did not care if you had a fake Social Security number. They needed women familiar with sewing needles, with fabric and stitches.

When my mother was pregnant with me in the mid-1970s, she could start a family in the United States. Our lives were possible because of the story told about citizenship at the time. Since then, so many lives have become impossible, not for any factual reasons but because Americans began telling a different story about citizenship. The story alleges that Latin American immigrants are the problem. The story forgets the United States has committed crimes south of the southern border. The story declares that we are foreigners even when, in 2022, a majority of Latinx in the United States (68 percent) were born here. This Latinx—the one born here, the one spoken of in the Constitution, the one with birthright citizenship—is not one white Americans can imagine, or perhaps they can, which explains the efforts to terminate our birthright citizenship.

Stories require repetition. We tell the story over and over again. We teach it. We put it in films. We photograph it. We document it. We share it. Then one day, we hear they all lived happily ever after, though we know they all lived at odds with one another, and this time, we question the stories we were told, and we begin asking questions. We wonder what it would mean if we recognized the United States as an empire whose political members are to be found across the globe. We consider how citizenship requires and sustains white supremacy. We draft a story of citizenship as obsessions, as mythology. We start to imagine a new story and maybe even a new country. We turn to one another, to the stories not yet on paper, the stories at the back of our throats, the stories that will set us free.

AJEDREZ

TÍO JOSÉ HAD a round brown face like the center of a sunflower. He worked at a paper factory in New Jersey, and when I was in middle school, he brought me huge stacks of white paper that, for official purposes, was defective in some way. I turned these rejects into books, filling them with poems about love that I hoped to experience one day. My tío approved. He had married into our family, married Tía Dora, my mother's sister, and José was nothing like the men I knew. My uncle spoke in courteous, measured tones. He never wore workman boots, opting instead for dress shoes and ironed polo shirts buttoned to the top. He came from Perú, which, from what I could glean at the time, was nothing like Papi's Cuba or Mami's Colombia. A ceremonial knife made of copper, its handle decorated with the face of an Inca deity, hung on the wall of my tío's apartment, and I took this as evidence of a glorious Indigenous history to which my uncle belonged, which was exactly what he and the government of Perú wanted me to think.

José was different in another way. While everyone in our family took public buses, my sunflower uncle drove a car. A Mercury Cougar. He was a man in charge of his destiny, the most American among us. The keys sang in his hands.

One Saturday when I was in sixth grade, José drove my auntie, mother, sister, and me to Tops Appliance City, an enormous store in Secaucus. The women paused at the long row of washing machines with their lids propped open, their vast, circular insides promising a cleaner, easier life. I stayed close to my uncle, who was buying a VCR that day. My own father worked every Saturday and never took us shopping, so being with my tío offered me a rare glimpse into the world of men, and there José stood that afternoon, calling out in his accented English to a white man whose uniform included a thick tie and a name tag. My tío talked with the man about the prices of the VCRs, because at Tops prices were not numbers but tiny parcels of land men scrutinized and frowned upon and debated. Finally, my uncle and the man settled on a figure, and we took the invoice to the cashier.

Waiting in line, José brought out his leather billetera, and I pulled on his arm. I wanted to see what men kept in their wallets, since Papi had nothing in his except for a Social Security card and pictures of me and my sister in Catholic school uniforms, our dark hair in pigtails.

José handed me the wallet. Inside, a white card had been placed beneath the plastic cover. The elaborate blue lettering on the card announced *United States of America*. I thought briefly of the cover of the textbook from my social studies class. A picture of my uncle's familiar sunflower face formed half of the card, except that his eyes looked almost startled, and above his forehead hung two words: Resident Alien.

I stared at the card, then shut the wallet. Without being told, I knew I had done something wrong. I had made my uncle show me a secret about himself. Somehow I knew I was not supposed to see this card or to know that the federal government had designated my tío an alien.

Tapping my sneakers on the store's linoleum floors, I made an excuse. I wanted to find Mami. Maybe she had circled back to the washing machines with my tía and sister. I slipped away and found her near the blenders, and when my auntie took my sister to the cash register, I grabbed my mother's arm. I had to know about the card in my tío's wallet, but I stumbled in Spanish because I did not know the word for alien in my mother's language. I only knew that it meant something very bad, that on the news, on the English-language channel, which I watched every weeknight, the white men in suits spoke of aliens. I did not know who the aliens were, but I was very sure I had never met one and that we were not supposed to be one of them. I asked my mother why my tío had a card saying he was not from here.

My mother sighed loudly, as if I, at the age of eleven, had heard a vague definition of sex and now she had to explain the whole endeavor to me, and she did not want to do it. She looked up and down the aisle. We were alone.

I don't know, she said quietly. Then, her mouth full of anxiety, she whispered, He's fixing his papers.

Arreglando sus papeles is what she said. By that time, I knew that in Spanish papeles was not a word but a song. Its meaning depended on the person who spoke, whether they lowered their voice or not. Sometimes the song had to do with lawyers, and other times it only referred to a sheet from a notebook. Sometimes the song moved quickly. Papeles was a cumbia, a salsa, a merengue. Other times it turned into a wistful ballad.

Arreglando sus papeles, Mami said. I did not appreciate the many definitions of the verb arreglar, and so I did not consider that my uncle was tidying up a stack of papers or organizing documents or getting the situation with his status resolved. I thought of his papers in only one way: The papeles were teacups that had cracked, the papers had broken and needed to be repaired. My tío was working to have his papers restored, and for some unspoken reason, this made my mother afraid.

South Africa's former poet laureate Keorapetse William Kgositsile, known affectionately as Bra Willie, observed, "In my language there is no word for citizen." In Tswana, people speak of a moagi, which, he wrote, "has nothing to do with any border or boundary you may or may not have crossed."

Moagi means "inhabitant." It also refers to a person who builds. Think of carpenters and construction workers, of sculptors and poets. Think of fingertips callused, the curvature of the body, the towels dipped in cold water. Think of your father, your cousin, your tío, yourself.

My elementary school, St. John the Baptist, occupied almost an entire block in our town. Every classroom had blackboards and white chalk and a row of hooks for our jackets. A wooden cross hung at the front of the room with Jesus nailed to it, naked except for his privates, which were covered by paint that looked like a dollop of cream. In the mornings, we recited the Our Father, facing the cross, and then we pivoted a few inches toward the flag, which hung in the corner. We stood by our desks with our hands over our hearts, chanting the Pledge of Allegiance.

The social studies textbook situated the start of citizenship in the United States with a picture of George Washington standing in a boat, the moon casting a shimmering white on the gray clouds. His hair had been curled and tucked under a funny hat. The river looked choppy, and I thought it was the Hudson River, but it was the Delaware, which I did not know and which sounded far away. George Washington's dark boots reached his knees. I wondered if he was cold, and why he couldn't take the Lincoln Tunnel if he was trying to reach New York.

I do not remember that any teacher said, Here is the definition of citizenship, and yet somehow I knew it meant membership, and that because of it, I had a right to live in this country and the government would protect me even from itself. I knew citizens had a duty to defend their particular country against other countries, and I figured that if the moment for battle came, I would be given a gun, though I had never seen a gun. I knew citizenship was a status, like being someone's girlfriend, and it was different from having rights. You might be the girlfriend, but it had only been two weeks, so you did not have the right to call every day or ask why they were talking to so-and-so during homeroom. A month later, you had those rights. Your status had not changed. You were still the girlfriend, but your rights had grown. You had discussed it after school. You had negotiated. You had won.

I would soon learn that none of it—neither the status nor the rights—meant the girlfriend would be treated well. Notes would be ignored. Calls unreturned. Rumors spread. Some girls in high school had it worse: boyfriends who slapped them, boyfriends who raped them. There was the theory of citizenship, and then there was the practice.

When I searched my computer's thesaurus for a synonym of citizen, it offered a few suggestions. If I was thinking of myself as a citizen of a particular country, then I might consider national or, strange as it sounds, passport holder. If I was thinking of myself as a citizen of a city (the online thesaurus suggested Atlanta), then I might try resident, householder, or native. If I wanted to be "humorous" about citizenship, the thesaurus proposed I name myself a denizen.

Scholars have searched for new language to recognize that you can have citizenship but still be treated badly. The political scientist Elizabeth Cohen describes this as a case of semi-citizenship. Another scholar suggested reviving the term denizen and adding specificity, so that Denizenship Type I would refer to people with green cards, while Denizenship Type II would refer to those who have citizenship but are denied basic necessities like healthcare and food. Under this scenario, you might think you are about to naturalize as a U.S. citizen, but you find yourself with a limited citizenship.

Social media and scholars and even the United Nations speak now of a crisis of citizenship, except they call it a "refugee crisis." My computer's dictionary defines a crisis as "a time of intense difficulty, trouble, or danger," and the crisis largely appears to be that the people on the move are Black and Brown people, and Muslims of all hues, traveling from the Global South into western Europe and North America. The movement of more than six million people from Ukraine, the vast majority of them white, does not inspire similar headlines about a refugee crisis.

The narrative of trouble and danger is not supported by the facts. Yes, by 2020, the number of migrants worldwide had almost doubled over the previous forty years, but according to the Migration Policy Institute's analysis of U.N. data, less than 4 percent of people live outside the country where they were born. Four percent. Another way to say this? The vast majority of us are at home right now.

My uncle José taught me to play chess probably that same year I was asking about his citizenship.

He set up the chessboard on the coffee table in the apartment he shared with Tía Dora on 75th Street in North Bergen. They were the kind of couple who believed in dining rooms, in an entire room devoted to the act of feasting, an entire room decorated with cabinets of ornate dishes used once or twice a year. Their rent-controlled apartment, though, had no dining room. Whoever had designed it expected the occupants to eat in the kitchen next to the stove. And so my tío and tía stuffed a large oval dining table into their living room. We had to squeeze around it or leave the living room and slide past the bedroom to reach the kitchen. My auntie hung lace curtains. My tío managed to find a coffee table that fit the room, and on this particular night in December, he moved it so he could reach the entertainment center and pull out a long rectangular box. I'll show you how to play, he announced with a smile, and placed the box on the coffee table.

The squares on the chessboard had been painted the color of cigars and canela. I plopped on the rug, crisscrossing my legs, while my sister, five years younger than me, her hair still in pigtails, stood next to me. One by one, my tío introduced us to the pieces: el rey, el caballo, el obispo, la reina. Each has its position, he said, and he showed this to us on the board. Some pieces could only move in straight lines. The horse jumps, he instructed, but it does not only spring forward. It gallops sideways. The smallest pieces, the pawns, formed the first line of defense. I shook my head. Why were the most vulnerable the first ones to be sacrificed?

My tío wore Coke-bottle glasses, the lenses so thick a family member teased that he looked like E.T., but I thought the glasses made him look smart, especially now with this game that had more rules than I could follow. He pronounced the name of the game as if it did not come from Arabic, and originally from Sanskrit. He pronounced it as if it were the name of a man he knew in Perú: ajedrez.

My sister picked the word up immediately, but I stumbled. My uncle repeated it: ajedrez. I said it quietly to not embarrass myself. Ajedrez. Then I tried again aloud and failed.

Here is what my uncle never told me: He had married a Puerto Rican woman to get his green card. He paid her. It was probably thousands of dollars. In 1985, when he married my auntie in a Catholic church, in all probability he was still married to this other woman. Or maybe he had started divorce proceedings.

Here is what my auntie never told me: She was under a deportation order from the federal government in 1982. A man in a suit at the immigration office in Newark told her to leave the country. A voluntary deportation. She hired a lawyer. She had only overstayed her tourist visa because she had a parasitic disease called Chagas that had almost killed her in her twenties, and here in New York City, she had undergone several surgeries to avoid dying. The disease made it so she didn't even weigh a hundred pounds. On good days, she looked like a pixie from a fairy tale, her thin hair framing her face. On bad days, she couldn't get up from bed. It didn't matter. She had to leave the country. The papers said so, but she stayed, and a few years later, in her early thirties, she met my tío in an English-language class.

Here is what my auntie did not have to tell me: My tío loved her. He loved her in the old-school way I only saw on Spanish soap operas. He held the doors open for her. He drove her to parties. He dressed up in suits to take her to parties. He paid for her lipstick and perfumes and eventually her college classes. He murmured to a friend: If I had known it would be so wonderful to be married, I would have done it sooner.

Here is what the schoolteachers never told me: My uncle was like Aristotle—another man who did not have citizenship in the place where he lived.

The social studies textbooks often introduced ancient Athens with a photograph of rocks arranged in the sun, as if democracy required only daylight, enormous stones, and an empty hilltop. The story stayed the same year after year: A citizen was a man who could vote in the assembly and serve on a jury. It sounded clean and precise, akin to numbers in a ledger. The textbooks never mentioned slaves or women or anything about the race of the men with citizenship. Whiteness was not named but understood.

The textbooks celebrated Aristotle, creating the impression that he was the ideal citizen, that when I thought of being a citizen, I should think of this man. But Aristotle was not a citizen of ancient Athens. Born in northern Greece, he moved to Athens to study, and the citizens there considered him an immigrant. Technically they called him a metic or metoikoi—meta meaning movement and oikos referring to the house, so that Aristotle was a man who had moved his house, or his household. Metics had to be sponsored by Athenian citizens. They were required to pay a tax and register with an office that oversaw all things metic-related. The status was like having a green card with no option of citizenship. But no one knows exactly what Aristotle experienced as a metic, because if he wrote anything on the subject of his status, the text did not survive.

Ancient Athenians changed their minds over the years about who could be a citizen. For a time, you were granted citizenship if your father was a citizen. That meant your mother could be a metic or a freed slave. In the middle of the fifth century B.C.E., however, a shift occurred that scholars have not been able to explain. Maybe too many foreigners moved to Athens. Maybe too many mixed marriages took place, with elite men from Athens choosing elite metic women. Maybe all the talk of the ethnic purity of those born in Athens took hold. Surely the causes were many; the effect was Pericles's Citizenship Law, which declared that to be considered a citizen, a person must have two parents with Athenian citizenship.

I wonder now what the Athenian general Pericles thought of the law that bore his name when he fell in love with a metic woman, an immigrant woman, a few years later. He apparently banished his citizen wife, and after his two sons from that marriage died, he demanded that an exception be made to the law so the son he had with his immigrant wife would be a citizen entitled to his inheritance. The request was granted because being a general in any century and in any community entitles a man to change the story.

Aristotle offered an extensive theory of citizenship in *Politics,* but he focused on a single understanding centered on the administration of political life. This was not the only story of citizenship, notes the classics scholar Josine Blok. Despite the widespread view that women were not citizens in ancient Athens, she points to Pericles's law dictating that a person could only become a citizen by having two citizen parents. A woman then had to be considered a citizen. Also, and equally important, religious life mattered a great deal during that time period. It structured how people spent their days and their riches. Only citizens could make certain divine offerings to the gods or hold the keys to the temples or feast on the best sacrificial meats. Women were central to these religious practices, and so they were citizens in ancient Athens, Blok writes.

But attention to the divine was not the story of citizenship Aristotle wrote. Did he want to avoid mixing politics and religion? Did he have another reason? The result was a single, uncomplicated story of citizenship as political administration. The story was recorded. The story was repeated and translated. And then the story was shelved.

When the white men of western Europe and the United

States considered Athens in the late 1700s, they mocked its form of government. In *The Federalist Papers,* Alexander Hamilton wrote that he found it "impossible to read the history of the petty republics of Greece and Italy," whose governments were often in armed conflict. The United States would not be like that, he insisted. It would not be a failed political project. The ancients, Hamilton wrote, did not know about certain principles that were clear in "modern times." These included the system of checks and balances and courts staffed with judges who were on "good behavior."

Historians returned to the citizenship of ancient Athens in the 1800s, and since the United States and France and Haiti had proved that a government without a monarch could endure, the white men picked up the story Aristotle told. They liked what they read about women and slaves and foreigners not qualifying for citizenship. In her book *Athens on Trial,* the historian and classics professor Jennifer T. Roberts observes that "numerous southern landholders discovered in the glories of the acropolis hard evidence that slavery and freedom were more than compatible."

White men had found a story they wanted to tell.

Here is what a family member told me: My Tío José had been a radio announcer in Perú. No, she did not know if he reported the news or if he introduced folk songs or if he hosted a call-in show, but still I love the idea of my uncle on the radio, his clear, gentle voice transmitted to thousands or even millions of listeners. Or maybe I am drawn to this story because of what happened with my tío and our local radio station.

In the 1980s, Radio WADO aired a popular program in Spanish on Saturdays featuring an immigration lawyer who took questions from callers. Out of necessity, the callers learned to tell their lives in a few sentences: I came in December. I worked with my brother. He had a green card. . . . And then the story swerved. The person paid a lawyer to help them with their deportation order, but he had vanished. Or it had been two years, and their lawyer had made little progress. Or they wanted to bring their sister or their daughter to the United States but . . . the sister had been deported or the daughter was twenty-three now.

By 1986, the calls to the Radio WADO lawyer were becoming more urgent and complicated because the Senate had approved what would become the Immigration Reform and Control Act—legislation that President Ronald Reagan would sign into law, granting a pathway to citizenship for almost three million people, most of them from Mexico. People wanted to know what the law would mean for their particular case or that of their mother or their brother.

Rarely did I understand the lawyer's answers, which struck me as dull and technical compared with the lives the callers shared and the emotions in their voices, often equal doses of frustration and fear. But I appreciated the lawyer. He spoke a fancy Spanish, enunciating each word the way my teachers did in school with English, and he paused at the end of his sentences as if what he had said carried so much weight that he had to proceed with caution. Always I imagined him at the radio station dressed in a three-piece suit with an expensive pen and a yellow legal pad.

One morning, while my mother scrubbed the oven and her sister, Tía María de Jesús, washed dishes, the lawyer on

Radio WADO took a new caller. I must have been preoccupied with listening to Madonna's *Like a Virgin* on my Walkman, because I did not notice that Mami and Tía paused and leaned toward the radio. The caller's voice rang with a certain familiarity. My auntie turned up the volume. She wondered if it could be him, and then she was sure of it. The caller's voice belonged to José, my tío. He told the lawyer that he had married a woman for his green card. Maybe he said it was an arrangement. Maybe it didn't need to be said. His question was this: If the amnesty bill became law, should he apply?

No one remembers what the attorney said. No one knows if my uncle had to call every weekend to get through to the station or what questions the screeners asked. They only remember his voice on the radio and that until then no one else in the family knew anything about his other wife or his papeles. He didn't talk about them. Tía Dora did not talk about them. And no one had ever asked.

Because citizenship has always been there—or should I say here?—because citizenship has always been presented as a fact of life, a status a person has or does not have or is on the way to having, it is easy to forget that the word itself has origins.

The vocabulary of citizenship began in cities. In ancient Athens, a citizen was called politês, a man who belonged to a polis, a city-state, and this probably came from acropolis, a fortress on a hilltop. Herodotus, often cited as the first historian of the Western world, preferred writing out the definition, so that a citizen was "a man belonging to the city." The tradition continued in Old English, where citizens became ceaster-waru, the men who lived in the city. The Romans themselves expanded the term for citizens (cīvitās) to refer to large towns. In Spanish, la ciudad, the city, is firmly rooted in citizenship: ciudadanía. The French adopted cité for city, which led to citeain, and it apparently leapt from there to English. The first recorded use of citizen in English came in 1325, when it was included in *The Statutes of the Realm,* a collection of the laws of England written in Middle English. A citizen at the time was one who lived in a city or town and held "civic rights and privileges."

I find it curious that the vocabulary of citizenship sprang up in cities, where people often make their living away from the land and where the proximity of bodies cannot be denied. Cities force a person to know the nearness of a grunt or murmur or shout a few feet away in the middle of the night. Cities insist on intimacy with strangers, on being close to bodies that do not belong to a mother or sister or cousin. Maybe citizenship, even in its earliest days, spoke to a preoccupation with the body, our own and that of others.

I never gave much thought to the fact that my uncle was not a religious man, since ours was a typical Latin American immigrant family: The men worked and drank cervezas, and the women worked and attended Mass. It had been this way for my grandmother in Colombia, and if my father's mother had not died during childbirth in Cuba, I am confident she too would have been at Mass. I did not question this social arrangement around gender and faith, in part because I took it as further evidence for a theory I was already developing in elementary school that women were superior to men and so were the ones to be trusted with divinity. Priests, in other words, were much like bus drivers. You needed someone to drive the bus, and it was not going to be me, since I had no interest in driving a bus, and it was not going to be my mother, since she did not know how to drive any vehicle, and so that was why the church had a priest. The only request made of the man was the one my mother and I made of the bus driver, which was that he show up on time.

Before I learned that our town had a library and that I could borrow books, I spent a fair number of weekend mornings when I was young reading my children's Bible. The stories about Jesus brimmed with magic. He could raise the dead and turn water to wine and make a feast out of a few fish and so on. I loved that Jesus liked the underdogs, that in a game of chess he would be fighting for the pawns, not the monarchs, and that he insisted we could be rich in our spiritual lives, which helped since my parents were always worried about money.

There was also this: Jesus was a migrant. He left his family and found a bunch of friends and together they created a new community and traveled together. I was not exactly clear about how far he had moved from Bethlehem, but in the children's Bible, he was rarely at home. One day, he arrived in such and such a city. The next, he appeared at a temple in another city. And because we had to rely on mass transit, I noticed very early on that Jesus did not have a car. The man walked everywhere, like my parents and me and my sister and my Tía Dora before she married my uncle.

Being in church was almost as good as reading the Bible.

Anyone could walk into the place. You did not need papers or money. You did not even need the same language. My mother and her sisters prayed in Spanish. The older women prayed in Italian or Croatian. The priest and the second- and third-generation Italian Americans prayed in English. Here was a true citizenship, I felt. A citizenship of the soul. When I reached eighth grade and the teacher tasked us with drafting reflection papers on the Sunday homily, I rushed home after Mass every week to write essays on the scripture and Father Carroll's sermon. My most memorable one stressed how women should be treated like valuable pearls, though I had no idea why that ugly jewelry was worth so much.

In all those years, I never once considered which political community Jesus and the apostles claimed. No teacher mentioned it either. I took it for granted that any such earthly citizenship did not matter since the true kingdom, as everyone knew, could be found in heaven with God. Yes, of course, I was informed about Rome and the emperor and giving to Caesar what belonged to Caesar and all that, but those were temporary, even petty, concerns. Jesus, after all, chose his Heavenly Father. He gave up his own life, and so did the apostles. Perhaps this is why it shocked me decades later to learn that Paul—the apostle, the one who founded the Church, the one whose words I heard so often in church—he cared about his papeles.

Paul initially did not believe in Jesus. After his conversion, when his eyes were literally and figuratively opened to the story that Jesus, a fellow Jew, was the Son of God, Paul traveled a great deal throughout the Roman Empire. He preached about Jesus. He baptized a man who jailed him. He pulled spirits out of an enslaved girl. When a man fell out of a window one night, he brought him back to life.

In Jerusalem one year, Paul faced a group of angry men. They dragged him out of a temple, their mouths full of accusations. Paul had betrayed Jewish traditions. Their fists and fingernails dug into his body. "Kill him!" the men shouted, and the Roman soldiers whisked Paul onto their shoulders, the sunlight surely bathing his face. The local officer permitted Paul to make his case to the city's Jews, but his talk about Jesus sending him to preach to non-Jews only led the men to call again for his death. Confused over the nature of Paul's offenses, the Roman officer ordered his soldiers to whip the apostle until he confessed.

Paul asked one of the soldiers if it was legal to torture a citizen. He knew the answer. Noncitizens in the Roman Empire could be tortured until they admitted their wrongdoings, but citizens first had to be tried and condemned. The officer in charge walked up to Paul in the barracks and inquired about his citizenship. The officer himself had the right papers, the Roman papers. "I paid a lot of money for this citizenship of mine," he told the apostle.

Paul squared his shoulders, or maybe he rubbed his bruised arms. Maybe he looked the man in the eye when he said, "I was born a citizen."

The translations differ slightly on this biblical passage. In some versions, Paul says, "But I was free born." In others, he asserts, "But I am a Roman born." In the earliest translation to English, he announces, "And I was born a citizen of Rome."

Paul knew citizenship was a story that could keep him

alive. It was a story about his body. And the story did, in fact, let him live, at least for a time. The officer shipped Paul to a governor, who detained him for two years and eventually granted him a choice: He could return to Jerusalem and most likely be murdered on the way by people who hated him for following Jesus's teachings, or he could, as a citizen, appeal to the emperor to consider his case. Paul chose his earthly citizenship. Paul chose the empire.

In Rome, he spent another two years under house arrest. Scholars suspect the Romans beheaded him, since a quick death would have been the right held by a citizen.

The law professor Catherine Dauvergne wrote, "Whatever else citizenship is or is to become, it remains tied to national legal texts."

Thomas Jefferson's first draft of the Declaration of Independence did not refer to Americans as citizens. Sitting at his portable writing desk in the summer of 1776, he used another word, then thought better of it and wrote citizens over the original term, leaving historians to speculate for the next two centuries over what it might have been.

In 2009, the preservation scientist Fenella France journeyed into the subbasement of the James Madison Memorial Building in Washington, D.C., where the Library of Congress kept its new spectral imaging technology. She spent hours teasing apart the chemicals of the ink of the word citizens in the Declaration of Independence. She worked her way back through time until she found the text that had been carefully tucked underneath: subjects.

Jefferson lived in between stories in 1776. All his life, he had been the subject of the king, and so at first, he reached for the story he knew best. In a list of offenses by the monarch, he referred to himself and his fellow settler colonizers as subjects. He must have paused while revising the text. He wanted a new story. He dipped his quill into the inkwell and wrote citizens.

Media outlets celebrated the finding. Here was the truth of the story. The science of it. The nonfiction of the story. Here was citizenship born from the body of a man. But I read the story and thought: Here is the fiction of citizenship. One white man named us subjects and another citizens, and when I was a child in the 1980s, one white man, Ronald Reagan, signed a law that granted citizenship to undocumented immigrants, and then in the 1990s another white man, Bill Clinton, signed laws that turned undocumented immigrants into criminals.

The author Joan Didion famously observed that we tell ourselves stories in order to live. A clarification: We tell ourselves stories to live the lives we want.

In 1857, Frederick Douglass spoke to the American Abolition Society on the Supreme Court's *Dred Scott* decision denying citizenship to all Black people in the United States. He offered a close reading of the Constitution: " 'We, the people'—not we, the white people—not we, the citizens, or the legal voters—not we, the privileged class, and excluding all other classes but we, the people."

I thought of Douglass's words often. The Constitution uses the word citizen eleven times without hinting at what it means or who might qualify for the status. The Constitution preoccupies itself with pragmatic matters such as declaring that you must be a citizen for seven years to serve in the House of Representatives, nine to be in the Senate, and a "natural born Citizen" for the presidency. Most revealing, the Constitution speaks of citizens primarily to talk about our bickering. The courts have power over disputes between a state and the citizens of another state, between citizens of different states, between citizens and their own state, and so on. The Bill of Rights, the first ten amendments to the Constitution, speaks only of the people. It is the right of the people to assemble, to not have their homes searched without a warrant, to not testify against themselves, and to not be subjected to excessive bail.

The constitution New Jersey adopted in 1776 made no mention of the word citizen. It spoke instead of the people and also of the inhabitants. Anyone could vote in elections if they lived in the colony for a year and were "worth fifty pounds." This meant that unmarried women, Black or white, could vote. Free Black men could vote. The state's constitution ignored the gender binary system and spoke of voters with the pronoun they. If there were questions about gender, a 1790 law clarified it by adding the pronoun she, saying a person could only vote in the town "in which he or she doth actually reside at the time of the election."

New York adopted a constitution that invoked the term citizen just once, and that was because it wove in text from the Declaration of Independence. New Yorkers preferred the phrase "the people," turning to it a total of nineteen times in their constitution. Any "male inhabitant" there, including Black men, could vote if they paid taxes and owned property.

Every national legal text is a story. The story can be interpreted. The story can be revised. The story can wound. In 1807, New Jersey banned unmarried women and Black men from voting, and in 1821, New York revised its constitution, making it so that white men could vote regardless of whether they owned property, while Black men had to own even more property than before to cast a ballot.

The Declaration of Independence announced that men had the right to life, liberty, and the pursuit of happiness. Almost a hundred years later, in 1868, the United States added a fourth privilege: the right to migrate. No one altered the original document, but the United States signed the Burlingame Treaty with China, agreeing to "cordially recognize the inherent and inalienable right of man to change his home and allegiance."

The Civil War had ended, and businessmen needed other men to work for low wages on the railroads and in the canneries. So the Burlingame Treaty was signed. The men from China continued arriving, and white supremacy speech began surging from politicians until, in 1882, Congress passed the Chinese Exclusion Act, eliminating the inalienable right to migration for Chinese people and, later, for anyone from Asia. The law would not be completely reversed until 1965, when Congress lifted all racial quotas on migration.

On paper, my uncle married my tía the year I turned twelve, about a year after Ronald Reagan signed the amnesty bill into law. On paper, he was a legal permanent resident. On paper, she asked for permission to reapply for residency after a deportation order. On paper, she was now a wife and homemaker. She had not been able to leave the country in the early 1980s because of medical treatments. On paper, my uncle with his green card swore to keep her from becoming a public charge. My mother did the same and so did my father. My uncle submitted a letter from his bank showing his account balances. On paper, someone stamped an approval. My auntie could have a green card.

The apostle Paul did not write the story of his own citizenship. Someone named Luke did. Maybe it was Luke the Evangelist. Maybe not. A number of religious scholars have reservations about whether Paul was a Roman citizen, though many are in agreement that the texts attributed to Luke (his Gospel and the Acts of the Apostles) address the question of whether Christians could be good citizens of the Roman Empire.

The story of Paul's citizenship began in Luke's mouth, and so it is curious that in 1998, when scientists and religious leaders opened the coffin in Italy where the body of Luke the Evangelist was said to be, they found a headless corpse. A single tooth in the coffin matched a head buried elsewhere and attributed to Luke. The scientists read the text of the Evangelist's body and published these facts: The DNA from the tooth revealed that the body most likely belonged to a man from Syria.

Were he alive today, Luke would perhaps be called a refugee, a citizen driven from their home. Or maybe, because he was a physician, he would have stayed in Aleppo when the bombings began. Or he would be dead by now. Or he would have recorded interviews with NPR and sent voice memos to his mother, whom he sent out of the country days before the skies exploded.

Or he would be like the man I met at a community event near Chicago: still shaken by the decisions he had been coerced to make. This man, Palestinian, recounted to me the start of the war in Gaza in 2023. The Israelis forced him, his wife, and their children, along with neighbors and friends, to evacuate their homes in northern Gaza. His was a mixed-status family: He had a U.S. green card, his two grown sons held U.S. citizenship, and his youngest three children and wife were stateless. The United States embassy offered to evacuate his eldest children, the ones whose papers bore the words and dates and stamps declaring their birthright citizenship to this country. They would have to leave everyone else behind. The boys, this man's boys, were men. One was married. His wife had no papers from the United States, and neither did their nine-month-old son. He would have to abandon his child, his wife, his parents, and his siblings. He refused. So did his brother. Their father pleaded with them: "You have to go. If we die, someone will continue the journey. Someone will carry the name."

The father wept telling me this. He wept in Gaza and drove south and watched his two sons board a bus in Rafah bound for Egypt.

The next day his name appeared on the evacuation list. He had a green card. He was an almost-citizen of the United States. He could leave. He could live. He could flee the killing fields of Gaza, though not with his wife, two daughters, and youngest son.

The man did not leave; he spent the next fourteen days emailing the U.S. embassy in Cairo and every person he could think of who might be able to advocate for his family. It was almost forty days into the terrible war. Fuel was running short and food becoming more scarce, and every day more agonizing. Then the list appeared online with the names of his wife and daughters but not his son.

Here, his mouth stopped, his face collapsed. It had been forty days, he told me. Forty days. He wanted me to know why he left, why he took his younger daughter and fled, why his wife and elder daughter followed days later, why they spent weeks upon weeks trying to get his son, his stateless son, out of Gaza. But the why of what he did drowned in the weeping.

We sat in brutal silence and also in the blessing: He and his family managed to bring his son to Cairo more than a month later by paying the right people at the border.

When I asked him what he thought of citizenship, he said, "I was born stateless." He entered the world in a refugee camp in 1964. He told me that a homeland is the land and the people, and he had concluded he could live on any land as long as he had his family and felt safe.

His grandchild was able to leave Gaza at nine months old because the boy's mother had Russian citizenship by way of her mother. At the Rafah crossing, officials bestowed upon the little one his first papel with his name, his picture, and his date of birth. It was a makeshift document of citizenship until he reached Russia.

The first time I saw the two photographs, I did not consider that they were of the same person. In one, the young man named Tom Torlino wears a dark suit with a high collar and silk bowtie pinned in place. His short, dark hair has been carefully combed. The man could be from the nineteenth century or the 1950s. He might be South Asian or Mexican or Italian.

In the other photograph, the same man has long, dark hair. Hoops dangle from his ears, a beaded necklace adorns his neck, and he has a blanket over his shoulder. In this photograph, he has spent hours in the sun. His face is a warm copper. He might be a citizen of Mexico or Perú, Colombia or the United States, and he is also a member of an Indigenous nation.

The photographs document the before and after of cultural genocide, the before and after of what the United States did to Indigenous nations when authorities removed thousands of children from their families during the nineteenth and twentieth centuries and shipped them to one of more than five hundred boarding schools. Teachers and administrators changed the names of the children and punished them for speaking their own languages and practicing their traditions. Hundreds of Indigenous children, maybe more, died in these schools.

The cultural genocide was not, at the time, called a genocide. It was referred to as citizenship training. At a convention in 1892, Richard Henry Pratt, the founder of the Carlisle Indian Industrial School in Pennsylvania, which became a national model for these institutions, asserted that Black Americans had been taught about U.S. citizenship by being in close proximity to whites while enslaved. The same, he insisted, was happening for Germans. They could not be taught about U.S. citizenship in Germany. They were learning about it here through cultural immersion. From there, Pratt concluded: "Neither can the Indians understand or use American citizenship theoretically taught to them on Indian reservations. They must get into the swim of American citizenship. They must feel the touch of it day after day, until they become saturated with the spirit of it, and thus become equal to it."

This was the same speech in which Pratt proclaimed, "Kill the Indian in him, and save the man."

Tom Torlino came from the Diné (Navajo) Nation, one of close to eight thousand Indigenous children who were taken to Carlisle. The school promoted its part in the cultural genocide by disseminating to white Americans before-and-after portraits of the children. The photograph of Tom in the suit was taken after he was forced to spend his days and his nights at the school for three years.

The photograph of the young Diné man in the suit with his hair neatly combed made me think of Tío José—my tío who ran errands dressed in slacks, my tío who groomed his nails, my tío who pulled on button-down shirts for family gatherings on the weekend, my tío who played ajedrez. I thought as a child that my uncle strained at respectability for private reasons. But nothing is private. The dress pants and the dry-cleaned shirts and even the car, all of it drew attention away from my tío's Indigenous face.

My uncle never told me what he knew of his family's history, and I never asked. His wife, my tía, did not want to know. She was a white woman with Indian ancestry. She was the one who scolded me for being impertinent, for not smiling, for being what she called una india. My uncle must have heard this racist accusation against me, but my memory falters. Maybe Tía never said it in front of him. Maybe she held her tongue. Or maybe he heard it and did not object.

In the United States, citizenship is often spoken of and taught as a coda to state violence. The story begins with slavery and genocide, and it ends with citizenship on paper. Or the story begins with Jim Crow laws and immigration quotas, then ends with the Voting Rights Act of 1965 and citizenship in practice. Over and over again, citizenship is the prize and also the apology.

The same year that the United States imposed racial quotas on migration with the intention of making the country white again, it extended citizenship to Indigenous people born within the country's borders. The Indian Citizenship Act of 1924 is told as a story of progress, of civil rights, of white Americans coming to their senses and doing the right thing. But by then two-thirds of Indigenous people were already U.S. citizens, albeit with serious limitations, as evidenced by how they had become citizens. They had married or served in the military and naturalized. Some were citizens because treaties had been signed. Some had become citizens when Congress passed a law in the late 1800s allowing the federal government to grab Indigenous land, then assign it to those who would leave their tribes and farm the land alone, like white men, apart from their communities.

While the 1924 law had Indigenous supporters, some leaders objected, insisting on the citizenship they already possessed. Clinton Rickard, chief of the Tuscarora Nation, protested at the time: "Our citizenship was in our own nations. We had a great attachment to our style of government. . . . There was no great rush among my people to go out and vote in the white man's elections. Anyone who did so denied the privilege of becoming a chief or a clan mother in our nation."

A year before sixty-eight thousand children showed up at the U.S.-Mexico border in 2014, I drove north from Miami, past car washes and jewelry stores and bus stops, until I reached a low concrete wall enclosing a few administration buildings, a church, a smattering of palm trees, and a cluster of plain houses with beds for two hundred children, including about forty or fifty the federal government labeled "unaccompanied alien children." Since 2008, the government had contracted with the faith-based organization His House Children's Home to feed and clothe and look after these children alongside those who had birthright citizenship in the United States and had been removed from their families. The houses, in other words, had become temporary homes for children in the foster care system.

I joined the other volunteers at the back of the church behind rows of metal chairs facing a simple pulpit. The volunteers all spoke Spanish, and several were getting graduate degrees in education. Some had come with enFamilia, a farmworkers' organization based in Homestead, Florida. Because I was new, one of the organizers explained that His House gave us an hour with the children. There was a lesson plan, she told me, but when the children arrived, I should tag along with Diuver. He was good with the kids. He was a sculptor and a refugee from Cuba.

The children filed into the church. They were boys, some with the face of my tío: brown faces, Indigenous faces. They huddled in pairs and groups of three. They teased one another. They leaned into one another's bodies. They lent one another pencils. A few called out Miss! and Good morning! The girls numbered about six. They wore mood rings and friendship bracelets and smiled shyly at us.

The immigrant children at His House sometimes stayed for two weeks, sometimes five months. Lately few of them had been here longer than twenty-one days, because, according to the rumors, Barack Obama's administration had decided that the children needed to be moved more quickly through the foster care system. Some of the children were twelve years old. Some were fourteen or sixteen. No immigrant child here wanted to turn eighteen. Crossing that threshold, starting at the chime of midnight, a child stopped being a child and turned into an adult the federal government could deport.

The lesson plan that morning was about preparing for the future. We could do anything that fell under that broad category, and Diuver nodded. He was tall with muscular brown arms, and in his baby-blue polo shirt, ironed white shorts, and baseball cap, he walked with the confidence of a man who owned a local business and planned on franchising one day. After the obligatory announcements, he marched up to a group of boys as if they had been friends for years and said, Let's go outside.

The heat descended on us. Diuver led the boys a few feet from the building to the shade of a tree and showed us how the game would be played. He placed his hands behind his back and instructed one of the boys to do the same. They each decided silently how many fingers they would reveal to the other. On the count of three, they pulled their hands from behind their backs. The first one to add the number of fingers his opponent showed plus his own won the round. Diuver won. The boys cheered. He ran through the game several more times, and when a lanky boy named José won three times in a row, Diuver declared him the capitán.

Our teams need names, Diuver announced. He was smiling and the boys laughed. What names should we use? he asked the boys, then clarified. Like the names of fútbol teams. Like Real Madrid.

Chelsea! a boy called out.

Diuver nodded and said, Real Madrid versus Chelsea.

I grinned despite myself. Here was the absurdity of citizenship and empire. The United States had colonized Central America for decades through private corporations and the CIA and the Marines and the infamous School of the Americas, which trained the men who led the death squads in Latin America. Here now were the children and grandchildren and great-grandchildren of U.S. colonialism, the children forced to flee their homes, and what they knew best, what all of us knew best, was the empire itself, the soccer teams of imperial powers, of Spain and England: Real Madrid and Chelsea.

The boys organized themselves in two lines facing each other, but they turned out to be an odd number. The last boy lingered on the edge of one team, the toes of his sneakers digging into the sandy grass. Diuver called out, You're going to decide who wins. The left-out boy would be the juez, the judge. He had soft eyes and wide shoulders. I wondered if he was fourteen or sixteen or eleven.

I moved to the sidelines, aware that to the boys I was a grown woman, an auntie, and because I knew the joys and the tenuousness of women-only spaces, queer-only spaces, BIPOC-only spaces, I recognized that this patch of land was a Brown boy space, an immigrant space. I was the citizen. I was the foreigner.

On the count of three, Diuver whistled. The boys' hands swung from behind their backs, and numbers crowded the air: Six! Thirteen! Ten! The boys laughed, glancing from Diuver to the judge, who called the first round for Chelsea. And the second one and third too. Suddenly a woman's voice rang out from the church door. She needed the judge. Time halted. The boys fell silent, and we all watched the judge slowly trudge toward the door, then disappear inside. The day was growing brighter and hotter, and I wanted to ask what was happening. Maybe the children did too. But one of them said, Let's play again, and they did, their arms and hands and fingers spinning through the air, their mouths shouting the sums.

When the judge returned, only minutes had passed. His eyes watered. His lower lip trembled. He didn't speak to us, and none of us asked, but I knew from the organizers that the children had disclosed how it hurt to stay and how it hurt to leave their new friends. All language bruised in this place. It hurt to hear, You're leaving on Monday, so have your things ready. No, not Monday. Thursday. Next week. Soon. Time was not time here. Time was an empty plate passed back and forth.

Diuver whistled to start a new round. The judge swallowed his tears and watched the flying hands and tilted his head toward the numbers tossed about. Chelsea, he decided. The children cheered.

We're going to switch this up, Diuver told the boys, and he traded players from one team to the other, so that in the next round, Real Madrid won. The hour almost over, Diuver asked the boys, What can you take from this game and apply to real life?

Mathematics, said the capitán. It's addition.

Another boy suggested, In real life, you try to win.

Diuver nodded. I like that, he said. In real life, we're on a team. You have friends, people who support you, and you work with people who oppose you. You might show up at a job and not like someone there or someone might pick a fight with them. Are you going to quit your job? He paused to look around the circle. No, he said. You're going to stay focused on your plans. There are goals and there are hopes. Your goals depend on you. Hopes depend on other people.

The boys nodded. I did too. Diuver said, Let's go around the group. What plans do you have?

The answers sprang without hesitation: Learn English. Get a job. Help my family.

He reached the judge, who said, I want to build something back in my country . . . a house or a business.

He looked at the tree trunk, which maybe now was not a tree but the future, where he had constructed a store with a wide doorframe and he could see himself at the cash register, the register popping open, the triumphant faces of the local children. He could see them—the children lining up in front of his store to buy Popsicles, caramelos, chewing gum. He could see their hands full of coins.

Hannah Arendt described citizenship as "the right to have rights," and she pointed to the absurdity of this situation. Documents like the Declaration of Independence recognize that certain rights belong to all people—these rights are self-evident—but you only have these rights because you belong to a specific country.

If your country bows to an imperial power and leaves you with little to feed your children, if your country murders your children during a traffic stop, if your country declares your gender to be the work of devils, if your country forces you to climb into a boat or the back of a truck, then you have no self-evident rights and no citizenship. You become a person marked with another story, which is to say that you are called a migrant, a displaced person, an asylum seeker, an undocumented person, or a refugee. The vocabulary list is long.

If officials, who still have their citizenship intact, decide you have no country to call home, that your country denies you political membership because of your race or religion or language, then the officials classify you as stateless. More than twenty countries, including Jordan and the Bahamas, deny women the right to pass their nationality on to their children. Unless they are legally recognized by their fathers, these children live without citizenship. More than four million people are stateless. Most of them were born and have spent every day in the countries denying them the right to be there.

Citizenship is an impossible story, a story of absurdities. The absurdity can be found in language, which means the absurdity of citizenship can be found right now inside your mouth.

On one paper, my tío was born in the 1930s. On another, he came into the world after World War II.

This is the part of the story I do not want to write. The part I have read now in other stories of immigrant families and papeles. The part about the illness, how one day my uncle was fine and the next day his friends at work rushed him to the emergency room, how that year of cancer moved faster than any other. It was my first year in college and my uncle's last year with us, except that by then I was desperate to leave my family, and I did not want to stay, especially not to watch him die. This is the part about how I have kept one or two photos of him from that last year, but that last year is not him.

This is the part of the story where I tell you that my tío was alive when my auntie sent the application to become a U.S. citizen. On paper, Tía Dora agreed that she believed in the Constitution and that she would be willing to "bear arms on behalf of the United States." On paper, she was a married woman. On paper, she had been in the United States for fourteen years. By the date of her citizenship interview, my tío had died. The immigration official amended by hand her application so it read "widow."

But that is not the story I carry with me. My tío's story is not a piece of paper. His story is that day when he taught me to play chess, both of us in thick sweaters because it was December, maybe Christmas Eve. We feasted on platters of yellow rice and lentils. My tía concocted an eggnog-like drink.

My tío and I sat cross-legged on the rug in front of the chessboard. I kept reminding myself that the bishops could migrate in ways the rooks could not. The horses could jump. There were so many rules, too many rules. I kept forgetting them, and my tío kept reminding me.

A PLACE CALLED NEGRO

I KNEW SOMETHING was wrong with me the moment I opened my eyes that morning. I was still in bed, my sixth-grade school uniform ironed and waiting for me on a hanger, the window blinds drawn so that I blinked several times, adjusting my eyes to the weak light. A weight pressed to the right side of my face, and I half-expected to see a woman towering over me, an auntie or maybe Mami, the back of a bony hand on my face. But no one was there, and yet my face—my chin, my jaw, my cheek—felt covered in gauze and adhesive, as if while I slept, someone had begun to mummify me, to prepare my face for burial.

My breathing quickened. I lifted my fingers to my cheek and found that my face was not my face. The skin had changed, turned into a coarse, almost reptilian surface. I sprang from the bed and rushed to the mirror. A thick layer of inflamed, dry skin covered the lower right side of my face. I ran to my mother in the kitchen, crying, Look!, as if she could avoid my half-lizard face.

Don't touch it, Mami warned, peering at my new face.

In Colombia, my mother had refused to attend nursing school because the thought of blood made her queasy, and also perhaps because, like me, she preferred a predictable life, and the body is never predictable. The body insists on chaos, on broken timelines, on abrupt endings. While I palmed my lizard face, my mother reached for the aloe vera plant on the windowsill. This served as her home remedy for burns and acne and now reptile skin.

I had not yet read the fiction of Franz Kafka and so I did not know the word metamorphosis, but I knew I had turned into a reptile and that we would need to see a doctor but it was expensive to do so. My world at the time was eerily silent on the topic of how other people paid to see doctors. On television comedy shows, no one handed cash to the doctor. In elementary school, no one spoke about their parents writing checks to the pediatrician. In social studies class, we read about the Pilgrims and how they would have died that first winter if it had not been for the labor and generosity of Indigenous peoples (the Wampanoag, I later learned), but no teacher mentioned how that cluster of white immigrants paid for medical care. By the end of the school week, the Pilgrims had become settler colonizers politely called colonists, the American Revolution had been won, and, from one paragraph to the next, the colonizing colonists turned into Americans—this invented citizenship being the spoils of war—but still no mention of how they paid for medical care.

I knew how we paid. At the pediatrician's office, my mother pulled out the bank envelope filled with crisp twenty-dollar bills when my sister and I needed vaccines. She did this until a Mexican mother in town told us that the health department vaccinated without charging.

That morning of the half-lizard face, my mother sliced open a leaf of the aloe vera plant and smeared its gelatinous innards onto my cheek. We pulled my hair into a ponytail, but strands still flew loose and stuck to the gel. I went to school like that, with a half-lizard face covered by a layer of sheen, and if the other children mocked me, I have blocked it from my memory. I remember only their curiosities: What happened to your face? And I remember the way they nodded in concern, as if I had lost a part of my face overnight, which basically I had.

The next day, my mother again applied the gooey aloe gel to my face. By late evening, the shiny material had dried, and the lizard remained. I began to tug at my skin, but nothing happened. I tugged harder. The lizard resisted. I ran my fingernails against the skin, digging along the dry scales. A tiny section loosened. Then another. But the skin felt too warm, too raw, too exposed under the lizard. I stopped, terrified that whatever lay underneath might be worse.

In the morning, the section of skin I had peeled away had already begun its return. The mirror tossed back what I dreaded: a half-lizard girl with dark hair.

We must have exhausted the aloe vera plant over the course of several weeks when my mother finally said, We're going to Nueva York. She had spoken to her women friends and my aunties. New York City had a health clinic that didn't charge and didn't care that we came from a different state. They took everyone.

At the bus stop, Mami wrapped her arm around her pocketbook, a bag the color of walnuts. She held the walnut close, as if she were afraid of losing it. Into the walnut, she had packed Juicy Fruit chewing gum, a sleeve of saltine crackers, and a plastic container of apple juice that came with its own straw. In the palm of her hand, she had folded the dollars for the New Jersey Transit bus.

We didn't know how long it would take to reach this clinic at a hospital in Nueva York. It could be hours. I stood beside her at the bus stop in the dazzle of the morning light. Don't touch your face, she implored. It was too late. I had already started tugging at the skin on my chin. When the bus finally arrived, stopping close to the curb, my mother motioned for me and my half-lizard face to board first.

Some two hours later, seated in the clinic's corridor, I swung my legs and tried very hard to not touch my face. My mother said I was lucky. In Colombia, I wouldn't even get to see a doctor. In Colombia, I would have to live with my half-lizard face all through middle school until we had saved enough pesos to pay a doctor up front.

The clinic's corridor did not have enough lights. We sat in stiff chairs, in the shadows, waiting. I grew bored. I did not have a book. I did not even have my Walkman. The bottoms of the nurses' loafers squealed on the tiled floors. The doctors' oxfords clicked past us. This clinic was nothing like I expected. The pediatrician back in Jersey, the one who charged too much, had an office with thick carpet and cushy seats and a bowl of lollipops. But we could not afford that doctor anymore. I didn't know why.

In the corridor, an overweight woman sat across from us with her husband or brother. They waited with tired faces and didn't speak, even to each other. My mother and I probably looked the same, and I realized, first slowly and then all at once, that we were only receiving medical care because someone had decided to pity us, to take care of us, to keep us alive.

Mami leaned into me and whispered in Spanish, Tell him you're menstruating.

Him was the doctor.

Why? I asked sullenly.

It might have to do with your face.

My mother clearly did not plan to see the doctor with me. I was almost twelve. I was almost all grown up. Besides, I was the only one in my family fluent in English. The only one who could fill out the forms. The only one who could deal with the nurses and doctors.

I sulked. I did not want to tell anyone about my period, least of all a grown man. I didn't see what it had to do with my face. But I knew I would follow my mother's direction. I would do anything to save my face.

The doctor had blondish hair and light eyes. He flipped through the paperwork slowly, then peered at my chin, my jaw, my cheek. He wanted to know when the reptile had arrived (overnight) and how long it had been (weeks, maybe two months). He grew silent. I didn't know the difference between a physician and a resident and a fellow, but I suspected that it was the man's first week on the job (he was hesitating too much), and I could see that I needed to take charge of the situation. I shifted on the exam table and the white paper crinkled under my legs, and that's when I announced, I got my period.

The man's eyes widened, but he managed to stammer, That's good.

My mother thinks it might have to do with my face.

He smiled a little. Do you chew bubble gum?

Yes.

Do you make big bubbles? Like the ones that burst around your face?

I knew he was thinking about the cool Puerto Rican and

Cuban girls back in Jersey, near Bergenline Avenue, the ones who had curly hair and tight jeans and boyfriends. They sat on front stoops and chewed their gum and blew balloons so marvelous they looked like goddesses with pink suns rising from their lips.

I was not that cool. No, I told the doctor sadly, and in that moment, I felt sorry for both of us. I knew he wanted to help me, and I wanted him to help, and yet it was clear that he did not know anything about my face. He sent us home with a cream that did nothing to make the lizard vanish.

Every morning, before I even reached for the mirror, I knew the lizard was still there. I could feel the weight of its scales, the coarseness of the dry skin. I ran my fingertips across my face, enraged, and burst into sobs.

My mother searched my face. It's still there, I told her, brushing my black hair forward so it covered a little of the lizard.

One day, Mami pulled out the envelope the bank gave her when her factory paycheck cleared on Fridays. She counted the twenty-dollar bills. They were a pretty shade of green, stamped with a string of numbers and the name of the country. The thin face of a white man had been imprinted on one side, though neither my mother nor I knew that President Andrew Jackson had enslaved Black people and signed the law that led to the Trail of Tears and the murders of thousands of Cherokee and other Indigenous peoples.

Mami tucked the envelope into her walnut pocketbook, and we boarded a bus that took us south on Bergenline Avenue to a medical office on the second floor of a quiet building. The waiting room had carpet and enough chairs for everyone. In the corner, a lamp stood on a table, regal, like ones in the living rooms on television shows.

The receptionist smiled at us from behind a dainty window that slid open. She gave my mother a clipboard, papers, and a pen. She spoke to us in Spanish.

We did not wait long. The dermatologist was Cuban, and he had the face of a beagle. He spoke Spanish but said very little, as if he were, in fact, a well-trained house dog. I did not tell him about my period, and he did not ask about chewing gum or anything else. He peered at my lizard face with a magnifying glass that made his own eyeglasses look enormous, and then he pulled out a small, square pad of white paper and wrote a prescription.

The dermatologist must have told us the diagnosis in Spanish (probably a severe case of psoriasis), but his words were foreign to us. My mother frowned at the prescription. It was another cost, and she worried that this treatment would also fail. We looked at each other, then walked to the pharmacy.

The gel he prescribed turned out to be a clear, sticky concoction, not unlike Mami's aloe vera plant, and it worked. The lizard began to disappear, a metamorphosis in reverse, until one day it was gone, and I was left with the knowledge of my mother's sacrifice: the dollars exchanged for my face.

I also learned that healthcare was not like the rights I was learning about in social studies class: the right to vote or to practice the religion of my choice. A terrible thing could happen to my face or to that woman in the clinic's corridor, and our fellow Americans would do nothing unless they felt sorry for us. What kind of citizenship let you turn into a reptile? I began to suspect that my teachers and the textbooks had lied to me. All men were not created equal. Some men—and twelve-year-old girls—had access to healthcare, and some did not. It was what the British sociologist T. H. Marshall called social citizenship.

Writing in the aftermath of World War II, Marshall saw citizenship as an evolutionary process of rights, at least for England and its white men. First came civil citizenship, or the right to have rights. So, you had a right to be free and to speak your mind and also to buy property because white men have apparently been obsessed with the ownership of land for a long time. Then came political citizenship, or the right to vote. Finally, social citizenship in the twentieth century brought the right to economic security and "to live the life of a civilised being." This meant that you could have civil citizenship and political citizenship but a terrible social citizenship, and so you could complain at a city council meeting, but not have the right to see a doctor when you collapsed on the floor of your kitchen.

Marshall did not comment on how his ideas spoke to the citizenships of women or queers or Black Britons or the children of Pakistani immigrants in London or the children of South American mothers in New Jersey. He was preoccupied with the experiences of white men in England. Still, there is a certain tidiness about his citizenship triad: civil, political, and social. At the age of twelve, I had not read Marshall's classic book, but I could see that when it came to social citizenship, some of us did not have it.

Almost ten years after the lizard face, I boarded another bus with my mother. This time it was for her. She said she did not qualify for Medicaid and neither her factory job nor my father's offered health insurance, so she relied on local health fairs to get her cholesterol checked. And her glucose levels. Sometimes even her eyesight.

This health fair took place at a park in Union City. The day was bright and sunny. Large blue tents had been arranged in a circle, and under their canopies Mami and I found tables covered with boxes of paperwork, needles, and vials. The volunteers, mostly women, all of them bilingual, greeted us with cheery smiles, and I tried to convince myself that this was a good thing, though by then I was in college and had met people whose parents had jobs with health insurance.

My mother glided into one tent and stepped onto a scale for her weight. Then she rolled up her sleeve. She detested needles and looked toward the cut grass while the technician wound the band around Mami's arm and tapped for a vein. I watched, fascinated and horrified, as the needle prodded her skin softly, and my mother's blood gushed into the vial.

We moved to another tent, where volunteers handed us plastic bags of healthy swag: low-fat cheese, low-sodium crackers, and shimmering red apples. Under a third canopy, a volunteer lectured on healthy cooking, and Mami settled into a folding chair, plunged her cracker into a startlingly good dip, and watched the volunteer slice cucumbers. The woman spoke of the virtues of salads. Mami marveled at the woman's swift hands, her ease with the enormous knife. Ellas son expertas, she murmured to me.

I agreed. The woman was indeed an expert with the knife

and on healthy eating, and as the mound of cucumber slices grew, I counted the years. In another decade, my mother would qualify for Medicare. We were lucky. Her citizenship in this country qualified her for Medicare.

The memory of the lizard face and the health fairs came rushing back to me in 2016 when I was interviewing a woman named Janet. She had tested positive for Chagas, a parasitic disease that can lead to cardiac complications and even kill an infected person, and when I asked if she had health insurance, I expected Janet to say no. Her husband worked in construction, and she took care of their kids. But I did not expect her to talk about time. I don't have the five years, she told me in Spanish.

Five years? I asked, confused.

Yes, I don't have the five years, she repeated.

We spoke in circles until she said, I don't have five years in this country, and at that point, I realized she had a green card but did not qualify for Medicaid because the 1996 federal welfare law, the Personal Responsibility and Work Opportunity Reconciliation Act, permitted states to deny legal permanent residents access to Medicaid until they had lived in the United States for five years. Before the passage of this law, a person with a green card could see a doctor using Medicaid, regardless of when they had arrived in the country. Karen Tumlin and Michael E. Fix, lawyers then at the Urban Institute, noted, "The law marks the first time in modern history that Congress has explicitly authorized states to discriminate against *legal* immigrants in the administration of their public benefit programs."

Congress was able to do this because it did not look racist. On paper, it looked like the new law was about citizenship. Only citizens, Congress members argued, should have a right to Medicaid and public housing and food stamps. But in 1996 everyone knew who the noncitizens were. Journalists and scholars and politicians were preoccupied with what they called the Latino "invasion" of the country, writes the anthropologist Leo R. Chavez. These men wrote op-eds and magazine articles. They authored books with blunt titles like *Alien Nation* and *Americans No More.* They ran photographs in their magazines of children who looked like me: children with black hair, wide smiles, and faces that grew dark if they stayed out in the sun.

The other political preoccupation was welfare. The Republican attacks on the welfare system had been rampant for two decades. Blaming welfare was one way to explain, in the early 1990s, why fourteen million people had full-time jobs but still lived below the official poverty line, and it had reached the point where Democrats also agreed that they did not want to use taxpayer dollars to support single mothers and their children. Congress members wanted the women to work out in the world away from their children.

The 1996 welfare law barred children, including toddlers, with legal residency from seeing a pediatrician with Medicaid dollars during their first five years in the country, unless the state wanted to fund such care with its own monies. Some states scrambled to do that, and in 2009, Congress allowed states to use Medicaid and the Children's Health Insurance Program to cover the medical care of children who were "lawfully present"—usually children who had legal residency but had not yet lived in the country for five years.

The Migration Policy Institute reported that in 2019 almost a million children nationwide could not get Medicaid because of restrictions on citizenship. More than half of them were Latinx.

In 1994, when Republicans won control of both houses of Congress, they liked what they saw that election year on the West Coast. California voters had approved Proposition 187, a ballot measure that would bar hospitals from providing nonemergency medical care to undocumented immigrants and would require public school teachers to turn over to la migra any child they suspected did not have documentation to live in the United States. While the courts eventually struck down the law, congressional Republicans started talking in new ways about immigrants. About all immigrants. The ones with papers and the ones without.

The historian Dorothee Schneider examined the congressional debates and proposals and reports about the 1996 anti-immigrant laws, and she found Republicans insisting that the United States only wanted immigrants who would work hard and never get sick and never need anything from their community, let alone the federal government. A good future citizen, Congress members posited, did not bring siblings and aunties to this country. They had only a nuclear family, and they took care of that family. They paid taxes and even ran their own businesses. They never needed Medicaid. They never broke an arm or felt a hard lump in their breast, and if they did—if they woke up with a terrible cough for two weeks straight—they paid for it out of their own earnings.

The Congress members were not talking about the undocumented. They were talking about those with legal residency, those who had been approved to live and work and raise families in the United States. By 1996, an immigrant with a green card was no longer someone on their way to becoming a citizen. They were no longer a "citizen in waiting." Researching health disparities and social policy, the physician Shantanu Agrawal reviewed congressional committee reports on welfare reform and learned that Republicans, during the 1990s, started referring to an immigrant with legal residency as a "noncitizen," and sometimes an "alien." Republicans equated those who did not have citizenship with those who had committed crimes. As if to underscore this point, the welfare reform bill that House Republicans passed in 1996 had a section titled "No More Welfare for Noncitizens and Felons."

What this meant—at least at the level of language, of the way people began talking and the way they are still talking now—was that citizenship changed. No longer did the United States have people with green cards and people without such documents and people with citizenship. Now the United States recognized only citizens and noncitizens.

One of my friends frowned when I told her about the five-year Medicaid ban for immigrants with legal residency who arrived in the United States after 1996. She was a journalist and well schooled in American politics. How did I never hear of this? she asked, then stopped. We both knew why. What happens to people without citizenship rarely makes the news, and neither of us had close family members with green cards who needed Medicaid.

At home, my sweetie frowned when I told them about the five-year ban. But people can get care at hospitals . . . they said, their voice trailing, a new doubt emerging.

By law, emergency rooms have to take patients, regardless of their citizenship status, when they are in a life-threatening situation, but what constitutes a threat to life has been debated since the 1996 welfare reform law passed. Is cancer and the need for chemotherapy an emergency? If the illness is labeled as chronic, then it's not an emergency, and hospitals are obliged to wait until you are on the brink of death to provide care in the ER. If you have kidney failure, you usually need dialysis several times a week, but if you do not have Medicaid, then the disease is not considered to be life-threatening at hospitals until the toxins accumulate in your body and your lungs fill with fluid and the only way to stabilize you—to save your life—is with emergency dialysis. In a 2018 study, researchers looked at the experiences of immigrants in San Francisco, where they had access to standard dialysis treatment paid with local government funds, and hospitals in Denver and Houston, where, at the time, only emergency dialysis was provided to immigrants banned from receiving Medicaid. The researchers found that people were fourteen times more likely to die from end-stage kidney disease when they had to rely on emergency dialysis.

Since each state can decide whether to provide healthcare to people without the right papers, the simple fact of your home address can dictate whether you live or die and how you spend your last days. In 2019, if your kidneys were failing and you did not have citizenship, people in your community paid for your care through state Medicaid dollars if you lived in Arizona or North Carolina or Virginia. Funds in these states made it so you could get kidney dialysis regardless of your citizenship status. In Texas, you might receive treatment if you lived in Dallas County, where a safety net hospital relied on a nonprofit to buy medical coverage for those without citizenship who had end-stage kidney disease.

The most common medical situation covered by Medicaid in emergency rooms across the country has nothing to do with kidneys or malignant cells in the body. It has to do with babies. In 2023, four in every ten births in the United States were paid for by Medicaid.

The more that I read about the 1996 welfare law, the more I thought about time, about how at the end of the twentieth century, President Clinton and elected officials serving in Congress reinvented citizenship, linking legal permanent residency to a person's ability to see a doctor. I found myself wondering how we did it *before.* I was not thinking about the 1980s or even the twentieth century. I thought about the years my social studies textbooks had focused on when I was in elementary school. I thought about 1776, when the Declaration of Independence was signed and the colonizing colonies began to create their identities as states and then as a federal government. When the notion of American citizenship was itself still new, how did we take care of those who fell sick and could not afford care?

This is what the documents suggest: By 1783, Phebe Perkins had stopped dreading the winters. She was twenty-three years old, and for years the cold months in Rhode Island had been a jab at the back of her neck. It had meant the harvest was over and, like other New England workers, she would need to find another farm where she could earn a living. It was not an easy task. The economy had soured in the wake of the Revolutionary War, and many poor people were on the move, all of them looking for work.

This year was different for Phebe. She had spent the last two winters working on a wealthy man's farm in Richmond, Rhode Island, and when December arrived, she got to stay. No, she couldn't afford to get her shoes fixed, and maybe she dreamt of a future where she could buy a new pair, but at least she did not have to leave and that was good. Maybe she boiled the tallow that winter, sculpting the wax into fat candles so the man of the house could read the Bible. Maybe she mended skirts and squinted at the field where she would pick greens and strawberries the coming summer. Maybe she felt lucky. She worked for the president of the town council. Everyone knew the man. Maybe she felt trapped.

In the new year, the white men of the Confederation Congress gathered in Maryland to approve the treaty ending the war with Great Britain, and some months later, Phebe's belly swelled. She might have felt the pregnancy in her nipples first. They were sore and flinched at the cotton of her work shirt. Or the full moon hovered in the sky, and she did not need a rag between her legs. Or she knew when the sex was over.

The white men who ran the town of Richmond panicked when they glimpsed Phebe's belly. She was unmarried. Who would take care of her when the baby came? And what if she became ill? If the fevers pooled in her armpits, her neck, between her legs? Who would take care of her then?

If you were poor and sick in New England in the 1700s, it was expected that your hometown would look after you. Your hometown was the place where you were born, though depending on the colony, a white man could also buy his way into a hometown by purchasing property or marrying a local property owner. Your hometown considered you a native, and everyone else a foreigner, which meant that in the eighteenth century, a woman born in Boston could be a foreigner in the Bronx.

Americans did not take care of foreigners in those years. They were not callous, just English. The new country had inherited English laws that required people to look after those who had a settlement, or property, in town. In her book *Unwelcome Americans: Living on the Margin in Early New England,* the historian Ruth Wallis Herndon writes, "Such legislation grew naturally from the official ideal of a static society rooted in the land: where community ties overlapped with kinship ties, and where everyone *had* a place and *knew* that place." Her book traces the plight of Phebe and other poor adults and children in Rhode Island during the second half of the eighteenth century.

As they do today, officials deported foreigners in the 1700s, except it was called "warning out." Sometimes a town official delivered a letter warning you to get out of town. If you didn't leave, a constable hauled you to your hometown, dumping you at the door of the constable there. Often, Herndon writes, the "warning out" came in December, when the harvest had ended and farmworkers were no longer needed.

At the beginning of this country, then, a woman's access to healthcare was tied to the place where she was born, and even that fact could be debated.

In Richmond, Rhode Island, town officials decided that Phebe—poor, unmarried, and pregnant—was a foreigner. She was born in Newport, about twenty-five miles away. That town should take responsibility for her and any medical care she might need. But Newport officials refused to receive her.

Richmond officials pressed on and tried the town of Hopkinton, where Phebe had been a bound apprentice for years. By then October had arrived. The baby was due soon. Would the good people of Hopkinton take in the poor, pregnant woman?

The men of Hopkinton met, and maybe they quarreled, but they concluded that, yes, they would step up. They paid a local family to board Phebe because this was before Section 8 housing, before CHIP, before TANF, before Aid to Families with Dependent Children. A family provided Phebe with a bed and were paid from the town's poor relief fund. They also spent money to repair her shoes.

The birth was difficult—awful, actually. Phebe must have been running a fever. The doctor came to the house with his surgical knife. He leaned the blade's edge to her skin, perhaps her forearm, and watched the blood pour from her body. He believed, as most physicians did in those years, that bloodletting—a practice called "breathing a vein"—could cure a person of illness.

Phebe spent the next three months bedbound, and the

baby? Her baby? The baby was lost. Or at least any documentation of the little one was. The records fall silent, though in 1784 it was not uncommon for newborns to die.

The people of Hopkinton had £22 in their treasury for poor relief. They spent £8 on Phebe, and I would like to imagine that when the white men met in January 1785, one of them stood in his sturdy shoes and reminded the others that they could surely come up with another £8 for their coffers. Not all had been lost. A woman's life had been saved. That was worth £8, was it not?

But when the Hopkinton men met to review the situation, they decided that they should not have taken care of Phebe. They sued the town of Richmond for what had been spent on her care, and the story ends there, as Herndon writes, because the records did not survive.

Phebe probably returned to the fields the next summer, plucking strawberries and eating her grief, while in New York, north of the Bronx, town officials in Eastchester decided they did not want to provide care for a local man who was blind. They declared that they did not have to do so. The man was a foreigner. He came from Rhode Island.

How does a government deport a man who cannot see the road?

In the heat of that summer in 1785, Eastchester constables accompanied the blind man, John Skyrme, five miles to Pelham, New York. There they placed him in the hands of another constable, who took him to New Rochelle. It went on this way for almost two hundred miles: one eighteenth-century police officer passing the man on to the next, most likely along the Long Island Sound, walking through oak forests and the cries of plovers and oystercatchers, pushing onward through Connecticut and into Rhode Island, until, twenty-one days later, the man who could not see the road was delivered to the town of Providence.

The next summer, in 1786, Charles Adams took his family to Walpole, a town some fifteen miles south of Boston. Perhaps he needed to leave behind a bitter memory. Or he wanted to start over and had heard there was work logging cedar trees in that town. Perhaps he had spent many days in Walpole, watching his children carefree and picking dandelions.

What did his children think when their father fell ill? When the future collapsed? When their mother surely told them to come along and hold their silence?

The town of Walpole paid the local doctor to examine Charles. It had become that serious. Maybe there was bloodletting. Or maybe the doctor refused to touch the Black father. Surely there was prayer. Nothing helped. A month later, Charles died, and the town paid for his burial.

Charles was born in Boston, in the area called Roxbury, a neighborhood that by the 1940s would become the center of the city's Black community. Born into slavery, Charles had fought in the war against the British and become a freeman. A number of Black men earned their freedom this way. They gambled on the American Revolution and won, at least on paper. But in Walpole, Charles was a foreigner. The local white men agreed on that. They had cared for him and buried him, and now they wanted their money back.

The town officials should have gone to Boston, but they did not. As the legal historian Kunal Parker recounts, the Walpole men turned to the state of Massachusetts, which covered the costs of foreigners who grew ill or died and had to be buried. Usually, such people were from Ireland or New Hampshire. Now the Walpole men declared that Charles was also a foreigner, and the state agreed, using its funds to pay for the cost of his medical care and burial.

Other towns in Massachusetts did the same, requesting to be reimbursed by the state for taking care of Black people who were poor, who were ill, who were too old to work. Local officials left out references to slavery and wrote in their petitions that the poor person hailed from Africa or Guinea, as if the person had freely chosen to leave their homeland for the crushing winters of New England. In fact, scholars estimate that by the start of the American Revolution, two-thirds of Black adults in New England had been born in the colonies.

Town officials conflated race with place to such a degree that a decade later, in 1795, Boston officials did not bother with references to the continent of Africa. In their records, they noted that the Black person in question was a foreigner who had been born in a place called Negro. On paper, Blackness became a country, a homeland, a point of foreign origin. Sometimes town officials contended the foreigner came not from a country called Negro but from one named Molato.

A pregnant woman, a blind man, a sick father. When Phebe, John, and Charles needed medical care and were penniless, their fellow Americans classified them as foreigners, as not-from-here, as noncitizens. Early American citizenship was contingent on a body that made no demands on the state, on the neighbors elected to local offices, which is to say that early American citizenship was contingent on a body that made no demands on white men and their money.

Texas was the only state in the country in 1970 that required a person to have citizenship before they could access Medicaid and talk to a nurse. Then again, the federal healthcare program, created in 1965, was still a new endeavor. Also new at the time was the world brought into being by the Civil Rights Movement and the backlash against it. Several white men in power, aware of the growing resentment among whites, spun stories conflating Black communities with the welfare state. It turned out to be profitable in political terms for men like Richard Nixon and Ronald Reagan to complain about the costs of welfare.

New York governor Nelson Rockefeller grumbled privately that Puerto Ricans and Black people from the South were not integrated into the state's economy. Such people lacked a "legacy of self-support," he told a deputy secretary at the time, ignoring how racism made finding a job or renting an apartment in New York and everywhere else so difficult, if not impossible, for Afro Puerto Ricans and African Americans. In 1971, when Rockefeller signed a bill into law requiring people to live in the state for a year before they qualified for Medicaid, he was not thinking about undocumented immigrant families. He wanted to prevent Puerto

Ricans and African Americans, all of them citizens, from using state money to see a doctor.

When I read Susan Sontag's words on illness—"Everyone who is born holds dual citizenship, in the kingdom of the well and in the kingdom of the sick"—I thought that some of us are not citizens but hostages. Some of us are being kept, against our will, in the kingdom of the sick.

At the federal level during those years, Nixon moved to slash the welfare state. He replaced the head of the Department of Health, Education, and Welfare (now the Department of Health and Human Services) with Caspar Weinberger. A Harvard Law graduate, Weinberger would go on to serve as Ronald Reagan's defense secretary and oversee what *The New York Times* in 2006 called the "biggest and costliest military buildup in peacetime history." As defense secretary, Weinberger would request billions of dollars every year to arm the country against the Soviet Union, and year after year, he would usually receive the money. In 1992, he would face felony charges for lying to Congress and obstructing justice in connection with the Reagan administration's covert sale of weapons to Iran to fund Nicaraguan rebels who were attacking their country's leftist government. Weinberger would avoid his trial with a pardon from President George H. W. Bush.

In 1973, however, none of that had happened. Nixon had just ended the war against Vietnam, and he occupied his days by denying Congress access to the recordings that would eventually reveal his involvement in the Watergate scandal and lead to his resignation. Weinberger and his team spent that year reviewing whether states could use federal Medicaid money for undocumented immigrants. The answer, they decided, was no. The sociologist Cybelle Fox observes, "The Nixon era, in fact, marks the moment when the boundaries of social citizenship—the line separating those with a right to social assistance from those without that right—were being redrawn. . . . Welfare became limited by the terms under which an individual entered the nation."

That summer in 1973—when the terms under which people entered the United States began to dictate if they could see a doctor—the Southern Poverty Law Center sued the Department of Health, Education, and Welfare for funding government programs that sterilized more than a hundred thousand poor women, many of them Black, Latina, and Indigenous, without their consent, for decades. The Alabama women at the heart of the lawsuit, which ended the department's funding of sterilization, were not women. They were two Black girls: fourteen-year-old Minnie Lee Relf and her twelve-year-old sister, Mary Alice. On paper, the girls were citizens. They had a right to healthcare and to become women and decide if they wanted a pregnancy. They had a right to welfare too. They had "entered the nation" through birth. They had been born here on this land. But it would also be accurate to say that Blackness constituted the terms under which they had entered the nation. A doctor whose work had been funded by the federal government sterilized both girls.

In 2020, almost fifty years after the lawsuit to end the sterilization of women of color, Karina Cisneros Preciado gave birth in Georgia. The entire country then was full of birdsong. The skies had quieted during the pandemic. The streets too. Fewer people drove to work or boarded airplanes.

The birds clustered in trees and on rooftops in Georgia as surely as they did everywhere else, and in the absence of car engines, their chirps and trills paraded through the towns.

At twenty-one, Karina was not alone with her baby girl and the songs of the warblers. The father of her newborn hovered nearby, and one day he punched Karina in the face. Everyone broke that year, and so did Karina. She called the police. They needed to take her abuser away. They needed to make the beatings stop. They would see her eyelid, blue and black, her newborn at her breast, and they would take care of her. How could anyone expect her to nurse like this, with her body a map of broken blood vessels?

The police did not care about the newborn. They arrested Karina and turned her over to Immigration and Customs Enforcement. She had entered the United States at the age of eight and did not have papeles, not the kind this U.S. government wanted.

No one spoke, at least not publicly at the time, about another set of missing papers. The federal agency tasked with contracting medical providers for detained immigrants had no written policy requiring doctors and nurses to seek a woman's consent before touching her body. Karina was in the custody of the Irwin County Detention Center in Ocilla, Georgia, when a gynecologist inserted a transducer between her legs for a vaginal ultrasound. He reported that she had an ovarian cyst. The condition typically resolves on its own, but this doctor told Karina she would get an injection, and that if the cyst remained, he would surgically remove it.

The class-action lawsuit that followed charged the federal government with carrying out unnecessary medical procedures on more than forty immigrant women. The Senate subcommittee investigating the allegations concluded that the accused doctor had been "too aggressive." Its report numbered more than a hundred pages.

None of this would have been documented had it not been for the whistleblower, Dawn Wooten, a Black nurse at the facility. After reporting the abuses, she found herself jobless. Other clinics apparently did not want to hire a woman who would speak up, and two years later, she told *The Guardian:* "I'm back on food stamps, I'm back on welfare, I'm back on Medicaid, I'm back trying to figure out how I'm going to make ends meet."

The following can sound like a pernicious riddle:

In 2024, if you were low income, you qualified for Medicaid or CHIP, regardless of your citizenship status, but only in California and Oregon. In New York, you had to be younger than nineteen. In Connecticut, you could not have celebrated your fifteenth birthday. In most states, if you were undocumented, you could not qualify for nonemergency Medicaid at any age. This included toddlers. In the first months of 2025, if you were a child but had lived in the country for less than five years, you were denied Medicaid or CHIP in eleven states, including Arizona and Tennessee.

If you were sixty-five or older, and also low income, in 2023, you could qualify for Medicaid regardless of your citizenship in Illinois, but only if you were one of the first 16,500 seniors to enroll. Low-income New Yorkers, sixty-five and older, got the right to access Medicaid in early 2024. In most states, it did not matter if you had turned eighty and didn't have the money to see a doctor for an injury or a persistent cough. Without citizenship or a green card plus those five years of residency, you did not qualify for Medicaid.

In all of these cases, you had to be what government administrators call "low income"—a designation that varied from one state to another. In New York, if you were a parent with a family of three in 2023, you could earn around $34,000 a year and qualify for Medicaid. In Texas, in 2019, you could not earn more than $3,626 a year.

My mother. She came to the United States in the early 1970s from Colombia. If she were arriving here today without papeles, the state where she landed would govern if she got to see a doctor for prenatal care. In New Jersey, she could earn less than $580.50 a week and qualify for state-funded prenatal care. In Iowa, if she was lucky enough to be in Iowa City, a community clinic would see her during the first twenty weeks of pregnancy. Then the clinic would try to enroll her in Medicaid, and the state would pay for prenatal care for about two months, until administrators figured out that Mami did not qualify because of her citizenship status. At that point, she would toddle back to the community clinic. Only when I was ready to burst into the world would Medicaid pay for my birth and my mother's care.

Since the Supreme Court's *Dobbs* decision in 2022, more Americans have become aware of what undocumented and poor people have known for decades: The state you call home determines if you can see a doctor and also if you can get insulin shots, prenatal care, or dialysis. The states completely banning abortion, including Texas, Louisiana, and Alabama, are the same ones where women are more likely to not have health insurance. The states refusing to expand Medicaid under the Affordable Care Act are clustered in the South, where more than 50 percent of Black people live. Texas and Florida combined have the highest number of Latinx in the country (a staggering 17.5 million people), and they have declined to expand Medicaid even to those with citizenship. These two states also now require hospital staff to ask about the citizenship status of every person who comes into the emergency room. This includes children.

In 2024, every state in the country had the option to offer prenatal care to women and pregnant people regardless of citizenship status. The states did not even have to wait for the birth. They could monitor the health of mothers during pregnancy because the federal government gave them the right to extend the Children's Health Insurance Program and treat a fetus as if it were a "targeted low-income child." Twenty-two states chose to do this.

It could be said that we are now, each and every one of us, citizens of a state more than citizens of a single country.

Not so long ago, a friend was surprised to learn that a woman we both knew who ran her own business had Obamacare. How did you think she had health insurance? I asked.

I never thought about it, my friend admitted.

Sometimes I wonder if one mark of social citizenship is a person's relationship to healthcare. If you have never thought about how you are going to pay for a doctor's visit, you have a certain kind of citizenship. To rephrase Sontag, you are in the kingdom of those doing well. If you have spent a lifetime paying out of pocket to see a cardiologist, or if you have relied on a man in a suit to tell you whether or not you can end your pregnancy, then you have another kind of citizenship, one by which you know the value others place on your life.

Before I knew anything about Terezita's citizenship, I knew her hands. Her marvelous white hands. They were always manicured, sometimes a bit plump, frequently lotioned and perfumed. Always confident and gesturing. I loved her hands.

Terezita had married my father's cousin. Or she was my father's cousin. The distinction didn't matter. In Jersey in the 1980s, everyone from Cuba was someone's cousin. I frankly thought that Terezita was too beautiful to be related to us. She was too white, too Spaniard. She belonged to a telenovela set in colonial times. I pictured her covered in a lace mantilla, her hair arranged in careful curls. But she also made sense in Jersey, where she wore cotton blouses and slacks the color of plums and ran a hair salon in her house.

The salon consisted of a tall chair in front of a large mirror, the air tinged with the floral chemical scent of hairspray. I climbed into the chair at the age of nine, grinning and intoxicated with nervous energy, and before I knew it, Terezita's hands draped a black cape around me and plucked my black hair out of the terrible ponytail holder. Tanto pelo, she boomed, her fingers stroking my hair, then my scalp. I didn't know why it was good that I had so much hair, but I understood that Terezita looked at my head with the same zeal that my mother, a seamstress, expressed when examining a roll of fabric, and in much the same way that my mother's hands changed when she reached for her scissors, once my hair was shampooed, Terezita's hands turned into those of a magical beast. One of her hands combed while the other measured the ends against the comb and snipped away half an inch, then a quarter, the blades grazing the back of my shoulders, the blades a song in my ears, her hands gliding through the black curtain of my hair, sending shivers into the palms of my hands.

Decades later, after Terezita retired to South Florida, we battled over the Affordable Care Act. I was in my thirties and she in her seventies. I was old enough to drink her Cuban coffee and to ask about her children and grandchildren. I was old enough to have opinions when we sank into her plush sofa. Terezita glanced toward the television set with the media pundits and their talk about healthcare, and she shook her still-gorgeous face and said in Spanish, with a certain bitterness, It's socialism.

My mother nodded politely.

What is? I asked, the cup of coffee teetering in my hands.

All of this, Terezita said, waving toward the television, toward the White House, toward President Barack Obama. They're going to ruin everything, she added sadly.

I tried to reason with her. I spoke about the necessity of taking care of people when they are sick. About the fact that Medicaid works. She said people abused the system. I hesitated, then I brought up her granddaughter who had moved to Texas. Terezita thought I was changing the subject and began chatting happily. Like me, her granddaughter had the sheer luck of being born in the United States. She was also now awaiting her first child.

She works at a hotel, I said. Does her job give her health insurance?

Insurance? Terezita scoffed. No.

I smiled. When it's time for her to have the baby, how will she pay the hospital? I asked.

Terezita paused, and I pressed on, saying, She'll probably be using Medicaid. It pays for a lot of women when they're having babies.

Terezita frowned, and my mother's eyebrows, the ones she now crafted every morning with burgundy eyeliner, rose in alarm. Mami had taught me that Medicaid and citizenship were private matters. We were never to speak publicly about such issues, not even with our cousins. But I wanted our cousin to know that the very policies she hated were the ones her granddaughter needed. The people in need of healthcare were not other people over there in other communities but right here in our own family. We already had government-sponsored healthcare for pregnant women, and it had not turned the United States into a socialist country. I wanted our cousin to know that the social citizenship we had, however fragile, could bear the weight of caring for the bodies of people we loved and the people we had yet to meet.

This was not the first time I had argued with a family member over social citizenship. The first time might have been in 1994, when I was a college sophomore and California voters were debating Proposition 187. In our family kitchen, Tía Dora told me that the initiative made sense. The one that would ban undocumented children from public schools. The one that would ban undocumented women from seeing a nurse. My auntie sighed. Es que son demasiado los que han llegado, she said.

She was thin and pretty, a younger version of Terezita, a woman who could be placed in a telenovela not as the protagonist but as her sister. A quiet, respectable woman. A woman who wore fake-silk blouses. A woman who had grown up with very little in Colombia and could now shop at Macy's.

My auntie's words rushed over me like ice water. They are too many. That's what she said. The ones who were arriving in this country were too many. She said nothing of her own arrival, nothing of her own papers, the ones I would retrieve from the federal government after she died, the papers saying the federal government had ordered her deportation. All I knew in 1994 was that Tía Dora had married a man with papers. She had done her naturalization interview that year and passed. She had raised her hand and sworn her allegiance. She was a new citizen, and if we had lived in California, she would have voted to stop a woman like the one she had been, a woman sin papeles, from seeing a doctor.

What did I say to my auntie? My memory stumbles here. Maybe I screamed. Maybe I stammered, They have a right to be here! What I did not tell her was that when I read about Proposition 187, I thought about the one-room public library in town where I worked. I thought of the children streaming into the library, bookbags dangling from their shoulders, their mouths politely asking if the new action movie video was available to rent. They spoke English, Spanish, Italian, Arabic, and other languages. Proposition 187 would have asked their teachers and maybe me as a city employee to turn over to immigration any child I thought might not have the right papers. I thought too of myself in kindergarten learning a nursery rhyme in English that was first recorded in German, and somehow I was sure that the teacher back then would have looked at me and suspected me of not having papers and turned me over to la migra, to INS, as it was called back then. I felt incredibly American but not exactly a citizen.

By the time I talked with Terezita about Medicaid, I had long been mourning this truth: I had grown up with people who could vote in hateful ways. I did not come from the families that Kamala Harris and Michelle Obama described at the Democratic National Convention in 2024. I did not come from a lineage of women who flung the doors open to abused children. I came from women who were scared and stubborn, who had convinced themselves that they could not trust anything soft in this world. What they could trust was a hard jawline, a slap to the face, and laws that punished anyone who went astray. Terezita was not the only family member who would vote against her own granddaughter to keep intact her story about the evils of socialism.

What I did not know in 1994—what none of us knew—was that Stephen Miller came of age in California during those bitter battles over immigration and Proposition 187. Twenty-one years later, during the first Trump administration, Miller devised the family separation program that took nursing newborns from their immigrant mothers at the southern border, and he pushed for banning Muslim immigrants from the United States.

What I also did not know in 1994—what no one could

have predicted—was that a ballot initiative viciously attacking immigrants transformed California. Almost two million people registered to vote in the state between 1994 and 2004, and close to 90 percent of these new voters were Latinx and Asian American. In the three decades since 1994, the number of Latinx elected officials in the state has tripled, and the number of Asian Americans and Pacific Islanders serving in the legislature has catapulted from one to more than a dozen. In 2022, California's governor signed a budget offering state-funded Medicaid regardless of citizenship status.

This does not mean that California will repeat itself on a national scale. The 2024 presidential election results clarified this point, with 43 percent of Latinx voting for Trump. What mattered in California after Proposition 187 was not the racial or ethnic designations of the voters but how they organized. The stories they wrote, the stories they told—these changed how people thought and felt and the policies that eventually came to shape people's lives.

THE WHITE MAN WHO LOVED ME

What is Person 1's name?

THE WHITE MAN. I never called him that, but when I read the political theorist Cristina Beltrán's book *Cruelty as Citizenship,* I paused on a section about the white men. Many of them were war veterans, divorced and alone, patrolling the bodies of immigrants on the U.S.-Mexico border. I thought immediately of the white man who loved me. He was not divorced but he was a veteran, and even in his marriage, he spent most of his time alone, and he wanted whiteness and all the delights that came with it—the job, the mortgage, the checking account, the lift of a waitress's chin toward him. The historian David Roediger, building on the work of W.E.B. Du Bois, called these privileges "wages of whiteness." The man who loved me, the white man, wanted to get paid in more than dollars.

He took the DNA test for me. Because he loved me. Because I ordered the test. Because I asked him to do it. I made it sound like a game. Vamos a ver de donde vienes, I said to him, as if he had been a gift delivered to me, and he agreed because he trusted me and never thought I would do anything to wound him. He had already forgiven me for the awful things I had said years earlier. He still loved me.

When the test kits arrived, we opened them on the deck at my sister's home in Maryland under a gray sky. I tugged at the tape on the box, then pulled out the tubes and the papers and read the directions twice. Vamos a ver de donde vienes, I said again, feeling almost giddy. I took the first test to show him how to do it. Puckering my lips, I said, It's all about the saliva.

He smiled at me, then opened his mouth and spit into his tube with gusto.

I sent the kits to the lab with a certain assurance that I was right about the white man who loved me. He was not *white* white. His birth in the Caribbean would surely reveal a strong genetic lineage to West Africa. I even imagined that he might be a quarter or more Black, and so I expected that when the DNA results arrived, I would have the evidence with which to mock him. That is what I wanted. The white man who loved me was a racist, and I wanted to humiliate him with science.

His DNA results came directly to me via email, and I stared at the screen in a silent, dull rage. The white man who loved me was white not only in his imagination and ambitions but also on paper. More than 86 percent of his ancestors came from Europe.

He had insisted on his whiteness from the start of our relationship. The first time he took me down the shore, he navigated the car out of Union City, New Jersey, and onto a highway that delivered us an hour later to Sandy Hook Beach. We had a bag jammed with juice, biscuit cookies, and Cuban bread. Under my T-shirt and shorts, I sported a one-piece bathing suit, a lurid pink affair. The white man who loved me was forty by then. Already balding, he was lithe in fitted swim shorts. He never wore sunglasses, so he squinted at the sunlight streaming into the car.

At the beach, he observed families arranging their towels

on the sand, swinging open the coolers, splashing one another in the low tide. He spotted an African American family. And another. And another. He stiffened. He gripped the car keys. He snarled that we could not stay.

I cannot say if I cried, if I startled, if I protested. I was a toddler, and the white man who loved me, my father, declared that we had to leave and we had to leave now. It did not matter that my mother had packed lunch. That her sister wanted to stay. We had to go, and that is what we did. Back in the car, we returned to Union City, which by the late 1970s had become a white Havana. The pediatricians were white Cubans and also the accountants and the bankers and the dentists. Even the funeral home had been purchased by a white Cuban.

Three years later, Mami knew better than to ask about a trip to the shore. When summer arrived, she plopped me in a plastic inflatable pool in front of the apartment building she and my father owned. A wrought-iron fence enclosed the narrow area, and behind me, in lieu of sand dunes, an opaque basement window rose from the ground. My mother filled the pool with water from the hose and invited my best friends, two sisters with pink beads and barrettes in their hair. There was enough room for the three of us to sit side by side in the plastic pool and stretch out our legs.

Maybe Mami told my father. Maybe she stayed silent. He worked long hours and was rarely home during the day. What was the use in telling him? Or she told him because he knew the girls. They were Cuban. They were from our block. I often played with them. Maybe he thought of the girls as Cuban, not Black. Or he didn't care that I spent time with them because they were Black girls, not boys.

I never called my father a white man, and I also never called him a refugee or an asylum seeker or a political exile. When I first heard those labels for immigrants, they belonged to English, not Spanish, and they sounded strange, like words from a third language. Also, when I read about Cuban exiles in newsmagazines, I did not see my father. I found instead wealthy white men from Havana, men who had other men work for them, men who had housekeepers and houses with more than one bathroom. But my father had been broke in Cuba. He had grown up on a farm without running water. He couldn't be in exile.

In Spanish, exilio sounded like the name of a country, of a place you could love. It implied that my father, the white man, had made a choice. He could have stayed in Cuba, near the town of Fomento in the center of the island, tucked away among lush green mountains, but instead he woke up one day before dawn, strolled into the sugarcane fields, and considered his options. It had been two years since the revolution threw the U.S.-backed dictator out of power. Every week about a thousand people were leaving the island. He heard the news. The men in town whispered that those who had fought against Castro's men, men like him, would soon be disappeared, even shot. He stared hard at the sky, the sun a golden orb coming over the hills. He decided to leave for the country of Exilio.

But this is not what happened. That white man, a man who chooses his destiny, is not how my father spoke of himself. He never narrated his contemplations. Of fighting against Castro's army, he only got drunk enough to tell me,

It isn't easy to switch sides once a war has begun. Of fleeing Communist Cuba, he said, I came the same week that the American embassy left. He made it sound as if he had been an employee of the State Department. He had not.

In 1961, in the early days of January, the United States and Cuba did indeed break off diplomatic ties. After my father's departure, the curtain fell on the island. No one could leave without the permission of Castro's government. It was not my father but his uncle who told me that after my father fled for Havana, then Miami, then the Bronx, some men arrived with pistols at the family home in the mountains. They wanted to know where they could find my father. His uncle shrugged and said, He's gone north.

On paper, Papi was not in exile. The Cuban Adjustment Act of 1966 only named refugees, which carries none of the romantic connotations of the political exile. As a child, when I heard about refugees, I thought of a person who was broke, who had to leave, who had no choice, who had to run in the middle of the night, who didn't have a home to which they could return, who would be a guest in whatever country offered to receive them. Exiles were welcomed; refugees: persecuted, unwanted. Everyone liked an exile, a person who had stood up for their political convictions. An exile was frequently a man, not a woman.

My father, as far as I know, never called himself an exile or a refugee. He referred to himself with only one word: Cubano.

The Cuban Adjustment Act of 1966 made it so that any Cuban who had arrived in the United States after January 1,

1959, and lived in this country for at least two years could apply for lawful permanent residency. In 1980, the residency requirement dropped to one year. On paper, Cubans had a way to become citizens of the United States.

On paper, the process for becoming a citizen is naturalization, which suggests that citizenship itself is a natural state of being and that a person is naturally a citizen of a place. This is an extension of the old idea that a person was, by nature, the subject of a monarch and that the monarch had been endowed by God with absolute power and that was natural. The term naturalization also springs from the notion that a person's birthplace determines their citizenship and that birth itself is the most natural of events. All of this suggests that when we speak of citizenship, of becoming citizens, we are in a way also talking about women's bodies, about reproductive rights, about every person being the child of a woman.

No one in my family ever used the word naturalization. Of my father, my mother said, Le salió la ciudadanía. He got his citizenship. I didn't quite hear it the way she intended. The verb salir could mean so many different stories. Sometimes it signaled that you were going to the supermarket. Other times that a bit of gossip had escaped from your mouth or that your friend took after her father or that everything had worked out at the doctor's office. In English, I had to pick a verb: leaving, slipping, emerging, resolving. In English, I had to say, She takes after her father, while in Spanish, it was simply Salió como el papá. When my mother said, Le salió la cuidadanía, I pictured papers pouring from my father's mouth.

The notion of naturalization has even confused people who were born in the United States and have spoken English all of their lives. This came to light most vividly when the Census Bureau asked about citizenship in 1980 on the long form mailed to a small number of households. Asked if they were naturalized citizens, 22 percent of people born in the United States said yes.

The Census Bureau staff wondered what had gone wrong with the citizenship question. Here it is worth noting that probably no other group of federal employees has contemplated the intricacies of the English language more than those who work for the Census Bureau. It took time, but the staff learned what had created confusion. The agency had begun mailing the long forms in 1980. In the past, enumerators would have knocked on doors and asked the questions and clarified that to be naturalized meant you had been a citizen of another country and petitioned to become a citizen of this country. The Census Bureau spent the 1980s—that decade of MTV, Reebok sneakers, and the AIDS epidemic—testing the wording of questions about citizenship. Finally, the staff came to the conclusion that the most productive way to ask was to not make distinctions: "Is this person a citizen of the United States?"

The 1970 census would have been the first one to count my father, and it was also the first one to ask a sample of people, about 5 percent, if they were Latino, except this term was not used and neither was Hispanic. The long form queried, "Is this person's origin or descent—" and Cuban was the third option after Mexican and Puerto Rican.

I have every reason to believe that on the short form my father was counted as a white man that year, and not only because he himself would have chosen it. In 1970, 93 percent of Latinx were categorized as white.

Four years later, Papi became a citizen. His certificate of naturalization does not specify his race or origin, only that he had brown hair and brown eyes and that his complexion was "medium."

The United States Constitution does not talk about counting citizens. Nor does it mention enumerating white Christians or married women over the age of twenty. For the purposes of taxing and settling how many seats a state will hold in the House of Representatives, article 1 of the Constitution says that the country will count "Persons," of which there are two types: "free Persons" and "all other Persons." The latter referred to enslaved Black people who would not be recognized as a "whole Number" but instead as "three fifths." From the beginning of this country's formation, then, the voting powers of white citizens have been tied to the dismemberment of Black people, to counting in pieces the bodies of Black people.

The federal government did not follow the Constitution's direction. In 1790, it tallied three groups: slaves, free white people, and all other persons. The last category included free Black people and also Indigenous people who lived among whites and were taxed. It did not ask any person about the place where their mother had given birth to them.

The counting of Americans is found in the sixth sentence of the Constitution. This mandate, writes the law professor

Justin Levitt, "precedes the power to coin and collect and borrow money; it precedes the responsibility to establish defense forces and to declare and wage war; it precedes the conduct of foreign relations and the establishment of a judiciary." As of 2024, the federal government used census data to decide where and how it would spend more than a trillion dollars for programs like Medicare, Section 8 housing, and food stamps. Private companies used the data to determine where they would build new homes and whether they would advertise in a community. Since the data reveals whether states have lost or gained residents, it determines the number of seats each state receives in Congress and ultimately the number of votes a state has in the Electoral College. Based on the 2020 census, Texas gained two votes in the Electoral College, while New York, California, and Illinois, among others, each lost a vote.

The Census Bureau began tracking citizenship in 1820. Over the next 150 years, the question was removed, then added again, then removed again. In 1970, when the agency would have counted my father for the first time, it shifted the citizenship question to the long form, and that is where it stayed without contention until Trump was elected president in 2016.

What is Person 1's sex?

Our family photo albums are parades of faces I have never met: an old friend of my mother's, a cousin of my father's, a neighbor from Cuba or Colombia. Recently I started writing names on the backs of photographs and in the margins of the albums when my mother or auntie remembered them, but mostly I have accepted that our family albums document the contours of migration, the geographies of joy, and the legacies of the American empire in the Caribbean and South America. Many names I will never know.

One day, sitting at the kitchen table thumbing through a family album, I spotted a sepia-toned photograph of a young white man in military uniform. His black tie had been knotted without precision, and a cap fitted over his shorn hair. The white man had a thin mustache. A European of some kind, I concluded. Maybe an Argentine whose parents had been Italian immigrants. He was handsome, the white man. I wondered how my parents or aunties knew him.

Who's this? I asked, holding up the photograph.

Mami sipped her hot tea, her eyes locked on the television set featuring that night's episode of *Primer Impacto.* She glanced at the photo. Your father, she said.

I stared at the photograph, confused. Papi? This is Papi?

Who else is it going to be? she asked, exasperated, as if our photo albums were not an archive of strangers.

I examined the photograph again. The shape of the eyes now struck me as a little familiar. The fullness of the eyebrows too. But that's as far as I could go. The picture was that of a white man, yes, but I could not see in it the white man who loved me. The man in the photograph was in his twenties, maybe even eighteen. He looked young and bright, as if he had just been given the uniform, as if he had landed his first big job, as if he had spent his entire boyhood dreaming of this moment. He stared at someone standing to the side of the camera, a cousin, maybe, or a girl he fancied.

It took me years to realize that I did not recognize my father in the photograph because he looked happy, genuinely happy. He was not yet a man who had fired a gun, who had fled a country, who had spent decades abusing alcohol.

Because of my father's gender, the United States government sent him a letter three days after Christmas in 1962. On paper, he was living in the Bronx with his cousins. In truth, he was washing dishes at a Manhattan hotel in exchange for room and board. The letter dictated that he was to show up in the new year at the Army Building on Whitehall Street in Manhattan. Government officials mailed him a token so he could take the subway. He would have no reason for missing the appointment. He was expected at seven in the morning.

The Americans were drafting my father to Vietnam, where the United States government already had what it called eleven thousand "military advisers." While the Kennedys celebrated Christmas in Florida that year, the Marines airlifted shrimp, ham, and turkey to U.S. soldiers at three rural outposts in Vietnam. My father was to join these men. On paper, he looked like a good candidate for military service. He was twenty-five, unmarried, and healthy. He was a white man who had been in the country for about two years.

In January 1963, my father turned up at the Army Building in downtown Manhattan, his hair carefully combed, his face clean, his stomach probably clenched. Would the U.S. Army be different? What uniform would he wear? What firearms would he carry? Should he heed the warnings of the Puerto Rican men from work? The ones who counseled him against going to Vietnam?

Nothing went as he expected. They said I didn't have to go, he told me when I found his draft papers in 2024. Why not? I queried. He pulled the cigar from his mouth and replied, They said I'd already been in a war.

I have no doubt that this is what the military official at the Army Building told my father: You already served. Thank you for your service. Thank you for helping us to battle communism in Cuba. I am certain that he said these words to my father because this is how men take care of one another. They embrace the soldier, the warrior. You have served—this is what you tell a man who has been through war. You do not tell him what is on paper. You do not tell him that he is a refugee who doesn't speak English. You do not tell him that 1962 was the year with the lowest number of men drafted to Vietnam for the entirety of that decade.

Print name of Person 2.
How is this person related to Person 1?

At the age of twenty-five, I returned to New Jersey from my first trip to Cuba, and I ran to the yard to tell my father everything: how I spent almost every day outdoors in Havana and also in his hometown of Fomento, how the trucks doubled as public buses in the countryside, how I rode a horse for the first time and how dollars were illegal but one of my cousins introduced me to Havana's black market by sneaking me into apartment buildings for haircuts and homemade ice cream. I met the grandfather who abandoned my father as a child, and I spent hours with the uncle who raised him. My father had not been to the island in more than twenty years. I had so much to share.

It was still early in the summer that year. I found my father in a beach chair near the apple tree, smoking a cigar. I'm here! I cried. Look what I brought! I unwrapped the packet in my hands to show him a bundle of cigars his cousin had sent. He took the contraband, sniffed one, and then stared at me in a fury. I did not think anything of this. My father in those years often moved through his days with a bitter face. Maybe he was angry about the factories that had closed or the new job he had landed as a janitor or the smallness of his paychecks or the vast quantities of beer that did not blunt his anxieties. I was about to begin the story of all I had seen in Cuba when my father growled, Mandé una hija blanca a Cuba y regreso una negra.

The words smacked my ears. I did not have to examine my forearms, which, like my cheeks and nose and chin and calves and feet, were the darkest they had ever been, because in Cuba for three weeks, without my mother and tías beseeching me to wear a hat or duck under an umbrella, I had walked and sat and stood in the Caribbean sun for hours. My father's words ricocheted through me: I sent a white daughter to Cuba and a Black one came back.

That is how I heard his words, though years later I wondered if he had said the N-word instead of Black. In Spanish, the meaning of negra depends on tone and context. It depends on who is speaking and to whom and under what circumstances and if the mouth of the speaker brims with love or hate or indifference. Negra can be a statement and also an epithet and an endearment.

It was the first and only time that my father talked to me about the color of my skin. My aunties, my mother's sisters, were the ones who monitored my body in racial terms. They said I had been born so negrita they had bathed me with milk. They said I needed to be careful in the sun. They said my full lips were the kind men preferred. They said I shouldn't act like an Indian, which was apparently the worst thing a girl could do in Colombia.

And they said my father was wrong about Black people. They said he was a racist because he had grown up in the campo, because he had never finished elementary school, because he did not know any better. They told me to ignore my father's racism, to act as if it did not matter, and that is what I did that day in the yard when he told me I had come back from Cuba negra. I treated his racism as if it were a fact about him like his strong teeth or his balding head—a story I could not rewrite. I don't remember now what I said that day. I may have ignored him and continued my story of Cuba, as if he had never spoken. I may have snapped, Negra y bella. I did not do what I wish I had done, which was to start a conversation, to ask, Why are you angry? Why are you afraid to have a daughter with dark skin?

Here I want to list my father's virtues. I tell myself I want to be sure readers know him fully, not only his racism, but this is not true. I want, even now, to protect him. I want my father to be a better man on paper than he was in life. He was the first white man who loved me, and he was also the first white man I loved.

Thomas Hofeller was a white man. And a father and a war veteran. He sang tenor at the National Cathedral in Washington, D.C., and he probably arrived on time for practice, a briefcase in hand, his tie tucked into a pocket of his trousers. He nodded to the other singers. Maybe he joked with them.

Surely they spoke of holidays, birthdays, and family gatherings. Then it was time.

Taking his place among the other singers, Thomas opened the choir book. One beat, and the silence descended, heavenly and anticipatory. The pipe organ quivered. He closed his eyes perhaps, the music rising over him, his voice joining the others rising toward the stained glass windows, the vaulted ceilings, the seven-foot statue of George Washington, their voices, all together now, celebrating the god venerated in this temple of marble and glass, bronze and linden wood.

Thomas spent his days not singing but revising maps. I never spoke to him, but I imagine that like me he loved No. 2 pencils and reams of paper, that he appreciated how a blank sheet could serve as a canvas. He kept a large eraser near him as he drew his maps. The border could be here. The border could be there. He examined demographic data, then returned to the map and moved the border again. One day, he ordered large sheets of paper, pinned them to the wall, and plotted the new maps with Magic Markers.

His work began in the 1970s with maps of California. He was not a cartographer. He was a man who had studied political science and saw that maps were fictions akin to citizenship. A map was a story. A map of a congressional district was most decidedly a story, and a story could be edited, even deleted. Thomas drew new maps, new stories, new futures. If the borders of a district were here, not there, the results of the next election could change like this. Or like that.

The maps Thomas drew would alter whether the federal government funneled money to schools or the Pentagon. In the 1980s, he joined a Republican team that privately spoke with Black politicians in the South, encouraging them to battle in court for creating maps with majority-Black districts. The result was a map in which Black voters, who usually elect Democrats, were confined to a few spots in the South, enabling the GOP to dominate elections there. The journalist David Daley, who wrote the go-to book on Republican gerrymandering, refers to Thomas Hofeller as the man who "invented modern redistricting."

Thomas appreciated the power of paper. During his PowerPoint presentations on redistricting strategies, he urged Republicans to conduct their business by phone and schooled them about technology. "Emails are the tool of the devil," he cautioned. While such communication might feel informal, it was still a story, and a story could outlast a man. "The 'e' in email is for 'eternal,'" he warned.

He gave these presentations and he sang tenor and he drew political maps favoring Republicans, and then he drove home to his wife and probably wondered more than once where he had gone wrong with his daughter, Stephanie. Or he did not wonder. He blamed her. Blamed her for ditching college after a semester, for waiting tables, for stripping in clubs. He surely blamed Stephanie for vandalizing campaign signs for the 2004 reelection of George W. Bush, and maybe he shook his head when she declared herself an anarchist. Maybe he was too busy to know that she had moved to West Virginia, at the age of thirty-one, with her husband to live off the land.

In 2012, Thomas angled his car along the country lanes of West Virginia. Stephanie had spent the night in a shelter for abused women with her one-year-old son. The bruises on her face showed, but she could hide her chest, the tender places where her husband had burned her with a skillet. Nothing had been able to protect her. Not her father's money. Not her mother, the psychologist who authored two books on intimate partner violence. Here Stephanie was, forty-three years old, her body disfigured, her baby boy in her arms.

What happened next is the familiar narrative of intimate partner violence: Stephanie returned to her husband, Peter Lizon. She refused to testify against him. She protested that he did not beat her. Her parents received custody of her son. A year later, she gave birth to another child, a girl this time, but Child Protective Services took the newborn. Thomas returned to West Virginia. He had spent almost five decades fighting for Republican control of Congress ostensibly to create a government that would have a very limited role in the private lives of citizens, and then, faced with his daughter's life, he found himself very much wanting the state to intervene. He turned his grandson over to the foster care system. Stephanie later told reporters that she never saw either of her children again. She lost custody. She left her husband, who married another woman, one he burned and dragged down the road from his van, a crime for which he faced charges of "malicious wounding."

Stephanie did not speak to her father again. When he died in 2018, at the age of seventy-five, the *New York Times* obituary said nothing of his grandchildren in foster care, celebrating him instead as "the Michelangelo of the modern gerrymander," but Stephanie wondered if anything of her life had survived the man. Her mother permitted her to check their North Carolina home. Among her father's possessions,

Stephanie found four hard drives and eighteen thumb drives. She plugged the drives into her computer and saw more than seventy thousand files, including photographs of her children and a music recording of herself. She glanced at the documents. They were her father's work files, nothing more.

The files turned out to be a story about the maps.

The story began in 2015, when legal conservatives started to contend that the Constitution did not require the federal government to count every person who lived in the United States, only citizens of voting age. If this reading was embraced, it would change a great deal about American political life, including the distribution of seats in the House of Representatives. *The Washington Free Beacon,* a conservative news outlet, considered funding these lawyers, so they hired Thomas. He could show them how the legislative maps would change if Republicans adopted this interpretation of the Constitution, and what kind of legal arguments could be made.

Thomas set to work on Texas. The state had a population of almost 30 million, and Latinx were on the verge of outnumbering whites there. About 1.6 million of the state's residents, mostly from Latin America, did not have citizenship. What would happen to the political map of Texas if only citizens of voting age were considered when drawing legislative districts? Thomas concluded that it "would be advantageous to Republicans and non-Hispanic whites."

There was only one problem with pursing this legal strategy. The data on citizenship did not officially exist because the census did not ask everyone if they were citizens. The question had last appeared on the long form of the 2000 census, which was sent to only one in six households. To change the maps, the question had to be added to the census for everyone. The legal argument could not be that the Justice Department wanted to boost Republican votes by excluding Latinx residents, so Thomas asserted that having this data would help the federal government with enforcing parts of the Voting Rights Act. It was an argument similar to the one he had pitched to Black leaders in the South during the 1980s.

When Donald Trump won the 2016 election, Thomas contacted his friends in the new administration working on the census. While his study on Texas was never published, his friends used part of his legal argument, word for word at times, in a letter the Trump administration sent to the Department of Justice, whose officials would request having the citizenship question added to the next census. Multiple states and cities sued to block the federal government from changing the census in this way, but no one had any evidence of the racism motivating the administration until Stephanie turned her father's files over to a group of lawyers in North Carolina.

The feminist author Susan Griffin wrote, "I do not see my life as separate from history. In my mind my family secrets mingle with the secrets of statesmen and bombers."

Somewhere in the United States, in West Virginia perhaps, the grandchildren of the Michelangelo of modern gerrymandering learned to count to ten. They grasped the mechanics of adding and subtracting. They studied maps.

Surely, they studied maps. They spent months or perhaps years as wards of the state. Taxpayers, not Thomas, paid for the milk the children drank and the beds where they slept. If his grandson and granddaughter were lucky, and many are not, they stayed together in the foster care system and were adopted by the same family. One day, if they look for their origins, they will learn that their mother made it possible for the country to know that the first Trump administration tried adding the citizenship question to the 2020 census to limit the political power of Latinx communities.

The Supreme Court ruled in 2019 that the Trump administration had not come up with a good reason to add the citizenship question, and the census proceeded without it. On the same day, the court ruled that federal courts could not hear challenges to maps redrawn for political purposes. Democrats would have to pursue gerrymandering more aggressively across the United States or continue losing statehouses and congressional seats to Republicans.

My father and I never spoke about the citizenship question on the census, but when I was still a teenager, still living in his home, I already suspected that we would never be voting for the same presidential candidate. He only voted Republican. Cross-legged on my bed, a journal in hand, the first time Bill Clinton was on the ballot, I asked the white man who loved me, Why do you vote Republican?

He smiled and said, They have money.

But you don't have money.

He looked at me as if I were naïve and said, That's why you want to be with the people who do have money.

Is this person of Hispanic, Latino, or Spanish origin?

The Census Bureau first recorded my existence in 1980, which was also the first year it asked all Americans if they were Hispanic.

At the time, we were living in New Jersey, in Union City, where almost 64 percent of the people were Latinx, the vast majority of them white Cubans, and the Census Bureau was not alone in demanding to know about origins. My father had taken it upon himself to query me on these subjects despite the fact that I was only five. Actually, if the family stories are true, he had begun the questions when I started to speak as a toddler.

In our living room, a sheath of hard plastic covered the red armchair, where my father settled in after work, cracked open a can of beer, and pulled me into a not-yet-drunken hug. He kissed the top of my head and asked me about my origins: Eres Cubana, Colombiana, o Americana?

My mother smiled. Her sister laughed. They shook their heads. What a silly question to ask when the answer was obvious, when the answer was on paper.

Are you Cuban, Colombian, or American? I glanced at my mother. She may have been the one who whispered the answer to me the first time. By the time the census form arrived with its questions about origins and race, age and marital status, I already knew the answer to my father's question. When he asked who I was, I squealed, Americana! except that the polysyllabic word proved to be too much for me at that age. Each time my father asked me to choose an origin, a race, a nationality, I answered with two syllables: Me-cana.

I came to love that truncated word. Me-cana. I knew it

only indicated that I had been too young to pronounce a word composed of five syllables, but I interpreted it as a sign that even at that age I was refusing both the census and the white man who loved me.

The census did tally the number of Latinx before 1980. The first year for such a count would have been 1850, since the war between the United States and Mexico had ended, turning thousands of Mexican citizens into Americans. The 1850 census, however, categorized people as Black, mulatto, or white, and so enumerators had to stitch Mexicans to one of these labels. The phrase "country of birth" did not clarify the situation either. Some Mexicans said their birthplace was Mexico because that's what the land had been called on the day they were born, while others held that it was the United States of America because in 1850 that was the name for the land. It is still unclear where the Mexicans-made-Americans ended up on the census.

By 1920, the federal government was trying more desperately to hold on to the story that the United States was a white country, white like the English or the Scottish. Congress passed legislation in 1924 placing quotas on migration from eastern and southern European countries, which it deemed to be not white enough. The law did not halt migration from Mexico—a situation some Census Bureau staffers did not appreciate. They contended that the increase in immigrants from Mexico necessitated a counting.

To date, the 1930 census is the only time the agency has ever counted a nationality from Latin America (it had been tallying the Chinese in California since 1860), but the agency was not focused on people who had been born in Mexico. Representative James Slayden of Texas spoke about the situation years earlier, in 1921, writing that in his state "the word Mexican is used to indicate the race, not a citizen or subject of the country." It did not matter if the person or their bisabuela had been born in Texas. They were still Mexican. Slayden added that it was "just as all blacks are Negroes though they may have five generations of American ancestors."

The Census Bureau still had to give instructions to the men who traveled door to door counting people. On paper, the agency began by noting that "practically all Mexican laborers are of a racial mixture difficult to classify." The agency outlined two tasks: First, inquire if the person was born in Mexico or if their parents were. Next, determine if the person is "definitely not white, Negro, Indian, Chinese or Japanese." If the person did not fit into one of those five racial categories, then on the form they "should be returned as Mexican."

The census takers imagined Mexicans as "laborers," and as a series of *nots*—not white, not Black, not Indian, not Chinese, not Japanese, not a person who practiced medicine, not a person who reviewed books, not a person who created abstract paintings.

Over the next decade, during the 1930s, cities and counties and states deported more than a million Mexicans and Mexican Americans under the pretext that they were being repatriated to their country of origin, and some government agencies tried to classify Mexican Americans as "colored," noting that categorizing Mexican Americans as white affected the numbers. Take El Paso. On paper, the city during those years had a very high infant mortality rate among white babies, but it was Mexican babies, labeled as white, who were dying. "The segregation [of data] would give El Paso a lower infant mortality rate," the city's health officer, Dr. T. J. McCamant, wrote. He apparently only wanted this to be clear: White babies in El Paso were alive and well. It was the Mexican newborns who were sickly, who were dying, who were throwing off the numbers.

Mexican American community leaders at the time were like my father. They wanted to be considered as white as the founding fathers. They were cowards or they wanted to stay alive or both. Close to six hundred Mexican Americans had been lynched between 1848 and 1928 in Texas, California, and the Southwest, and that was probably an undercount. There was no Civil Rights Movement yet. There was no Brown Power. Not yet. The Immigration Act of 1924 dictated that if a person could not become a citizen, they could not enter the United States. As long as Mexicans stayed white on paper, they qualified for migration and a second-rate citizenship.

It was not only community leaders who wanted Mexican Americans to be white on paper. The White House did too. Franklin D. Roosevelt's administration was intent on protecting U.S. investments in Mexico, as well as its Good Neighbor image, and so it stuck to diplomacy, pushing for the Nationality Act of 1940 to include that "descendants of races indigenous to the Western Hemisphere" could become citizens. No one offered an explanation of who qualified as Indigenous in this case, but it was generally understood that the White House was speaking of Mexicans and also of Indigenous peoples, particularly those from Canada. In 1940, the Census Bureau told enumerators, who were tasked with deciding the race of every person in the country, that Mexicans were white "unless definitely of Indian or other nonwhite race."

The Census Bureau, though, did not give up on tallying the number of Mexicans in the United States. In 1950, working with a list of almost eight thousand Spanish surnames la migra had compiled, the agency's staff began calculating how many Mexicans lived in the Southwest, California, Colorado, and Texas by noting how often these surnames appeared on census forms. In 1970, the agency expanded the list by consulting phone books from Mexico City, San Juan, and Havana. If a last name appeared more than twenty-five times in a city's phone book, the Census Bureau added the name to its list.

My father's last name appears on the list. So does my mother's maiden name.

In the census of 1970, the agency asked a sample of Americans about their Hispanic origins. Question 13b offered a choice of answers, including Mexican, Cuban, and Central or South American.

The results did not give an accurate estimate of the number of Latinx in the United States. People thought they were "Central American" because they lived in Ohio or Indiana—the central part of the country—and some of those making their home in Texas thought they were "South American," given the state's location on the map of the United States.

The Civil Rights Movement changed the counting of Americans. The strategy was simple: Numbers could illustrate racist policies. With numbers, it was possible to point out when a neighborhood full of Black families was also the one to not have a grocery store. Or when a small city that was mostly home to Black families had only one bus line. Or when banks were closing branches in these neighborhoods, or when the state or federal government had sent limited funds to schools in these communities. "Numbers once used to legitimate relations of domination were leveraged to expose those very relations," writes the sociologist Michael Rodríguez-Muñiz in his book *Figures of the Future: Latino Civil Rights and the Politics of Demographic Change.*

To make these political claims possible, however, the numbers had to exist.

The Census Bureau admitted that its 1970 count missed around five million people and that these people were living in poor cities, which meant they were more likely to be African Americans, Mexicans, and Puerto Ricans. Decades later, in 2019, when the Trump administration pursued the idea of adding the citizenship question to the census, community advocates and lawyers and elected officials objected because such a question would lead immigrants and even their U.S.-born relatives to avoid the census. In that whirlwind of panic and fury, I myself forgot that numbers require narratives. Politicians can use data to call for closing the border as easily as they can use it to support funding a majority-Latinx school in Denver. Numbers did not make the Civil Rights Movement. The movement made of the numbers a story, a way of looking at what was happening and demanding change.

Cubans, like my father, almost did not become Hispanic.

When Latinx community leaders in the 1960s spoke of the hardships their students faced in graduating from high school, they were not speaking of Cubans. They were referring to Chicanx teenagers with Indigenous faces in San Antonio and Boricua teenagers with Afros in the Bronx. None of them were talking about my father in Jersey or my cousins in South Florida.

Yes, my father never finished elementary school in Cuba, but in a town of white Cubans in Jersey, he still qualified for a mortgage to buy an apartment building. When he was ready to sell that property, he bought a little house in a white community farther north without a problem since the neighbors thought he was Italian. The house had no basement and the living room only fit one armchair, and it might have been the least expensive house in our town, but that was not the point. He was welcomed into a community of white people descended from the English, the Irish, and the Germans, and so was I.

My father only became Hispanic in the 1970s because of President Nixon, but not in the way many people suspect. As the sociologist G. Cristina Mora chronicles in her book *Making Hispanics,* when Nixon moved into the White House in 1969, he inherited a committee tasked with advising the federal government on Mexican Americans. Puerto Rican leaders demanded to be included, and the two groups had a great deal in common. Both communities lived in cities and faced poverty. Their people wanted bilingual education. Their people needed job training and food assistance. Though they were separated by many miles—Mexican Americans largely in the Southwest at the time, and Puerto Ricans in the Northeast—they shared a biography.

The committee was renamed the Cabinet Committee on Opportunities for Spanish Speaking People, and when Nixon formed an advisory group for it in 1971, he and his staff added two Cuban Americans. Perhaps Nixon and his people thought: The Cubans speak Spanish. It's a committee for people who speak Spanish. Or perhaps Nixon wanted to work more closely with Cubans. He and an aide would soon hire three Cuban Americans, including a locksmith, to break into the Watergate office building.

Cuban Americans, though, did not share a biography with Mexican Americans and Puerto Ricans. Yes, they arrived in Miami during the 1960s to find rental houses with signs reading "No children, no dogs, no Cubans," but by 1985 the city had its first Cuban-born mayor. A white man, he was a Harvard graduate; his father, an engineer. With the exception of three years, the city has only had Cuban American mayors since then. The more powerful position—mayor of Miami-Dade County—was held by white Cuban Americans for almost a quarter of a century, until 2020.

The Nixon and Ford administrations, along with Mexican American, Puerto Rican, and Cuban community leaders, settled on the label of Hispanic as the least problematic of the many options. Latin American, they decided, sounded too foreign, while Latino invoked the idea of Latin. Spanish speaking would be strange for Mexican Americans whose families had been in the United States for more than a hundred years and did not speak the language. Hispanic it was, then.

What is this person's race?

The handsome boy visited me the summer I turned fifteen. A friend of a friend, a Dominican, he had short, tight curls and a lovely smile. Because it was warm outside, because our house had no formal living room, because I was embarrassed to bring him inside, where he would see how cramped our lives were, I invited him to sit at the picnic table in the front yard. The sky made everything appear more grand and possible. Also, the yard had a tree. It was a solitary affair, that tree, but I liked its soft bark, its quiet demeanor.

My mother turned into a bird when the handsome boy arrived, flitting nervously around the two of us. She looked at me as if she had a question, but when I stared at her blankly, she asked the handsome boy if he wanted something to drink. A soda or a juice. I scowled. She had never cared if my ex-boyfriend wanted a soda, and now here she was, acting the part of the anxious hostess. She scurried into the kitchen, and I wondered vaguely why she liked this boy so much, why she was trying to impress him.

The handsome boy and I talked. My mother brought the sodas. She remembered something in the kitchen: The rice needed to be started, the frijoles pulled from their overnight soaking. Again, she glanced at me as if I might now reveal an answer, then left. My sister, only ten, pranced out to meet the handsome boy. He was kind to her. I smiled at him and wondered what we would discuss when we ran out of things to say. The handsome boy and I didn't go to the same school.

My father worked nights at a textile factory a few blocks away. He usually left in the late afternoon and returned home the next day near dawn. He would not meet the handsome boy, because he never came home while he worked, not even for a meal. It would not have mattered if my father had been home, though. He had never said anything to my ex-boyfriend or to me. He was not the kind of Cuban father who spoke about purity, about saving yourself for marriage, about marrying up or marrying white or marrying anyone. He never spoke to me about love.

The handsome boy and I sat opposite each other at the picnic table, and he was speaking when I noticed over his shoulder my father at the gate to our front yard. My mouth filled with questions, but before I could ask anything, my father reached us at the picnic table and turned into a violent storm, screaming at the handsome boy to leave, to get off his property, to never come back, and when he called the handsome boy negro in Spanish, I knew the translation to English was the N-word.

The law professor Tanya Katerí Hernández observes: "When it comes to Latino racism, the family is the scene of the crime." I want to say that I defended the handsome boy, that I yelled at my father, that I called him a racist, that perhaps this was the day I bruised my father, the day I screamed at him in our front yard, I want you to die! The day you die I'm going to throw a party! That's how happy I'm going to be the day you die! But my memory falls silent here. Maybe I spoke up. Maybe I collapsed into complicity. I know the handsome boy ran out of the yard and my mother stayed in the kitchen. I know my father hollered at her that if she ever let this happen again, if she ever permitted a Black man to come near me or my sister again, that he would leave her, he would throw her out, he would divorce her, except he said all of this in Spanish and I remember it in English.

What I wanted to tell my father at the time was that he had made a mistake. The handsome boy was Dominican, not African American. I genuinely thought this distinction mattered, that my father's cruelty toward Black people was bound to the place where the child had been born and the language the child spoke. I thought of the handsome boy as Latinx, not Black, the same way that at the time I considered my father to be Latinx, not white.

My mother had given me those conspiratorial looks because she did know that the color of a child's arms and the texture of a child's hair affected how people treated them. She knew the handsome boy was Black first, Dominican second. She knew I was breaking a rule, and she thought I knew it too, but I did not. I was a child of the 1980s, of Black and white America, and in that binary racial landscape, I clung to a multiracial Latinx identity as if it were the land beneath my feet.

Later, on the phone, the handsome boy, his voice trembling, said, How could your father think that I'm Black? I'm Dominican.

The handsome boy told me that of everything my father had screamed at him that day, what hurt him the most was the accusation of Blackness.

On the census, Latino is not a race because in the 1970s no one wanted it to be.

Community leaders—Mexican, Puerto Rican, and

Cuban—hoped to keep access to the white category on the census form. They wanted better data but not the risk of being classified as Black or Indigenous. The Census Bureau, meanwhile, was thinking about white people who were not Latinx. One official told G. Cristina Mora that the agency worried about how a Hispanic race category would change "white data over time." If more than fourteen million Latinx stopped being white on the 1980 census, the agency would have had to figure out other ways of counting the whites who had graduated from high school over the last fifty years. It would have had to do this for a great deal of data.

The Census Bureau was concerned about newspaper headlines too. When it tested Hispanic as a race category in Arizona in 1975, the number of people reporting that they were white or Indian fell. It was possible that if Hispanic were a race category, an Afro–Puerto Rican woman in New Jersey might only report that she was Hispanic, not Black, driving down the numbers of Black people in the United States. In 1980, the director of the Census Bureau met with African American leaders about the new Hispanic category largely to assure them that Black Americans "would remain the nation's largest minority group." It was not a promise the agency could keep. At least not on paper. Twenty years later, the 2000 census reported that Hispanics outnumbered African Americans.

Since the 1970s, then, the Census Bureau has been tasked with both counting Latinx and not counting us. The agency insists that we can be of any race, but it produces demographic reports as if we are, in fact, a single racial group. This is why it is possible today to easily find the rates of Latinx homeownership and also how many Latinx live in North Dakota, but not the rates of Black Latinx homeownership or how many Indigenous Latinx are graduating from high school. In 2021, researchers, using datasets of newborns from the Centers for Disease Control and Prevention, found that Afro-Latinx newborns were more likely than white Latinx babies to be born underweight and were also more likely to die. The researchers warned that "a significant racial disparity is masked and not taken into account in setting healthcare priorities."

Even if the Census Bureau had never produced a single report on Latinx, it might still be understandable why some of us are confused. In 1980, when Hispanic debuted on the census, there were eight categories for Asian Americans, including Japanese, Vietnamese, and Filipino. The oldest race category on the census besides Black and white is Chinese because, as two Harvard political scientists observed, "nationality was consistently racialized in the case of Asians." It is possible to understand that a Latina might look at the Asian category and wonder: How are the Japanese a race but not the Guatemalans? Or the Cubans?

If the handsome boy and I had filled out the 1990 census together, he might have picked white. I have no idea how the handsome boy would have labeled me. I was old enough that year and in charge of everything in our family that had to do with paper, so I did act the role of a census enumerator and filled out the form for my family. My mother maintained that my father was white, as were she and my younger sister. I think we decided to not count my one auntie who lived with us because she was using an address in a different county for her food stamps and SSI, and everyone knew that even if the government said it would not use the census to persecute people, anything you put on paper could come back to punch you in the face.

My father would have counted me as white in the 1990 census, but I picked "other race." At the time, I had no idea that the Census Bureau was using a technique called hot-decking, whereby people, like me, who marked "other race" were reclassified by how our family members and neighbors identified. On paper, we had to be Black, Asian, Indigenous, or white. On paper, I became white by association with my parents. The same happened to about ten million people that year, most of whom also reported that they were Hispanic. It happened again in 2000. For anyone who wrote in Arab or Middle Eastern, association did not matter. The census counted all Middle Eastern people as white.

In the 2020 census, I joined the second-largest population group in the United States, officially called "some other race." More than 90 percent of the people in this category were Latinx, but what caught my attention was the demographic data on white Latinx. In 1970, when the Census Bureau did not offer a Hispanic option, more than 90 percent of us were identified as white. A decade later, in 1980, when everyone was permitted to choose their race, the number of white Latinx dropped dramatically, to 57 percent. In 2020, the bottom fell out: Only 17 percent of Latinx reported being white. In fifty years, more than 70 percent of white Latinx vanished.

One study from the 1990s might explain these vanishing white Latinx. Researchers surveyed more than five thousand young people and their immigrant parents in Southern California and South Florida. When asked about their race, Haitian children picked the same category as their parents. So did Jamaicans. But not so with Latinx children and their parents. While many Latin American immigrant parents reported themselves to be white, few of their children did. The sociologist Rubén Rumbaut noted the irony that "the children of Latin American immigrants, historically 'white by law,' should learn to become 'nonwhite' in the post–Civil Rights Era." Some of the widest racial mismatches occurred for children whose parents were Cuban or Colombian.

People presume that my parents look like me. The first time I showed a photograph of my mother to a co-worker, the woman gasped and cried, She's güera! I inspected the picture. My Chicana co-worker had just called my mother a white girl, and I wanted to say, No, she dyed her hair a light shade of auburn, but I stayed silent because I was trying to see my mother as my co-worker had, and also because I was thinking about the flip side to my co-worker's comment: You're not white.

No one had ever been so blunt with me before about how they saw my family. Then again, no one had ever told me that I looked like my mother or my father or my aunties or my sister, and I had never thought that strange, because I knew other Latinx families whose members did not resemble one another. I thought it was normal.

There are, of course, other reasons for the intergenerational racial mismatches among Latinx families in the United States. I grew up with a light-skinned Latina who could have been read as a white American, except that she could not be that, because white girls were the ones at school who mocked us for our culture and language. Television shows, newsmagazines, and teachers told us in implicit and explicit ways that anyone who was an immigrant and spoke Spanish was not white. Not white like American white. It would be reasonable to describe this as ethnic discrimination—bias about your ancestry, the language you speak, the cultural practices your parents teach you—but in the United States few people speak like that. Your origins here are about race. Yes, the Irish became white, and so did the Italians and the Germans, but not the Puerto Ricans or the Mexicans or the Egyptians or the Lebanese. Not as a group of people. And what does Latinx mean in this context? It refers to what the Census Bureau said in 1930 about Mexicans: We are a series of *not*s, as in "definitely" not white, not Black, not Asian, not Indigenous.

In high school, my friend's refusal of whiteness did not bother me; now it does. I worry about how the disparities among us are unreported and unexamined when it comes to health and education. I worry that we praise companies for equity when they only hire Latinx with light complexions and blue eyes. I worry that a college can now boast about being a "Hispanic-serving institution" when it does not recruit Black and Indigenous Latinx students, staff, or faculty. The literary scholar Christina León, describing her experience of race, observed: "I'm most often read as a woman of color in the academy, not in Target, not in stores, not on the streets."

Still, the first time I learned the Census Bureau might make Latino a race category, I was flooded with joy. There is no other word for it, and this startled me. I had no idea that I cared about the census. I had spent a short lifetime debating the race categories every ten years and also every time I filled out a new HR form, but I had learned to accept this situation. I had learned to be absent to myself, to never be able to choose "Latina" on institutional forms, and so my own joy surprised me. Here for the first time someone was saying that the way I had been describing myself since I was a teenager would now be on paper. It would start with the Census Bureau, but then it would be used across the federal government and state agencies and at colleges and at doctors' offices.

The Census Bureau had actually been working to add Latino as a race category since 2008 because it wanted to get people like me to stop saying that we were "some other race." The agency tested more than a million households to see how they reacted to a combined question that merged the existing categories of race and ethnicity so that "Hispanic, Latino, or Spanish" showed up alongside Black, white, Asian, and American Indian. This 2015 National Content Test was, according to an agency official, "the largest ethnicity-and-race content test we ever conducted at the Census Bureau." Of course, it could not have been a surprise to anyone that when Latinx saw a Latino category, it lowered the number of people who picked "some other race."

The most revealing part of the test was not on the test. Unlike in 1980, national Latinx community leaders this time wanted Latino as a race category. They didn't need access to the category of whiteness anymore, and in 2022 they teamed up with more than a hundred organizations, including the American Civil Liberties Union, the Muslim American Society, and the National Council of Churches, in drafting a letter to the Office of Management and Budget, the agency that decides which race categories the federal government recognizes. In the letter, they asked the government to approve the combined question for Latinos and also for Middle Eastern and North African people.

My joy about Latino-as-a-race faltered when I thought of that awful afternoon in the yard with the handsome teenager and my father. I thought the handsome boy was Latinx, and my father said he was Black, and maybe the handsome boy thought of himself as white. It was possible that my father and the handsome boy had spent decades picking the same categories on the census: white and Hispanic.

The problem might not be which race Latinx pick or how large the "some other race" category has become. The problem might be that the census is using one question about race to ask about two very different situations: how you see yourself and how others see you. The sociologist Nancy López has suggested that the federal government add a second question to the census focused on how others perceive race because "you can't capture two analytically distinct concepts with one question." In this scenario, the race section of the census might ask both "What is Person 1's race?" and "What race would others assign to Person 1?"

In a 2004 survey of four hundred Dominican immigrants in New York and Rhode Island, less than 7 percent identified as Black. When they were asked, "How do you think most Americans classify you racially?" nearly 37 percent said they were seen as Black. This means that if the census asked about both the race you consider yourself to be and the race others consider you to be, it would find that this one group of Dominicans was simultaneously 7 percent and 37 percent Black.

The two questions might also turn up more Latinx. One study found that 7 in 10 people who trace their origins to Latin America believe people who see them on the street would describe them as Latinx.

The poet Langston Hughes was familiar with this predicament. In 1919, when he was a teenager, clerks in a San Antonio train station mistook him for a Mexican. Jim Crow laws barred Black people from the whites-only bathrooms and the whites-only sections of the trains in Texas, but they were available to Mexicans. Langston spoke Spanish, and without calling himself Mexican, he ordered himself a sleeping car. No one asked if he was Mexican. No one had to. What else would a man with his color be? Upon reaching a St. Louis train station, doubts emerged. When Langston ordered an ice cream soda, the clerk asked, "Are you a Mexican or Negro?" He could serve Langston Hughes ice cream if he was Mexican but not if he was Black. Langston said, "Colored," and the man turned away.

In early 2023, when the Office of Management and Budget asked for public comment on making Latino a race category, a coalition of more than thirty-five organizations, largely Afro-Latino and organized by Afrolatin@ Forum, protested with the social media campaign #LatinoIsNotARace. Scholars and activists pointed out that the Census Bureau had not tested the question in areas of the country with large numbers of Afro-Latinos or consulted with Afro-Latino scholars and nonprofits. In an opinion piece for *The Hill,* Tanya Katerí Hernández warned that a Latino race category "not only situates blackness as foreign to Latino identity, it also encourages a view of the Black category as only pertaining to non-Latinos."

When I saw the #LatinoIsNotARace, my heart broke. This is what my father had said so many years earlier in the yard with the handsome boy. He had said, Latino is not a race. He's Black. I'm white. You're . . . Here language fails me. The first time my father called me Black, when I returned from the trip to Cuba with darker skin, was also the first time he referred to me as white.

For months, I contemplated the hashtag and the arguments of the Afro-Latino scholars. I thought about the many ways people, not just my father, assigned race to me over the years. I left my hometown in New Jersey twenty years ago, and since then I had lived in Manhattan, Northern California, South Florida, northern Virginia, North Carolina, Ohio, and Chicago. Journalism assignments had taken me across the country to talk with people, and I had spoken at dozens of colleges from West Virginia to Oregon, so I had also spent a fair amount of time chatting with Lyft drivers and baristas and the white men with whom I shared a hotel shuttle. People of every color had asked about my origins. They wanted to know if I was Mexican or Pakistani or Indian or Dominican. In my twenties, at a lesbian club in Manhattan, a woman wondered if I was Native Hawaiian. In my thirties, at a college in the Midwest, a woman asked if I was Black. A month after I moved to Chicago, my new hygienist informed me that I could be Palestinian.

I have now spent more than two decades asking people why they think I am this or that race, and I can say with a great deal of confidence that people choose the race category with which they are most familiar. I am Palestinian because the hygienist has a family friend from that country whom I resemble. I am Pakistani because the woman I've just met has a good friend who is from that community and I look like her. I am Dominican because the Mexican guy from the moving company says my Spanish sounds like that of the Caribbean women on the radio. I am Indian because the taxi driver is himself from that country and I am wearing a scarf a family member gifted me from a South Asian shop in London.

Nine years after we met online, I asked my sweetheart, What race did you think I was when you first saw my photo? We had met online in North Carolina, and at the time, my sweetie, a white American, lived in a town where more than half of the residents were Mexican American. I had selected my profile pictures with care, hoping prospective suitors would notice my smile. Now my sweetheart grinned and said, I thought, She's cute. I wonder if she's Mexican.

None of this was the case when I was growing up in Jersey. My hometown was home to the descendants of the British and the Germans, the Irish and the Italians. People did not know Pakistanis or Dominicans or Native Hawaiians or even light-skinned Black people. They assumed I was Italian or Greek or some kind of Spanish like Cuban or Puerto Rican. As I grew up and moved around the country, and as the United States became increasingly multiracial, the ideas people held about my race shifted. They stopped reading me as an ethnic white or even a Cuban. In California, they assumed I was Mexican, and after the terrorist attacks of September 11, more people in New York City began asking if I was South Asian. Again, this reveals nothing about my face or my hair or my mouth or my actual origins, but instead it corresponds to the communities with which people have contact or the communities demonized on media platforms. On the last census form, if I was choosing an answer based on the race others assign to me, I would have checked Asian Indian and written *Mexican* under "some other race."

During the seven years that I taught in Ohio, I asked students to write about a time when they had been afraid, and many of the white female students drafted essays about being pulled over by the police. The stories varied but followed a similar narrative arc: The student had just acquired her driver's license, and her friends had convinced her to take the back roads to the big party at a schoolmate's house a few miles away. She steeled herself and drove through the dark of suburban Ohio. A few blocks later, her friends chattering and laughing, a freedom let loose inside her chest. She was finally a grown woman driving her mother's car. She rolled down the window and blasted a Taylor Swift song, the summer breeze flicking her hair. She was happy until the flashing lights spilled onto the rearview mirror. She pulled over, her hands trembling, her friends now mute, the playlist silenced.

What happened next unfolded in all the essays I read during those years: A male police officer strode up to the car. He spoke in a familiar "Father knows best" tone. He pointed out the speed limit or the red light that had been ignored. Often the girl cried. Sometimes she invented a story and then cried. The traffic stop ended with a warning, and the young white woman quietly pulled the car back onto the dark street.

I must have read this narrative five times before I remembered the first night that the police pulled me over. I was alone in the Buick my boyfriend and I had pooled our money to buy. The radio blared with the news from an AM station. I was finally a grown woman. I had a car and I had started college and even landed two part-time office jobs, which meant I worked full-time and attended college full-time and kept everything in my car: textbooks, highlighters, deodorant, a good pair of black shoes. It was a life I could only have with a car, since the college was an hour away and so was one of my jobs.

On Kennedy Boulevard, I passed the old A&P and rolled down the window. I was four blocks from home when the police car's lights flared in my rearview mirror. I panicked. I didn't know what to do. I had grown up on the public bus system. I had never been in a car stopped by the police, so I imitated what I had seen on television shows. I slowed the car and pulled over. I lowered the window. I waited. My hands shook. I thought of my possible mistakes: speeding, maybe, or running a red light.

The blue uniform had a thick mustache and asked for my driver's license. I fumbled with my wallet. A second police car pulled up in front of my car. Slow night, I thought, because when I had worked at the supermarket, that's what the other cashiers and I did when the store emptied. We gathered to restock the paper bags but more so to share the minutiae of our lives: who had taken a trip down the shore, who was dating whom, whose baby had started walking.

The road was well lit and well traveled. Drivers slowed to glance at me, then moved on. A third police car pulled up. A uniform emerged from that car too. The men huddled by the first car with my driver's license. Finally, the first uniform returned. Do you know your taillight's broken? he asked, his voice gruff.

My what?

Your taillight, he said, pointing to the back of the car. It's out.

The uniform did not know that I knew nothing about cars, that I had no idea how a lightbulb worked in a car, that I thought he was telling me I would have to come up with more money to fix the used Buick that had already cost me more than a thousand dollars to purchase. The panic about the police vanished, replaced by fury. I was ready to curse out my boyfriend, who should have known better than to convince me to buy a broken-ass car.

I snapped, What do you mean? What's wrong with the car?

The uniform. On the boulevard that night, he peered at my anxious, angry face, at the thickness of my eyebrows, at the streetlights pooling on my forehead. He heard the way I pronounced the word *car,* the way the vowel drowned inside my mouth, my dialect as familiar as his here from Jersey. He noticed that I was not apologizing. I was not terrified. I was not silent. I wanted to know what the fuck was wrong with my car, and I spoke to him as if he had better tell me right now. I spoke as if I owned the man and his uniform.

He weighed the evidence with his buddies a few feet away, all of them armed, all of them in sheets of blue, all of them fluent in English, and he settled on what he thought of my race and my citizenship, shifting his mouth into that of "Father knows best," telling me it was an easy job to swap out the bulb, only a matter of minutes to do that job, and how I should get it done right away since it could be dangerous driving around like that with a broken taillight. And then it was over. He did not issue a ticket, and the police car in front of me pulled out into traffic. The uniform said good night, and I drove the few blocks home and crawled into pajamas and my bed in my parents' home, and for years afterward, I thought it was absolutely normal for three police cars to pull over a teenager for a broken taillight. I thought this constituted a good kind of citizenship. When I learned about what happened to Black folks stopped by the police, how a traffic stop could serve as the prelude to murder, I thought about that night on the boulevard with the police and how privileged I had been. How white I had been. Just three cop cars and a tight knot of white men. I thought this was the citizenship of white people. Until I read the essays of my white Midwestern students, I had no idea citizenship could offer anything better.

Now I suspect the police were out hunting that night. It was the mid-1990s. More Latinx families had moved into the neighborhood. The police were patrolling the border of what had been a white town, and when they spotted me, they probably read me as a new arrival: a Salvadoran, a Guatemalan.

Racial hierarchies produce citizenship hierarchies, and both require the existence of people like myself, people who are not Black, not white, not Indian, not Chinese or Japanese, people who interpret three-cops-in-the-dark as a good citizenship, people who can forget we have a limited citizenship until someone asks, Where are you from? No, really. Where are you from? Where are your parents from?

Population trends can feel very factual, but if tomorrow the Census Bureau decided to count those Latinx who marked "some other race" as white, the country's white population would become enormous, and all the talk about the vanishing white race could be moot if everyone accepted these Latinx as white. "It is politics—not demography—that governs what we think and feel about ethnoracial demographic change," writes Rodríguez-Muñiz. "As such, what we are confronting, therefore, is a political rather than a demographic phenomenon—one that demands ethical vigilance, not simply better data."

When I walk into a classroom of mostly Latinx college students, I expect to see rows of mirrors, and this is what happened one Thursday on the campus where I teach now. I stepped into a Latinx literature class, and the majority of the students had my skin coloring and my hair texture. They grew up speaking Spanish and Spanglish at home. They laughed when I said, I know someone who reads the cartas. They disclosed that they were navigating college by finding friends in their Spanish heritage classes.

The students and I are what the historian Geraldo Cadava, in writing about the census, refers to as the "mestizo-Latino majority" of the United States. Mestizo, as a term, has a complicated history in Latin America and the Latinx diaspora, but it generally refers to a person who is Indigenous and white or is read that way. Historically, Latin America's elite relied on this label to erase and exotify Indigenous peoples, and mestiza, or mestize, is generally what people mean now when they ask me, Are you Mexican?

In the classroom that day, I noted that few of the Latinx students would be read as Black or Indigenous, and I began to wonder what it would mean for us to acknowledge that in a country with almost sixty-four million Latinx, those of us seen as mestizes do, in fact, hold racial privileges. How would this change our understandings of ourselves and our political commitments? How would it shift the way we celebrate Latinx public figures?

Before joining the cast of *Saturday Night Live,* Marcello Hernández, a talented Cuban-Dominican American, did hilarious stand-up routines on how white people in the Midwest reacted over the fact that he looked like a white boy with floppy hair but was fluent in Caribbean Spanish. This routine vanished when he joined *SNL.* On set, his hair was styled so it appeared thicker, lusher, browner, and overall mestizo. His appearances centered his Latinidad and his Spanish to such a degree that it became hard to remember he was once the white boy joking about how he was the kind of white Latino Americans could not imagine.

In 2021, media outlets reported that the Census Bureau would be headed by a person of color for the first time. A third-generation Mexican American from San Antonio, Robert Santos might be called a mestizo. An NBC News journalist described his appearance as that of "a poet or Chicano studies professor," mostly, it seems, because of his ponytail and his last name. Santos was considered to be the first person of color to lead the agency since its only Black director, James F. Holmes, served temporarily in the late 1990s without Senate confirmation.

Better data is not the point, but if it were, the 2020 census did not get it. In March 2022, the Census Bureau admitted to undercounting Black, Latinx, and Indigenous communities. The Pew Research Center's analysis of the data found that the 2020 census failed to count more than three million Latinx, a threefold increase from 2010, and the National Urban League reported that the census may have missed as many as two million Black people. The highest undercount, as in the past, was of Indigenous Americans.

The census has a long history of undercounting communities of color, and the reasons provided are usually that we are hard to find. We are more likely to rent. We are more likely to be evicted, to move in with our sister or grandmother or auntie. We do not trust the government, let alone any papers the government issues. In the literature, we are called "hard to locate" and "hard to persuade."

The 2020 count proved to be different in that the pandemic slowed the Census Bureau, and the Trump administration, with the approval of the Supreme Court, stopped the agency's work in October ahead of schedule. In a hearing before the House Committee on Oversight and Reform in December 2020, Santos testified that communities of color were reeling from the disproportionate impact of the Covid-19 pandemic, and he also highlighted: "Litigation on the inclusion of the citizenship question and possible exclusion of undocumented immigrants generated fear in the immigrant population."

On paper, DNA testing revealed that my father was mostly the descendant of Spaniards.

White Americans tend to think of Spain as exotic, as the land of Antonio Banderas and summer vacations, and so for some white Americans, my father was not white. But this racial calculus is not valid in Latin America and its diaspora in the United States. To be a Spaniard in our communities, in whatever tiny fraction, is to be considered white. It is common to hear in certain families that so-and-so, despite her hair, has a Spanish abuela or that fulana's baby salió blanquita on account of a Spanish great-grandfather.

My mother, according to the same test, is about half Indigenous—a fact that makes sense to me in light of how often her sister scolded me as a child. When my auntie admonished me for acting, in her words, like "a damn Indian," what she actually meant was this: Don't act like a damn Indian, because you are one.

The census does not ask about DNA test results even though people use this to answer the race question. For my part, I never spoke to my father in detail about his percentage of Spanish blood. I did not want to admit that I had been wrong.

On paper, my father is dead now. He died six months after I finished a draft of this writing. He died in my arms, gasping for air, his lungs filled with fluid, the two of us alone and curled up on a hospital bed in a hospice unit for poor white Cubans in Florida. His kidneys were shot. His heart failing. His lungs compromised. He was almost eighty-seven years old and had avoided hospitals and basic lab work his entire life.

Weeks before passing, he asked my mother to donate a thousand dollars to Trump's 2024 presidential campaign. He wanted the man to win. My mother pretended to not hear. She pretended to forget. She did not oppose Trump as much as she opposed sending that much money to any politician. My father, the white man who loved me, died devoted to Trump, devoted to the way the man spoke about power and money. My father died thinking he could be white, that he was white, that he was a white citizen. On paper, he was. The Bureau of Vital Statistics designated him as Cuban and white.

QUEER KIN

IN SOUTH FLORIDA, early that morning, the sun towered over the front yard at my parents' home. My dog sniffed at a spot where the neighborhood cats had peed, and I greeted the man who arrived next door to work on his daughter's house. In his sixties, balding, and overweight in jeans and a white T-shirt, he shared that he was completely renovating the house. She wants to take out all the walls, he told me in Spanish. Everything's gonna be new.

His daughter had recently moved in, and he had installed a privacy fence around the property for the German shepherds and golden retrievers they bred. The man wanted to know if my small dog, a rescue, was spayed. She was. Why'd you do that? he complained. You could have had a good litter!

I smiled politely. I was still half asleep in pajama sweatpants, my graying hair in a loose bun, but I continued the conversation because it was our first meeting, and I lived thousands of miles from here, from my parents and Tía María de Jesus, who had all moved to Florida in their elder years. I needed to confirm that this neighbor was a decent person, someone I could call on if anything should happen: a bad fall or a memory lapse. So we talked about the house renovation and Cuba. He was Cuban. You married? he asked.

Despite myself, I smiled again. In other cities where I have lived, like Manhattan, San Francisco, and Washington,

D.C., people generally ask me what I do for work when we first meet. Here in South Florida, in Hialeah, where most residents are Cuban American, most people first query if I am married and how many kids I have. Later, sometimes hours later, or days later, as an afterthought, they will ask: You have a job?

The man next door waited to hear if I was married, and I debated whether I was awake enough for the conversation where I told the man that I was not technically married, but my sweetheart and I had been together for many years, and I used to call myself bisexual but pansexual was probably the right identity at this point, except I did not know how to say that in Spanish, and my sweetie was nonbinary and I also did not know that word in Spanish. I thought about my parents and my tía and that I did not know what it would mean for them if I came out to this neighbor. I did not know him well enough to gauge the potential for hostility. And worse, I was a coward. I did not want cruel words or even indifference directed at me, not this early in the morning, not when I had not prepared. I was as decent a spokesperson on LGBTQ matters as the next queer, but only when I had my internal notes lined up for the fight, when I had anticipated the pelea.

You married?

Yes, I told him.

Where's your husband?

I am not the kind of queer who grew up keeping a secret about myself. I did not spend middle school devastated by crushes on girls. I did not walk into the local Catholic church, my chest heavy with the shame of an unspoken sin.

I was, as a teenager, boy crazy, the walls of my bedroom festooned with magazine clips of young white actors like Michael J. Fox and Tom Cruise. I began college anticipating that my romantic life would follow the plotline of the Harlequin romance novels I consumed: he and I enduring trials and tribulations before a blissful wedding day. When I met lesbians and queers in college and found, to my astonishment, that my body and my heart had been a secret even to me, I rewrote the romance novel in my head. It was the late 1990s, and I trusted wholeheartedly that the hard fights for queer rights had been fought and won and were done.

My entry into New York City's queer community in 2000 was an incredible joy. On weekends, I boarded the bus for Manhattan, where I danced at Henrietta's and the Clit Club alongside women who had already found the freedom to pierce their lips and tattoo their necks. I chopped my hair and dyed it pink. I ditched my bra and makeup. I made new friends who fit all the lesbian stereotypes: bookish, feminist, and male-hating. I attended my first Dyke March, convinced that it had been happening for decades, though it had only been organized a few years earlier by the Lesbian Avengers, whose name I adored and who were battling for lesbian visibility.

The day of the march, I joined my friends and hundreds of other women, and when a pack of us reached the line of police officers, we plopped ourselves on the street, refusing to move. The police had known we were coming, and we knew they were going to let us march, or at least that's what the older lesbians said and they had done this before, and it turned out to be true. The police conceded. It was a protest and a not-protest. No one got arrested. No one expected to get arrested. Other women had already done that work so we could march—no, waltz! We waltzed south under a glorious sun. We were women in glitter, women bare-chested, women in leather, and one day some of us would have top surgery and change pronouns, and some of us would say, Don't call me a woman, but that day we waltzed and pranced and skipped.

To speak of queer citizenship is to speak in plural—queer citizenships—since it has so much to do with where and how we grew up, the ways in which we experience our hearts and our bodies, the multiple ways in which our bodies and faces are read by strangers and family, and queer citizenships have so much to do with the jobs we have, the schooling we did or did not get, the policing of the streets we call home, the passports we hide under our mattresses, and the papeles our primas and mothers and hermanos hold in their hands. It has so much to do with the particular place we call home.

During the seven years I lived in southwest Ohio, I braced myself every time a new neighbor or the emergency plumber or the barista asked about my husband. I chose the pronoun *she* instead of *they* when making medical appointments for my sweetie to avoid a long conversation with the receptionist. When I told a new therapist that my sweetie is nonbinary, the woman fumbled through a series of questions until finally, frustrated with her own understandings of gender, she demanded to know if my beloved wore a skirt or pants.

Often during those years, I counted my blessings. Spotting a pride flag, even a tiny one, in a front window in my College Hill neighborhood was a blessing. So were the smiles when strangers complimented me on my T-shirt emblazoned with the phrase "Mighty Queer." When my sweetie moved in, and our neighbors, Black and white, working-class and middle-class, embraced us, I concluded that we had won a private lottery.

Now I live in a white gayborhood in Chicago. I buy caramel lattes at a coffeehouse full of gay white men and frequent a gift shop full of rainbow flags and pins with ironic phrases. At the local tea shop, I indulge in nostalgia, observing the queer BIPOC youth flirting with one another. In the summer, gay young men and middle-aged men walk by holding hands, and gay men push baby carriages. I chat at the park with a lesbian couple who, like us, have adopted a rescue dog, and in conversations with new neighbors and friends, I learn that it is possible to hire a gay real estate agent, a gay lawyer, and a gay accountant without leaving the area.

This gayborhood would not have been possible at one time in Chicago, and it is still not possible in many corners of the country, and so while I treasure this place, I have no delusions about it. This exists precisely because so many other communities still do not welcome us, and at the same time, this gayborhood has come to replicate white America. Houses here now sell for more than a million dollars, and even small condos fetch close to $400,000. Once a haven for lesbians, the neighborhood is home more often these days to gay white men and straight married couples with white-collar jobs, luxury cars, and finished basements.

To be queer and confined to one area of a city or a state or the country is to be reminded that full citizenship, full political and social membership, remains out of reach, and that racism and capitalism take the highest toll on the most vulnerable among us, which means that walking home one day, I notice a bundle of trans pride balloons tied to a wrought-iron fence across the street at the Walgreens parking lot. My throat tightens. I tell myself to calm down. It's probably a Trans Pride event, now that the days are growing warmer. Folks are ready to show off their short shorts, their open-toed heels, their political T-shirts. I wait at the corner for the cars to let me cross, silently pushing myself into anticipating happiness, and then I am on the other side of the street and reading the flyer, which announces that the street will be renamed for Elise Malary, a Black trans woman and advocate who was known here for years, and who, I later learn, had recently moved farther north, out of the city, and whose body turned up in Lake Michigan, her death ruled a drowning. Whether dying was her choice or someone else's, the medical examiner could not say.

To be queer is to think of safety—its proximity, its tenuousness, its illusion. But that does not mean that every queer is concerned with safety in the same ways. Before Elise died, two gay white men in my condo building said that I was wrong about our neighborhood. It's not as safe as you think, one told me. He wanted to add security features to the building: a camera and a gate that locked.

In Hialeah, I told my parents' neighbor, the one who wanted to know if I was married, that my husband was in the Midwest. I had done the seventeen-hour drive alone with the dog. The neighbor looked confused. He had probably never met the kind of man who let his wife drive by herself for two days. A wife with no children. A wife with a dog small enough to fit in a tote bag. A dog that could no longer reproduce.

A year later, the city renamed the cross street near my parents' home President Donald J. Trump Avenue, and the man next door or his daughter hoisted a blue flag above the roof of their house calling for Trump to win the 2024 election. This was before anyone knew that Supreme Court justice Samuel Alito and his wife had bickered with their neighbors and hung the American flag upside down in front of their Virginia home in support of Trump. In Hialeah, the neighbors agreed with one another. A good number of them raised flags blaring Trump's name over their one-story houses, shouts of "Make America Great Again" floating among the terra-cotta roofs.

The city of Hialeah is a reminder of what a civil war can do to a place. In the 1950s, white people filled the homes of this city northwest of Miami. Residents spoke English and played baseball. Then, a few hours south, the war arrived. Everyone chose sides. Everyone argued. The revolution in Cuba cracked that country open, and those who could fled to Miami, then to Hialeah. Multiple U.S. presidents and Congress members decided that the Cubans had escaped communism and needed to be welcomed. The federal government produced new papeles. The Cubans could stay. The Cubans could become citizens. The Cubans could buy houses in this city that had once belonged to the Seminole Tribe.

More than sixty years later, in 2020, 95 percent of Hialeah residents were Latinx, giving the city the distinction of being home to the largest concentration of Latinx in the United States, tying only with Laredo, Texas, which sits on the border with Mexico. Hialeah has been labeled the fourth least diverse city in the country—after towns in West Virginia and South Dakota. It is what working-class Havana would have looked like if the revolution had never happened. SUVs clog the main streets and battle for parking spots in strip malls. Bakeries sell pastries for less than a dollar. Residents work shifts at the local hospital or Walmart or the nail salon. They fix cars and toilets, air-conditioning systems and ceiling fans. They drive for Uber and Lyft and take classes at the community college. The women here don't leave the house without lipstick, not even for a quick car ride to Sedano's to buy plantains.

The one gay person I knew in Hialeah was my cousin, a man I will call Primo. Nestled in a wide armchair in his living room, Primo looked like a movie star from the 1950s. He had skin so clear and luminous that it was hard to believe he was already in his sixties. When I asked for his facial regimen, he smiled and said, Soap and water. It was not only his skin and his bright eyes that made him look young. He had a pianist's hands, a calligrapher's hands. He had the kind of hands meant for cradling the flute or transcribing scripture. It was easy to imagine him in a high-end hotel in Berlin or Buenos Aires, a glass of chilled white wine in his hand. Instead, he opened the door for me in Hialeah in a white T-shirt and blue cotton shorts.

Primo and I did not grow up together. When we first met, I was in my twenties and making my one trip to Cuba, where he lived. He was almost forty at the time. A year later, in 2001, he and his boyfriend escaped from the island—escaped because Cubans were not permitted to leave the country without government approval until 2013. Now it had been more than twenty years, and Primo was still not a citizen. His papers were making their way through the vast bureaucracy of the U.S. immigration system. He wasn't sure why, or he didn't want to tell me.

Citizenship so often revolves around years and months, and so dates dictate where a person will live and how they will work and where their children will grow up. If my cousin had arrived in the United States in the 1960s, he would have joined my father and the nearly 400,000 other Cubans who came during that decade and were automatically eligible for a green card after a period of residency, thanks to the Cuban Adjustment Act of 1966. He would have had this easy access to citizenship because the United States held firmly to the idea that it could win the Cold War against the Soviet Union by offering refuge to exiles from a Communist country in the Caribbean. This would have also been true if Primo had come in the 1970s and '80s. If my cousin had come in 1995, he would have needed to reach dry land first. President Bill Clinton's so-called wet-foot, dry-foot policy required federal authorities to turn any Cuban intercepted at sea back to their home country. Those Cubans whose feet touched U.S. soil could qualify for legal residency as they had for decades. If my cousin had come after 2017, the condition of his feet would not have mattered. President Barack Obama ended the Clinton-era policy, requiring Cuban immigrants to apply for political asylum. Deportations of Cubans shot up dramatically. In 2017, the United States expelled 388 Cubans from the United States. Two years later, it deported more than 24,000. Still, nothing stopped the migration. In 2022, more than 200,000 Cubans arrived at the southern border.

In 2024, Primo was still waiting, still fixing his papeles, but if he had a paper granting him citizenship in this country, he would have voted for Trump in the presidential election. In theory, a gay Latino without citizenship would never vote for Trump, but political life is not theoretical. It is the memories we carry and the stories we tell.

At the start of the twenty-first century, while I traipsed into my first women-only sex party in Lower Manhattan, the sociologist Kenneth Plummer observed: "Everywhere we look we can now find new kinds of citizens: multicultural citizens, diasporic citizens, postcolonial citizens, flexible citizens, cultural citizens, global citizens, technological citizens, intimate citizens, radical citizens, consumer citizens, critical citizens, dissident citizens, and the like. It is not at all surprising, therefore, to find that we now also have 'sexual citizens.'"

When scholars first began writing about sexual citizenship, they were preoccupied with economics. The sociologist David Evans, who coined the term, was thinking about citizenship as a social, legal, and political experience from which even the well-off gays were excluded. For so long the places to which gay men belonged, the places where they could be open, where they had a right to speak freely, had been confined to cruising spots and underground bars. Those were the sites of gay citizenship. In the 1970s, as states began overturning sodomy laws, the bathhouses and the gay bars flourished, and by the 1980s travel companies started catering to the spending habits of wealthy gay men and lesbians too, promising to transport a gay accountant from San

Diego to a place like Amsterdam, where he could be out and about in ways still not possible in his own country. It was a citizenship a well-off gay man could purchase.

Feminists, of course, had been talking about sexual citizenship before Evans. The second wave of feminism in the 1970s centered the ways that a woman's social, financial, and political rights were tied to her gender and whom she loved in the middle of the night. Many women today still do not marry for love. They marry for papers. They marry for rent money. Sometimes they don't marry. They move in with the boyfriend. They stay with him. They look the other way. They have a place to sleep. Their kids have clean underwear. They don't have to go back home to their awful fathers. The sociologist Diane Richardson put it bluntly: "Sexual citizenship operates as a form of poverty reduction."

Citizenship has always been bound to race, to gender, to sexuality, to the ways that others make of our bodies a text, a document read according to a vocabulary created by a small group of people we've never met. In the seventeenth century, British law dictated that citizenship be controlled by the father. If your father was a citizen of Britain or its colonies, then so were you. In Virginia, a group of white men agonized over this. What were they to do with the white men raping Black women? How could the biracial children of these men also be citizens?

In 1662, Virginia's rich white men answered this question by barring white men from granting citizenship to their children. The Grand Assembly infamously declared that citizenship would go "according to the condition of the mother." An enslaved Black woman could no longer birth a citizen. Citizenship could only be inherited through the body of a white woman, and white men could continue raping Black women without harming their own citizenship.

I did not think about my auntie's white body when I urged her in 2014 to move from New Jersey to Florida. Or I did. In the seventh decade of her life, Tía María de Jesus's body started a new metamorphosis. She began to shrink, the hem of her pants grazing the floor. She still walked or took the bus everywhere, but she teetered at times, and at least twice she lost her footing and fell on the sidewalk. The Bell's palsy returned, paralyzing the left side of her face. I knew she loved her one-bedroom apartment, but she couldn't live alone. Not anymore.

It would be accurate to say that I thought about my auntie's body but not her sexual citizenship. She was, after all, a naturalized citizen of the United States. I thought that was enough. She would move in with my parents, who had transplanted themselves from Jersey to South Florida after my sister and I left home, and I figured Tía would get the same food stamps and later we would figure out a Section 8 apartment. I was wrong on all counts, for I failed to appreciate how Ronald Reagan's obsession with the anti-citizen in the 1970s and '80s crawled across the political aisle, so that by 1996, Bill Clinton signed the welfare reform law, granting states more control over the spending of those funds. In 2021, at least ten states were diverting this money to subsidize anti-abortion clinics, and earlier, in 2016, the investigative reporter Krissy Clark uncovered that Oklahoma was using its Temporary Assistance for Needy Families dollars to offer marriage coaching to couples who had high-paying legal jobs. The couples had no clue that their local marriage program was actually welfare.

On paper, my auntie was unmarried and childless. She moved to Florida and her monthly food stamps were slashed. She was blessed. She lived frugally and managed, but still it could be said that she moved to a different country.

Primo did not want me to write about him. You need this book, he told me. I don't.

He was right. I was the one contemplating citizenship and the political times in which we were living, not him. For the purposes of this writing, I could have turned him into my uncle. I could have told readers on the page: He was not my uncle, but let's call him that. Let's call him Tío, the tío who lived in Hialeah. But everyone has an uncle with shitty politics. A cousin is different. A cousin is supposed to sneak you out of the house and into parties where the rap music makes you love poetry. A cousin is supposed to tell you about queer movies and books and all the other creative works your parents do not know. A cousin is supposed to be a portal to magic. A cousin is supposed to agree with you about politics.

Primo stayed on the page as a cousin. I wrote, then scrapped, entire paragraphs about one part of his life, which made him distinctive, and I changed the name of his boyfriend, and I wrote nothing of what his boyfriend did for work. I wrote nothing of my cousin's childhood. Nothing of his parents. But I kept him as my cousin because I wondered if writing about our relationship would help me to answer a question about citizenship that I had begun to contemplate when I heard college administrators and political commentators imploring Americans to speak to those with opposing political views, to find common ground, and to move past the awful and divisive talk marking political life. This call to civility sounded reasonable. It was what a good citizen would do.

This emphasis on political reconciliation made me wonder how and when and under what circumstances a person comes to know that such an outcome is possible. It made me wonder about the exact opposite too. How do we recognize when the political divide cannot be bridged? How do we know when to walk away? How do we reckon with such a grief? What was possible for me and my cousin?

Primo was born on the eve of the Cuban Revolution. He was among the first children to come of age during the years when literacy rates boomed in Cuba, and when seeing a doctor, a good doctor, one with medical supplies, was possible regardless of family income. These children chanted new patriotic songs. They studied a new political history. They came of age in a country whose economy floundered but managed to stay afloat with the aid of the Soviet Union. While poor children in Caracas and Mexico City and Lima were kept from classes to beg on the street or to rummage through trash, Primo and the other first children of Cuba's revolution learned to read and write and, later, to study the Russian language.

All of this came to a crushing end in the early 1990s, when the Soviet Union splintered into more countries than I could name. The Cuban economy reeled from the shock of losing that financial support, and like other Caribbean nations, it turned to tourism for revenue. Still, I often wondered about the revolution's first generation, the one most familiar with its best years. What kind of citizens would these children grow up to be?

What Primo told me was that they learned about surveillance. Fidel Castro's government relied on neighborhood watch groups called Comités de Defensa de la Revolución, or Committees for the Defense of the Revolution, to monitor their neighbors. The committees had to report anything they found to be anti-government. Being gay was anti-government, and so in the early 1980s, when Primo was asleep, two government officials knocked on the front door of his family's home. He was twenty-three. The officials told Primo to come along, and they promised his family that he would be back soon. He was in prison for the next four years.

The first time Primo told me about being imprisoned in Cuba, he made it sound like fun. I was his little cousin, his little sister, his American cousin. I was to be entertained, not told the truth. They put me to work in the office, he said, smiling.

He handled documents. He typed letters. He managed some of the bookkeeping. He had a chair and a desk. The job was almost classy. And because of his beautiful hands, the skin smooth and alabaster, the kind of white European hands Leonardo da Vinci might have sketched, it was easy to picture Primo in an office at a desk tapping away at a typewriter as if it were a musical instrument. Maybe he overheard prison officials discuss what the U.S. newspapers were reporting during those years about a new virus killing gay men, but Primo never mentioned the AIDS crisis to me, and I never asked.

The second time my cousin told me about being imprisoned, he was explaining why he could never be a leftist. He had seen the worst of what a leftist government could do. He was explaining why he could never be like me.

Queers have long been considered bad citizens. Whom we have loved and fucked and dreamt about at night—this has made us bad citizens at different points in time in different places around the globe. When my cousin talked with me about being imprisoned in Cuba, I thought of the gay men jailed here in the United States, the men arrested in gay bars, in local parks, in public restrooms. Later I thought of the borders, of the fact that even if my cousin had been able to avoid prison in Cuba and had arrived in Miami during the 1980s, if he had called himself a gay man, or if an immigration agent had designated him in that way, he could have been denied entry.

On paper, gay men and lesbians and anyone queer were prohibited from coming into the United States prior to 1965 on the grounds that they had a "psychopathic personality." The Supreme Court clarified that the government did not mean "psychopathic" in the language of psychiatrists. It was the way immigration officials referred to "homosexuals and other sexual perverts," the court wrote. Congress members concluded that the terminology was insufficient. In 1965, they declared that anyone "afflicted with . . . sexual deviation" was barred from entering the country. The ban continued until 1990, while the one on HIV-positive immigrants lasted for twenty-two years and was only lifted in 2010.

The admission of queer immigrants to the United States resulted from the work of lesbian, bi, trans, and gay activists across this country. They had spent the better part of a decade battling the AIDS crisis and demanding a new citizenship. There would be no more hiding. There would be no more shame. There would be no more silence. These activists embraced the "bad citizenship" they possessed by celebrating the families they had created, the people they had buried, and the ones they were keeping alive. They began calling themselves queer, which did not have to do with whom you were fucking but rather with fucking up the systems of power that had made lesbians and gays and trans folks and bisexuals and everyone nonhetero hide for so long. On the streets and in court, gay men and lesbians had once said: We have a right to do what we want in private. By the end of the twentieth century, they were saying: We have a right to be in public.

As the years inched forward, white gay men and lesbians began to quarrel about citizenship, about whether they wanted to stay radical and deviant or act like straight, white Christians. They didn't talk explicitly about citizenship. They debated instead the possibility of being seen as normal or virtually normal—what the American studies and queer studies scholar Lisa Duggan named "homonormative." They wrangled over whether or not to embrace the option of enjoying the social, civil, political, and religious rights of white, hetero citizenship—an option that was only possible thanks to the activists who had organized and marched and protested for years in T-shirts and high heels, in blazers and boots, in English and Spanglish and Black English.

What citizenship did the white gays want?

On an island more than two thousand miles from the continental United States, an answer began to take shape in 1990. A woman in Honolulu woke up that year with a terrible earache. She had no health insurance. If only she could marry her girlfriend and be added to her health plan at work. Another lesbian and her girlfriend wanted to have a family. If only they could tell the child welfare agencies: We're married. A local lawyer convinced both couples to join him, and together they went to city hall, along with a gay couple, for a marriage license that was denied. Three years later, in 1993, Hawaii's supreme court ruled that gays and lesbians could marry.

The battle for gay marriage that ensued across the United States hinged on arguments about citizenship. Those supporting gay marriage stressed that a citizen, a full citizen, a good citizen, a valued citizen, got to marry whomever they wanted. They got to marry whomever they loved. They got to have the life they wanted. A decade later, in the early 2000s, advocacy campaigns paraded the gay couples eager to marry. These were often couples who wore cotton T-shirts and slacks in shades of beige and gray and sometimes coral. The couples were similar in height and weight, the two of them with tidy haircuts, their bodies free of piercings and tattoos and any evidence that they could not afford clothes that fit them well. Every gay in the ads was a good citizen—the kind who could move in next door and keep to themselves.

At the time, I understood that gay marriage was not going to win supporters if anyone suggested that the couples to be married were broke and needed rides to work from their neighbors. Or if the gays to be married had student loans they couldn't pay back and needed Medicaid and were trying to get their aunties into Section 8 housing. Or if the gays to be married had left prison last week with felony convictions. In other words, I was in my twenties and well acquainted with racialized capitalism. To win on gay marriage, advocates had to present couples who paid taxes and made no demands on the federal government or even the city council. The gay couples who wanted to marry had to be post-welfare citizens.

Maybe I should have been thinking about marriage. I was not. I was thinking about my mother. She was still living in Jersey at the time, and the factories had turned into sweatshops. She and my father owned a home and were convinced that they did not qualify for Medicaid. Besides, they did not need to see doctors; they had made it this far without any doctors. The free mammogram clinic in Harlem was good enough for my mother, and the health fairs in the local parks in Jersey told her and my aunties about their cholesterol and diabetes. Let me be clear: The women in my family were lucky. Their numbers were good. Their cholesterol never swung too high. The diabetes kept its distance. Still, I read the stories in the papers. I knew a medical catastrophe could take a family's house. I was twenty-two years old, and I knew financial ruin could be averted if the health insurance plan at my first job after college would add my parents as my dependents. And my aunties too. It didn't work that way, the lady from the insurance company patiently told me over the phone. My mother could not be my family. But that's what I wanted. I didn't want to marry my girlfriend, who had a job with health insurance. I wanted to marry my mother.

It mattered very little that I had become a good citizen, that I had a college degree and an office job, sick pay and vacation pay and health insurance. I could share none of it with the people who had raised me and made this life possible. Legally and politically, the country insisted on one kind of family and only one kind, and it was this kind of marriage gay activists fought for and eventually won—and I was happy for them, but in my twenties and then in my thirties, it did nothing to change my own tiny life. My gay friends married. My gay friends had children. My gay friends divorced. And I was still not able to add my mother or my auntie or my father to my health insurance plan.

Because our country does not offer a robust social citizenship, marriage is still largely the mechanism by which we are cared for when we get sick or when we lose our jobs or when we become disabled. For those of us who are unmarried, who are childless, whose families of origin offer no sanctuary, let alone care, we turn to friends. It is a friend who drives you to the emergency room. A friend who shows up for the next round of chemotherapy. A friend who makes room for you on the sofa and copyedits your résumé. A friend who finds you a new gig.

Marriage and family and friends are how we negotiate financial insecurity in this country, and because women and femmes are so often the ones tasked with caretaking, this work, this social citizenship, becomes our labor.

Facebook classifies Primo as my friend. Or that was the default and neither of us changed it. Primo recounted that we are cousins because two brothers in this one spot in Cuba married two sisters and all of us are the descendants of them. All of us are cousins now. Second cousins. Third cousins. Cousins once removed. Twice removed.

More than one person has tried to teach me how family members are removed, and I still do not understand it. In English, language offers an astonishing hierarchy of relations. In Spanish, informally, we speak only of primos. My father's primo is also my primo. If I had children, I would tell them: This man with the beautiful hands? This man who wanted to vote for Trump? He's your primo.

Or, in English, I might say: Kin. We are kin to each other. We have a kinship. We are queer kin. *The Merriam-Webster Dictionary* says that to be kin is to be part of a clan or a family, but also to be of a "similar nature or character," as in the familiar phrase "a kindred spirit."

Primo and I are kin but not kindred spirits. We do not have a similar nature, a similar character. Or as he told me about my citizenship: You were born here, so you don't value it.

What I loved most about my cousin was his love story. He met a handsome man at a bus stop outside Havana. Let's call him Miguel: Miguel with the caramel eyes, the long lashes, the gentle smile. Miguel who moved to Havana, who couldn't hold Primo's hand in public. Miguel who arranged his life around Primo's. They drank coffee together in the mornings and eventually began to plan their departure from Cuba.

In 2001, Primo and Miguel boarded a plane in Havana. This part of the love story was familiar to me. I had heard different versions of it from different Cubans over the last twenty years: Relatives in South Florida pool together money for the plane ticket, the flight bound for Central America, where people make their way to a country that has a policy of not deporting Cubans. Then they wait. They eat pupusas for the first time. They walk around the neighborhood. They hide under kitchen tables when earthquakes strike. They have nightmares. They call their families in Florida every day.

In Central America, Primo and Miguel drank coffee together in the mornings. They cooked for each other. They met children on the street begging for food. The days collapsed into weeks. Then, finally, they boarded a plane destined for Miami. They were two men in love, and they had practiced what they would say when they reached immigration officials: I'm a Cuban. I'm seeking asylum.

At the Miami International Airport, the uniformed woman listened to Primo's asylum claim, and then her mouth churned out rules and regulations. He would be restricted by these laws and have a right to this but not that, and god knows what else the woman said. A new fear gripped my cousin. What had he gotten himself and Miguel into? The woman, a Cuban American herself, finished the cruel speech and burst into a laugh. Don't worry about all that! she exclaimed in Spanish. Welcome to America!

Primo had no idea of all that was to come. There would be the year when he found work managing a gas station.

The many years when Miguel worked every day of the week. The year when Primo fell ill, seriously ill, and needed to be hospitalized for weeks. He prayed harder perhaps than he ever had, and when the surgeons opened his body and carried out the necessary procedures, he said, Thank you, thank you, thank you. Back home, Miguel hired women to take care of Primo when the hospital discharged him. The women fed him and watched him take his medicine and helped him to the bathroom while Miguel himself had to be at work. When I visited, Primo had lost a lot of weight. His cheeks were sunken, but he was alive.

On the apartment balcony, where Primo could not hear us, I told the home health attendant how good it was that she could be here and how blessed my cousin was to have Miguel. She sighed, and then, wistfully, she said, It's incredible—to be loved like that.

Her words spun inside me. To be two men and have been together a lifetime when the world did not want you to be together or to even exist, and then to not only be together but be loved with such devotion, such commitment. It was the stuff of fairy tales, of romance novels, of the telenovelas this woman and I had watched our entire lives. It was what we had been told as women to need and want and hope for our entire lives—to be loved like that.

In Florida elementary schools, my cousin and his beloved, my sweetie and I—the four of us could not exist in classrooms after the state passed the "Don't Say Gay" law, officially known as the Parental Rights in Education Act, in 2022. The law's wording was so vague that teachers and students did not know if they could talk publicly about being gay. A kindergarten teacher had to presume that she was forbidden from reading to children a story about two men who loved each other so much for so many years that they crossed many borders together. The law declared that "sex is an immutable biological trait," so my sweetie could not work in the K–12 public school system and request that co-workers and students refer to them by the pronoun of their choice. A judge temporarily blocked this part of the law in 2024 while a lawsuit made its way through the courts, but the fact of the law still bruises.

Lawyers for the state and civil rights groups in Florida reached a compromise on the "Don't Say Gay" law two years after its passage. Teachers could say they were gay. Students too. Teachers could talk about books with queer characters as long as they did not "instruct" students on sexuality or gender identity, which suggested that state officials still championed the impossible idea that grown queers can recruit young people to be gay. Meanwhile, Illinois joined four other states mandating inclusive curricula for public schools. These states now want children to learn about the Stonewall Riots, which kick-started the gay liberation movement in the United States. In fourth grade, Illinois children can discuss, in the past tense, questions such as "Why did LGBT people have to hide in society?" In ninth grade, they are encouraged to consider: "What might the 'American Dream' mean if you identify as LGBT?"

What might the American Dream mean if you are a gay Latino immigrant?

By 2024, Primo's sweetie had become a U.S. citizen after waiting more than twenty years. Miguel held up his right hand in Florida, pledged allegiance to this country, and became a man with papeles, and Primo did what my mother, pregnant with me, had done decades ago: He married a man with papers. He planned to become a citizen in this way and eventually to vote for a man like Trump.

In the months after the terrorist attacks of September 11, I glimpsed how differently my cousin and I experienced political life. The United States was bombing women and children in Afghanistan, and I was having nightmares about planes chasing girls across open fields, but in Hialeah, Primo shook his head at the absurdity of his life and mine. We're at war, he said, smiling sarcastically, but it doesn't feel like we're at war.

Primo had a point. No one worried about being drafted. No one rushed to the supermarkets to stock up on bread and canned soups. No one was pressured to buy government bonds. Our family had no one serving in the military, and no male relative born in a Muslim country who had to register with the federal government. For Primo and me and so many people in the United States, our day-to-day lives did not change when President George W. Bush declared war on al-Qaeda and the Taliban. When my cousin said, It doesn't feel like we're at war, I recognized the queerness of my citizenship in a new way.

My cousin made me aware that in Cuba, where food was rationed by the government, a declaration of war would have been felt immediately. He would have received bread staler than usual or none at all. He would have expected fewer eggs available and higher prices on the black market. He would have known there would be less of everything, and he would have worried about him or Miguel or someone they knew being sent to fight.

Within a year of declaring the War on Terror, the United States opened a detention center in Cuba at Guantánamo Bay. Since 1903, the United States has required Cuba to lease it this land. It would be akin to forcing New York City to rent a section of Brooklyn to Cuba for military purposes. The base at Guantánamo is the oldest U.S. military installation in another country and a reminder of the many ways in which the United States remains an empire. No, it's not the British Empire or the French or Spanish ones, but it is an empire in the authority it holds over other countries.

At Guantánamo, beginning in 2002, the United States detained about 780 Muslim men and teenage boys in a military prison. Nine of them died there, and dozens more lost their lives after being transferred off the island. By 2024, a military commission had only convicted two men, and the United States government still held fifteen men at the base, all of them largely forgotten by the world despite the headlines over the years about interrogators torturing these prisoners, stripping them naked and forcing them to bark like dogs, depriving the men and boys of sleep and smearing fake menstrual blood across their faces.

At Guantánamo, citizenship vanished. While the Constitution guarantees the right of habeas corpus, which prohibits the government from tossing people into prison indefinitely and without charges, the Bush administration held that this did not apply to the detainees at Guantánamo. The men and teenagers had no right to go before a judge, the administration contended. The detainees were not even on U.S. soil. They were in Cuba, on foreign land.

Borrowed from Latin, habeas corpus means "you shall have the body." It directs the government to bring the prisoner to court before a judge. For the men held at Guantánamo, hundreds of lawyers had to sue for this right. The Supreme Court declared that the base was under U.S. jurisdiction. In another case, the court declared that the men held at Guantánamo had a right to habeas corpus. Our national legal texts did, in fact, protect the bodies of these men and boys.

In 2003, a year after the United States began torturing Muslim men at Guantánamo, the Supreme Court heard arguments in *Lawrence v. Texas* about the bodies of gay men, about whether gay men should have the right to have sex with one another. Lesbians too. Gay rights organizations had been fighting sodomy laws at the state level since the 1950s, but when a case of theirs reached the Supreme Court in 1986, the justices ruled that the Constitution did not protect the privacy of gay men since no connection existed, the majority wrote, between the sex lives of gay men and "family, marriage, or procreation." If a police officer showed up in a man's home and the door to his bedroom was open and the police spotted him making love with his boyfriend, he could be arrested.

That kind of arrest happened in 1998 on the outskirts of Houston. A white man called the police to report that a Black man was "going crazy with a gun." He did not tell the police that he and the Black man, Tyron Garner, were in a relationship, that neither of them had a home address, that they loved each other maybe or surely that they needed each other. He did not tell them that they were drunk that night with a white man, John Geddes Lawrence, and how maybe Lawrence and Tyron were flirting and this hurt him, so he ran out of the apartment to call the police.

The sheriff's deputies arrested Lawrence and Garner and charged them with "deviate sexual intercourse," even though the four officers could not decide what exactly they had seen of the men's bodies inside the apartment. Two declared they never saw any sex; the other two couldn't agree on what type of sex they had witnessed. What they agreed on was that Lawrence and Garner were gay, and a law existed to lock these men up.

The case reached the Supreme Court in 2003, and a great deal had changed by then. The gay liberation movement and AIDS activism had made it possible for lesbians and gay men to be open about themselves at work and in their communities, and even in Texas, gay and lesbian couples were not technically barred from legally adopting children. This visibility had reached the Supreme Court, where gay clerks were no longer closeted, and Justice Sandra Day O'Connor felt comfortable enough to send a gift to a former clerk who was having a baby with her girlfriend.

In *Lawrence v. Texas,* the court ruled that gay men and lesbians, like anyone else, had a right to a full social citizenship. We had the right to choose to whom we would make love. We had a right to "choose without being punished as criminals." The court acknowledged too that the world itself had been transformed. Even other nations, it wrote, were protecting the rights of gays and lesbians.

Citizenship is a social construct. We can change its meaning over and over again. We can make of it what we want or need, which explains how at the very moment when the United States expanded the parameters of queer citizenship, our country was also torturing Muslim men, violating their bodies, at a military base less than two hours by plane from Miami. It also clarifies why in the first months of 2025, while finishing this book, I woke to the news of men's bodies again at Guantánamo. The Trump administration shipped 290 immigrants to the base mostly on chartered flights. The men had traveled to the United States from twenty-seven countries, and at the base, they were shoved into solitary cells. They were taken to shower once every three days, shackled. They were given water that tasted strange. They were, in photograph after photograph, young men, their bodies shown not in court but on airstrips, their wrists bound, their bodies handled by soldiers and ICE agents. More than half of the immigrants were deported to Venezuela, and others were returned to detention centers stateside by way of Louisiana.

During those same weeks, ICE agents handcuffed a white woman at the border checkpoint in San Diego. A U.S. citizen, Lennon Tyler was traveling back from Mexico with her German boyfriend, who was on a tourist visa. La migra refused him entry into the country, then placed him in a detention center, where he stayed for two weeks before being allowed to return to Europe. That day, at the border, after detaining her boyfriend, ICE agents subjected Lennon to a body search and handcuffed her to a bench. She sat there asking aloud: "Why am I being detained? Is this legal? Can you do this to a United States citizen?"

Primo did not understand me. He wanted to understand me. Your mother is from Colombia, he said to me. Your father is from Cuba. How did you turn out to be a leftist?

I did not have an answer for Primo except that his question hinted at one possibility. I did not grow up with two political refugee parents. My father's rage about communism in Cuba was his own. My mother looked upon it as a bruise my father had. It was not her wound. She could return to her home country whenever she wanted, and of the civil war in Colombia, she only shook her head and murmured, It's terrible, as if it were happening to someone else's homeland. Her parents and brothers and sisters and cousins had been spared. They were too poor to be kidnapped, but mostly they were lucky. They had never been in the wrong place at the wrong time.

Or maybe it had nothing to do with the political histories of my parents. I witnessed at a young age how strangers disparaged my mother for not speaking English. I noticed the people with us at the dental school's free clinic: women who were tired and short on money, women who didn't speak English, women who snapped at their children. At the same time, I consumed multicultural television shows emphasizing the reconciliation of Black and white America. In elementary school, I believed Jesse Jackson would be the first Black president, and in high school, I saw that California's Proposition 187, which would have denied public education to undocumented children, targeted people like me: Latinx.

Or maybe, to answer my cousin's query, it had to do with faith. I came of age in a Catholic school whose teachers told me over and over again that we were here to take care of one another. We were here to help the least among us.

We were here to love one another. Everything could be forgiven. Everyone could be forgiven.

I did not give all these answers to Primo. I thought of them later. I listened to him blame the Cuban government for the years he spent in prison and the poverty that had dogged his country for decades. I respect everyone's ideas, Primo said, but I can't have leftist ideas.

When I suggested that it was not about the Left or the Right, that a dictatorship can take hold in any country, he retorted, Every leftist government is a dictatorship.

My cousin worried that people like me would stop Trump from running in the 2024 election. This was neither illogical nor incomprehensible. In Latin America, and many parts of the world, a candidate might be a presidential candidate on Sunday, and then on Monday, the same candidate is banned or exiled, imprisoned or dead. Primo did not take it for granted that a person running for the presidency would, in fact, be allowed to do so. He knew there was nothing solid about a country. A country could fall apart. A country could be lost. A country could turn into memory.

My cousin did not understand me, and white media pundits, electoral strategists, and my friends did not understand my cousin. Why would a gay Latino with a green card want Trump for a president? The confusion arose only because when Americans say Latino, they are thinking about the Latino they imagine. They are thinking of Brown people crossing the desert on foot. They are thinking of Latinx who protest anti-immigrant legislation. They are thinking of Latinx like me. They are not thinking about the ones who have been here for twenty or fifty years, the ones who see themselves as white and who like the powers that come with that race category. They are not thinking about the Latinx who have green cards and want the "white again" country Trump promises.

But Primo is gay! I can hear someone gasping this somewhere, and they too are thinking of the gay man they imagine: the gay child bullied through elementary school, the gay teenager who flees rural Idaho for Brooklyn. They are thinking of someone who is only a victim, not someone who might enjoy the power of his whiteness, of his maleness. They are not thinking of a man who associates the persecution of gay men with the work of a Communist government.

A gay Latino without citizenship wanting Trump in the White House is not a contradiction. He only appears that way because many of us ignore the complicated dynamics created by a long history of white supremacy in the United States. In *Caste: The Origins of Our Discontents,* Isabel Wilkerson points out that many working-class white people were not voting against themselves in 2016: "The people voting this way were, in fact, voting their interests." It just happened to be that their interests were in maintaining a racial hierarchy for the privileges it offers them.

The psychiatrist Jonathan M. Metzl spent five years with white voters in the South and the Midwest trying to understand why they would support politicians whose policies made their health worse. These voters often opposed the Affordable Care Act, even though they themselves were broke, chronically ill, and desperately needing medical care. One white man in Tennessee told Metzl that he "would rather die" than sign up for Obamacare. The man could not tolerate the idea that the program would also benefit "Mexicans or welfare queens," and so he supported politicians who refused to expand Medicaid in his state. This man was willing to lose his life to preserve white supremacy. Metzl concluded: "I found that Trump supporters were often willing to put their own lives on the line in support of their political beliefs. As a result, when viewed more broadly, actions that may have seemed from the outside to be crazy, uninformed, or self-defeating served larger political aims." He titled his 2019 book on this subject *Dying of Whiteness.*

White supremacy, combined with capitalism, often propels the most vulnerable Americans to fight among themselves. In 2023, in Chicago's Brighton Park neighborhood, close to a hundred residents blocked the city from building a winterized camp for immigrants. They threw signs at an alderperson and her aide, sending the latter to the hospital with injuries. They told the police they were ready to be arrested. The neighborhood was 80 percent Latinx and 10 percent Asian American. Protesters chanted, "No los queremos aquí, de ningún lado." They did not care where the immigrants were coming from; they did not want them. A Chinese resident told local reporters, "We are not racist. Almost everyone in this neighborhood is an immigrant."

The Latinx and Chinese protesters understood the racial hierarchy under which they lived. Here was the city, ready to spend more than $90,000 a month to build temporary housing for immigrants. "They could have spent it on our school, on our education for our kids, on our senior citizens for the community," a Latino from the neighborhood told reporters. He seemed to recognize that the problem was not the immigrants. The problem was the racial and economic inequities to which he and his family and community had been subjected, and he had had enough. The immigrants had to go elsewhere. I don't know if this Latino voted for Trump, but I could see how he might think that doing so would be in his interest since Trump promised to shut the border.

Writing for *The New Yorker* in the wake of the 2024 election, Keeanga-Yamahtta Taylor, a leading Black scholar on housing policy, enumerated the many inequities facing Black and Brown Americans: soaring inflation and median incomes that did not budge; savings that dropped to drastic lows and credit card debt that surged; twenty-two million people using a third of their income to pay for rent; and between 2015 and 2022, a 48 percent increase in the number of people sleeping in their cars, on the streets, in abandoned buildings, and out in the woods. None of Trump's policies would alleviate this dire reality, she noted, but he provided a narrative of blame that people understood.

Many college-educated white Americans think of Black and Latinx voters as the people Trump targets with racist and anti-immigrant language, but these voters don't necessarily see themselves that way. Primo did not see himself as a despised immigrant at the southern border. He had been in this country for more than twenty years. He did not think of himself as one of the undocumented immigrants Trump blamed in 2023 for "poisoning the blood of our country." Primo had papers, if not citizenship. He did not see himself as remotely akin to the transgender people Trump attacked from stages across the country. Primo saw himself as a regular man, a manly man, the kind of man Trump was.

In Texas, a Lyft driver, a white Dominican woman, informed me that Biden was not a man, not the kind of man she liked, a man who could take control of a situation. She did not tell me the rest of the story, but I am a woman and I knew the rest of the story. She wanted the privileges that came with being attached to a man who had power, the kind of power so often denied to women at work and at home and in our communities. She would not be voting against herself if she picked Trump; she would be voting for what she wanted, because white supremacy is not the only story to which people are so loyal that they would choose it over their own well-being. Patriarchy has a powerful pull.

When the *GQ* writer Daniel Lefferts spent time with gay men who voted for Trump in 2024, he found that they thought he was "the gayest president we've ever had." As evidence, they pointed to Trump's cattiness, to his hair and makeup. These gay MAGA voters considered themselves the "normal gay guys" JD Vance had hoped would turn out on Election Day. One of them, a twenty-seven-year-old, put it this way: Gay men like him "want to do our jobs and make our money, and have our family." They did not need big government or any government. They were convinced that they were safe now as gay men. There was no contradiction in how they voted.

None of this is new. In 1979, Stuart Hall, the father of cultural studies, observed: "The 'swing to the Right' is not a reflection of the crisis: it is itself a response to the crisis." The crisis in those years was the social movements of the 1960s, which produced a new crop of citizens in formerly colonized countries and also in Britain and the United States, with the rise of queers and feminists and people of color demanding institutional changes. People who liked the old social order were taken aback, and the economy was tanking, which made it politically prudent to point at all those women, all those queers, all those Black folks—all those bad citizens—and declare a need for law and order and the restoration of family values.

A similar situation has developed now. During the last two decades, young people have organized their undocumented communities, and they have taken to the streets to defend Black lives, and they have battled for the protection of transgender people of all ages. The #MeToo movement brought women into the streets and onto social media and into more intimate conversations with one another. The people in these movements have expanded the collective understanding of who constitutes a citizen, of who can be considered a member of a political community, and they have made a great many people uncomfortable. What is disturbing, then, is not that a political leader can tap into resentment and fears about these social and political changes, but that voters are there for the taking. Voters are ready and willing to preserve a system where they might keep, at the very least, a modicum of power, be that around gender or race or their pocketbook.

Primo, like a number of Cuban Americans, wanted the presidential candidate who vowed to keep this country free of communism and socialism, but I found it more important to consider what Primo had to protect. No, he did not have citizenship, but he had a green card and a good life in the United States. He had married his beloved and was driving an SUV. He had enough money for trips to Los Angeles and Europe. He had, in fact, a great deal to protect—his whiteness, his masculinity, his capitalist consumptions—and Trump promised to protect all of it.

In Catholic elementary school, a science teacher told me the story of Pompeii. It was a tragic, romantic story. Almost eighty years after the birth of Jesus, a volcano erupted in Italy, pouring ash and pumice over the city of Pompeii, choking to death whoever did not escape. Women perished holding their children. Women perished embracing their sisters. Entire families lost their lives together under the onslaught of volcanic rock, their arms and faces and their love for one another—their kinship—frozen for centuries.

This story of the families was not true, at least not in the way my teacher and archaeologists thought. In 2024, geneticists reported they had pulled mitochondrial DNA from the bone fragments of fourteen people who died in Pompeii. The woman with the gold bracelet on her arm, the woman holding a child, was not related to that child. The man near them, the man long presumed to be the father, bore no maternal relation to the woman or the child. The three were kin and not kin. The woman with the gold bracelet had black hair and what the scientists called "dark skin." The woman was, genetically speaking, a man, and maybe a slave. The data suggested their origins and that of the other adult and child could be traced to North Africa or the eastern Mediterranean.

The two women who died holding on to each other were long thought to be sisters or a mother and daughter. One had a graceful, slender head, the crown of a woman. The new study showed this person was genetically a man. Perhaps a trans woman. Perhaps another way of being. The geneticists did not speculate on gender beyond the binary, concluding only that "modern assumptions about gendered behaviors may not be reliable lenses through which to view data from the past."

It is strange now to think that if I was about to lose my life and I grabbed onto my neighbor or my neighbor's child, my life too might be interpreted through the most heteronormative lens. My schoolteacher and the archaeologists and I myself—none of us had dared to imagine another kind of kinship, another formation of family, another way of living in the body and in community.

My cousin was not the first family member who disagreed with me about politics. My entire life I had been surrounded by such family members. I did not think of it as a strange arrangement, or even divisive, because it had always been that way. My father was a lifelong registered Republican and voted for Trump in 2016 and 2020. My one auntie supported denying undocumented children a public education. My childhood best friend, who had become a sister to me, voted Republican and told me, when I pressed her, that she had been happier with her investment portfolio under Trump's first administration. In 2016, when most of my friends discovered for the first time that they had uncles and cousins and co-workers who voted an accused sexual predator into the White House, I nodded in sympathy. I had already known for more than a year that Trump had the support of the people I loved.

Kinship was not about agreement for me then. Over the years, I'd had conversations about elections with my father and my childhood friend. I understood the stories they carried about political life. I understood the conclusions they had reached. I didn't agree with them, but I understood them. The same was true now with Primo, except that we had not grown up together. We had not had the chance to talk often and at length. I was curious to see if that would make the difference: more conversation.

Primo agreed with the Florida law that sex is "immutable" and "biological," and he did not understand how my sweetheart could be nonbinary. What is that? he asked one day in his favorite armchair. What does nonbinary mean?

They don't identify as a woman or a man, I answered.

What role do they have?

My cousin was asking if my partner topped or bottomed, if they took a feminine or masculine role during sex. I felt confident that my cousin did not know how offensive it was to make this query. He was trying to understand gender through the binary system familiar to him, so I cracked a wide grin and said, They do their role really well. Primo laughed.

Later my cousin asserted that gender is natural, that a person is either male or female. Then he added, I come from farmworkers. These were men who worked the land, for whom men were men, so that influences my thinking.

But you're smart, I countered. Realizing that was a stupid response, I clarified, You can have different ideas.

He paused, then quietly he replied, I don't know. I don't know that I can.

We both grew silent. I realized what he was saying. He

could change his perspective, but he did not know if he wanted to.

We talked about political nightmares. My cousin knew that during the 1970s and '80s the United States supported the military dictator Augusto Pinochet, a man who overthrew the democratically elected president of Chile and then proceeded to kill more than three thousand people under the guise of defeating communism. Thousands fled into exile. Primo knew all of this. Of Pinochet, he told me: He killed many people, but he saved his country.

I stared at my cousin, dumbfounded. It had never occurred to me that he believed slaughtering thousands of people could be considered a political necessity, that he could support a man who would order such a butchering. I began to sense that Primo did not want to have different thoughts about this either. He liked his thoughts. He believed these thoughts would keep him safe, would keep him alive, would keep him out of prison.

I don't recall what I said, in large part because what I said did not matter. Something broke in me that afternoon with my cousin. I appreciated that "hurt people hurt people," and that Primo, imprisoned for being gay, had continued in a prison of his own making, but I understood something new too. People like my cousin did not need more information, more facts, more data. I didn't know what they needed. Maybe they needed to hear their neighbors protesting on the streets and at their doors. Maybe they needed to see the people who usually stayed out of politics risking their comfort and speaking up in their quiet voices. I did not know.

What I did know was that my cousin and I had spoken to each other. This was not a situation in which divisive language had kept us apart. Primo and I had talked in a civil manner. We had discussed our queer citizenships, and we understood each other perfectly well. He wanted to live in a country where a leader could murder whomever he pleased in the name of ideology, and I did not. We wanted to live in different countries. There was nothing to reconcile, in much the same way that there had been nothing to reconcile with people who wanted to maintain Jim Crow laws and the lynching of Black Americans and Mexican Americans.

The grief that came next was blunt and clarifying, for I had to admit that Primo and I did not have a relationship to salvage. We did not grow up together. We were not in each other's lives day to day. We had stark political differences, yes, but we did not have a relationship that could bear the weight of these differences.

I began to wonder if public calls for civic engagement, for building bridges across political divides, were a way to avoid grief. I myself had found a certain comfort in the notion that this democracy could be fixed if only we spoke plainly to one another, if only we listened to one another. It had soothed me to think that my cousin and I, in our little corner of the world, could do our part to find consensus. But since this was not true, what else was there to do but to sit with this grief? To stare it in the face and to keep protesting and writing toward a better world for all of us?

Leaving my cousin's home, I drove slowly. It was after dark, and when I waited at a stop sign, I wondered: If a civil war broke out in this country, the kind with different flags and militia and machine guns, would my cousin hide me in his home? Would I shelter him in mine? Would we keep each other safe if the idea of citizenship collapsed?

CHINGONA CITIZENSHIP

The Shoe Store

ON BERGENLINE AVENUE, I lingered outside the shoe store on a Sunday morning. I was in my twenties and trying to convince myself that I did not need a pair of Nikes. I promised myself I would only take a look.

The store brimmed with working-class Latinx, with Spanish and English mashed up in their mouths. It was the same all along Bergenline, a two-mile strip in northern New Jersey of clothing stores, restaurants, bodegas, florist shops, and doctors' offices. The area had been home to Cubans in the 1960s, and by 2000 it had become a United Nations of Latinx. There were still a few Cubans but many more Dominicans, Salvadoreñes, and Guatemalans.

The store stocked the women's sneakers next to the kids' section, and so I found myself inspecting footwear alongside a four-year-old Black girl in a white lace dress with a tutu skirt that made her look like a tiny bride. The girl had the most radiant smile. Put these on, her mother instructed, and the girl, obedient and delighted, climbed onto a bench and extended her foot, so small and dark under the layers of lace. The red sneakers fit perfectly, and the girl's face turned serious. These fit well, she said in her most grown-up voice, and I told her mother, She's beautiful. We spoke long enough for me to learn that it is never easy to find the right shoes for a toddler and that the mother was from the Dominican Republic and the girl was named María Concepción Altagracia.

The child's name was longer than the child herself, and grinning, I wanted to tell the mother that the child needed a shorter name for navigating the ordeal known as elementary school. Before I could say anything, however, the woman, also smiling, added, She's Americana.

Of course she was. María Concepción Altagracia on Bergenline Avenue in New Jersey had been named after the Virgin Mary in multiple ways, named in such a way that the connection to Latin America could never be doubted, and she was an American, by which I believe her mother meant that the child had birthright citizenship, that the child had been born within the borders of this country.

Chingona

The official dictionary of the Spanish language, published by the Royal Spanish Academy, does not have much to report on chingonas. It offers this single definition for chingón, the masculine version: someone who is "competent at an activity." In contrast, the academy offers a robust and more lively definition for the related word chingar, which means "to fuck," as in to have sex and also to fuck with someone, like when your joke annoys a person and you end up being told, sometimes in a crude way and sometimes in a friendly way: No me chingues. Don't fuck with me. According to the dictionary, chingar can also indicate that you drank too many whiskeys or beers, and in parts of Central America, it can refer to cutting off an animal's tail.

In 1950, Octavio Paz, Mexico's famed poet and winner of the Nobel Prize in Literature, called chingar "a magical word: a change of tone, a change of inflection, is enough to change its meaning." He wrote at length about the chingada, which can refer to a fucked-up place, "a country of broken and worn-out things," and also to women. Paz, like other men, conceived of women as the chingadas, the ones who are fucked over or just fucked. He pointed to a historical figure, an Indigenous woman named Malintzin, as the first of the chingadas.

In the early 1500s, when she was a teenager, Malintzin was taken as a slave, along with nineteen other girls, by the Spanish colonizer Hernán Cortés and his men. Fluent in Nahuatl and Yucatec, the languages of the Aztecs and Maya, Malintzin became Cortés's interpreter, often negotiating on his behalf with Indigenous leaders and making his military prowess possible. She also gave birth to their child. On paper, after her death, the Spanish empire forgot Malintzin, and then, in the early 1800s, as Mexico gained its independence, the leaders of this new country realized they needed a story. They turned to a novel about Malintzin, a fictional account in which she seduced Cortés, betrayed her people, and became the symbolic mother of the first Mexican—her son being both Indigenous and Spaniard. In the novel, she was the one who had been fucked and the one who had fucked over her own people.

Across the years, in both public and private discourses, Malintzin became a traitor, and chingona turned into the worst remark that could be made about a woman. It became akin to calling a woman a bitch but much worse. A boy could be celebrated for being a chingón. It meant he had taken a risk. He had taken what he wanted and acted like he didn't give a fuck. A girl, a good girl, was never to behave that way. She was never to be so careless, to want so much.

My family was not Mexican, so no one called me a chingona, just an Indian, as in qué india when Tía Dora arrived at our house early in the morning and I did not greet her with kisses and a polite smile. Qué india when I took the cereal box and did not offer any to my tía. Qué india when I walked out of the room without excusing myself because the conversation bored me and I wanted to read my book instead. Over and over again, when I did what I wanted, I turned Native for my auntie.

My mother never said this to me. It was her sister. Her one sister. Tía Dora. She was obsessed with Indigenous women. She located all female desires and boldness and demands there in la india, and often she puzzled over the fact that her admonitions meant nothing to me. She had grown up in a country where you could see Indigenous women mistreated on the street and in private homes and on television. She was perhaps terrified of becoming one of them, of being treated as if her life held very little value for others. She wanted me to feel the same fear. Maybe she thought it would keep me safe.

But I was growing up in Jersey, not Colombia. I did not know another girl who was told to not be an Indian. When I grew up and heard the word chingona, when a Chicana feminist told me, It means you're a badass, I thought, Here they are. Finally. The girls like me, the ones who make trouble simply for being who they are.

Chicana feminists reclaimed the word chingona along with Malintzin. They ditched the nonsense about a betrayed people and pointed instead to her intellect and linguistic talents, to the ways she grabbed power in a man's colonial and colonizing world. Malintzin was a survivor, a fighter, a chingona.

On social media now, memes turn up from Chicanas and Latinas claiming "I'm chingona like my mother" and "Note to self: be chingona." The term has been so embraced that when the activist Alma Zaragoza-Petty wrote about navigating the racism and sexism of higher education as a graduate student and professor, she titled her book *Chingona: Owning Your Inner Badass for Healing and Justice.* I can now purchase T-shirts, mugs, and tote bags announcing to the world that I am a chingona, and I don't cringe at this reclamation-for-sale, because these are not big-box stores capitalizing on the word. These are Chicana women running small online businesses. They are designing the earrings and hoodies they want to sport themselves.

In Oaxaca, Mexico, the Zapotec never had to recover Malintzin from history because they had celebrated her life across the centuries through ceremonial dances. In the essay collection *Tres Veces Tres. En Clave Malintzin,* the Mixe linguist and writer Yásnaya Elena Aguilar Gil recounts that for one village it is such an honor to dance for Malintzin that "it's necessary to add the girls, as soon as they are born, to a long waiting list" so when they come of age, the girls will have a chance to perform in *Danza de la Pluma.*

The woman in the shoe store, the woman who named her daughter after the Virgin, the woman who blessed her daughter with three names in Spanish and called her una Americana—that woman was a chingona, and if she had given birth to her daughter among the Zapotec, I am convinced that she would have offered her baby girl to dance as Malintzin.

Chola, Chonga, Cholita

The chingona has linguistic sisters across borders. In working-class Southern California, cholas were the Chicana girls who didn't take shit, who wore winged eyeliner and painted their lips a dark red and pulled their hair into tight ponytails. This began in the 1960s. The media conflated them with gangs, with their cholo boyfriends and brothers, but the journalist Barbara Calderón-Douglass points out that the origins of chola fashion are to be found in the 1940s pachucas, the femme counterpart to the Chicano teenage boys in those years who wore zoot suits, the long blazers over the high-waisted trousers. The pachuca was part of "a rebel subculture that rejected assimilation into the white, hyper-patriotic spirit of WWII," writes Calderón-Douglass, and the girls had a reason to reject that patriotism. Before the war, in the 1930s, the United States had deported more than a million Mexicans and Mexican Americans, many from Southern California.

The chola has a long history. A Nahuatl-Spanish dictionary from 1571 indicates that xolo referred to a servant or a slave. In the casta paintings that the elite Spaniards used to label the racial mixtures of colonial Mexico, a cholo was the child of an Indigenous woman and a mestizo man, one who was himself Indigenous and European. In Perú, one linguist traced cholo to Mochica, an ancient Indigenous language, whose people referred to a child as cyulo.

A new kind of chola called the chonga appeared in Florida in the early 2000s. Chongas were the girls who lived in the working-class neighborhoods of Hialeah and Miami. They squeezed themselves into tube tops and tight jeans. They sported two, sometimes three gold chains and hoop earrings emblazoned with their names. They believed, as I did in high school, in the necessity of long acrylic nails.

The chingona, the chola, the chonga. These are not the people who come to mind in conversations about citizenship. In *Aesthetics of Excess: The Art and Politics of Black and Latina Embodiment,* the gender and women's studies professor Jillian Hernandez observes that stereotypes of Latinas "in visual culture are measured against an imagined white/middle-class construct of U.S. citizenship. Latina bodies are read as out of control, and thus queer." And, I would add, as not citizens.

Bolivia offers a different story. In the capital of La Paz, cholitas are Quechua and Aymara women who don the garb of colonial Spain: the heavy, layered skirts, the shawls, and the bowler hats. For years upon years, restaurants refused to serve these women, and cities banned them from walking in their plazas. But the cholitas organized. As early as 1962, a cholita hosted her own radio program, and in 2005 these Quechua and Aymara women helped to elect the country's first Aymara president. The new constitution of 2009 officially recognized thirty-six Indigenous languages, and a 2010 law outlawed racism, at least on paper.

The traditional dress of the cholitas is now recognizable around the world. It has been adopted by daughters and granddaughters. In La Paz, Diana Málaga, a trans woman who runs a clothing shop, dresses like her grandmother, a cholita, complete with the bowler hat, shawl, and puffy skirt. She carefully placed a sign in her window that reads "All of us are equal before the law."

La Nena

In lessons on drawing the human figure, a teacher will say to begin with a landmark, one of those places on the body where bone thrusts against skin. Think of the clavicle, the sternum, the pubic bone. After the landmark graces the page of your sketch pad, the teacher will say to measure the distance. If the clavicle is here, the pubic bone must be here. The body is not art, not at first. The body is math. The iliac crest, the edge of the hip bone, is a landmark.

In fifth grade, I never saw this one girl's hip bones. She never saw mine. We were students at a Catholic school named after St. John the Baptist. Our classroom had linoleum floors, a cross above the blackboard, and rows of wooden desks. The girl and I arrived in the same uniforms every morning: maroon vests over white blouses and gray plaid skirts that shot straight down from our waists. The girl and I were like St. John the Baptist: floating heads. Nada de caderas. Nada de piernas.

That's not true. The girl had a glorious body, from what I could see: robust arms and a thick torso. She towered over me with short, uncombed brown hair. Unkempt, the tías would have said if they had spoken English. Untethered, I would have said if I had known the word.

The girl, whose hip bones I never saw, had skin like mine if my mother let me stay in the sun. She sat at the back of the class, and one day when I walked by her desk on purpose, to whisper hello, to learn if she was friendly, I saw what she had done to her arms, and I startled. I had never seen a girl do such things to her own body.

In English, I think of her as *the girl*. In Spanish, it's different. In Spanish, she is *la nena,* never *la niña,* because to call a girl a niña is to say that she knows how to pour the coffee and behave herself when company comes over. A niña keeps herself tiny and quiet. She is a sniffle from the corner.

The girl at the back of the class, the girl who did what she did to her arms—she was not a niña. She was a nena, a word that grows tall in the mouth, that goes loose and cracks open in the mouth. A nena. A chingona.

Cuban women taught me about nenas. On twenty-eight-hour bus rides between Jersey and South Florida, the women talked about nenas. Their nena had gotten into nursing school. Their nena was getting her license to cut hair. Their nena had gotten knocked up. A woman was either a mother who had a nena or she was the nena herself. Either way, a nena did not apologize. A nena kept her house spotless and managed her man's money. A nena knew to tell the bus driver that he had to pull over soon because everyone on the bus needed to stretch their legs and use the toilet.

I marveled at how a single word could sound so self-possessed and still be loved.

At the back of the classroom, a pencil in my hand, I gaped at the nena's left arm. She had taken a blue Paper Mate pen, the skinny ones, the point medium thick, and she had pressed the nib to the inside of her forearm. She had covered her skin with inky blue swirls, painting on her arm stars, moons, meteors, even crosses—and what I remember most is the look on her face: luminous, gratified. She had made of her body a work of art.

I did not know the word ligament. Neither did the nena. We did not know what binds bone to bone, girl to girl. But I panicked. There is no other word for it. Girls were not supposed to do that to their bodies. They were supposed to stay clean and good and safe. I bit my bottom lip and glanced at the front of the room. The teacher did not know. Not yet. I hurried back to my desk.

That was the first time. There were other times, other days, that I wandered toward the back of the class under the guise of needing the pencil sharpener but in truth to peek at the nena and her brazos and the imaginative worlds she was creating there on her own body. She arrived every morning, her arms scrubbed clean, and by the end of the day, there she would be, at the back of the class, arms covered by the blue cosmos.

The teacher scowled at the nena but said nothing. I wondered how the nena could do it. How she could sit at the back of the class. How she could stay so far away from the teachers and their power. How she could do that to her arms. How she could risk everything.

I was never the nena at the back of the class. Always, I chose a seat in the first or second row, my skin scented with the pink Camay soap Mami bought at the A&P. Always, my skirt was ironed with military precision. My mother insisted on this. She could not do anything about my dark hair or my thick lips, but she could make it so that I was dressed as required.

At the front of the class, I raised my arm as far as I could, sometimes even waving my hand lest the teacher think she could ignore me. It did not matter if I had started kindergarten with more Spanish in my mouth than English. It did not matter if my father beat me, if the police were called. It did not matter if one day people would ask if I had been born in this country. By fifth grade, I knew that if I intended to survive this world, I had to grab it by the throat at the front of the class. My tía might have called me una india at home; at school, I had to be una india, una chingona, if I planned to go to college on a scholarship. I had to take what I wanted within the prescribed limits erected by the white women.

The Cuban performance artist and activist Tania Bruguera has written: "At times, surviving is the wrong answer, the conservative answer." In fifth grade, I thought it was the only answer. The nena who drew on her arms—she lived by Tania's words. She did not care about the knowledge of the white women at the front of the classroom. She did not need their permission, their recommendations, their support. That is the reason I stared at her. It is the reason I have not been able to forget her. The nena did not want what this white country offered. She trusted her blue pen, her imagination, her body.

Or she was desperate, neglected, a riot of emotion. She inked her body to reclaim it from a violation no one could see. She had sunk into a depression, and the touch of the pen on her flesh jarred her into sensation. Or she was terrified of the white world, of the hard edges of the English language, and she marked her body so the white teachers would not want her, would pass her over, would disown her. She expected the rechazo, so she did it first, made of her body a work of art to scare the white teachers and even me.

She was the nena a school psychologist might take into her office. The psychologist would give her colored pencils and paper and invite the nena to draw her parents, her home life, her feelings. But our school did not have someone like that. We were not poor enough for state funding or rich enough for private child psychologists. We were expected to abide by the rules, to be good enough for admission into the girls' Catholic high school and one day a state college and after that a husband and two children, a house with a tree in front and a car of our own. We were expected to survive in that way.

I don't remember when the nena left. I don't remember if she was in our class for two months or six. I don't remember the sound of her voice, the words she used, or if she ever spoke to me. I don't remember if she said goodbye. I don't remember who took her seat or what the teachers said when she was gone.

I do remember that after she left, I felt her absence with an acuteness I did not shake for years. She had begun to show me another way of living, another way of being a girl, a chingona, a citizen.

Goodenough

A white woman created the Draw-a-Man test in the 1920s to determine the intelligence of children between the ages of four and ten. The directions for drawing the man went like this: "Make the very best picture that you can. Take your time and work very carefully. . . . Make the whole man." Up to fifty-one points could be awarded, including how distinctly a child distinguished the neck from the head and whether they had pinned nostrils to the man's face. A total of four points alone were granted for how a child drew the eyes.

Children were to only imagine a man. The inventor of the test, Florence Goodenough, had graduated from Stanford University with a doctorate in psychology, and she agreed with the argument used in medicine and science that men are less complicated than women. Imagine the chaos of allocating points to a child's drawing of a woman's body. One child might depict a woman in a pleated skirt, another in a wrap. How would a psychologist assign points to the placement of hemlines or the size of a bust? Goodenough concluded that the male body made grading the test easier. Children would know to depict their men in trousers, button-down shirts, ties, and hats. She urged caution that the neckties in children's artwork not be missed. They counted for a point.

Numbers preoccupied Goodenough. She prized quantitative results: percentages, means, table after table of data. She focused on methods that other researchers could reproduce, and it did work. Her Draw-a-Man test showed correlations with the esteemed Stanford-Binet IQ test, and it became so popular with clinicians studying child development that today she is credited with devising the "first systemic scoring system of children's drawings."

Goodenough developed the test by examining the drawings of almost four thousand children, most of them in schools in Perth Amboy, New Jersey, about thirty miles south of my elementary school. She excluded from her initial study schools where the majority of students came from Black or immigrant families. But she could not ignore these children for long. In 1926, two years after Congress instituted racial quotas on migration to the United States, Goodenough published her first book, observing that less than a quarter of the children from Perth Amboy were "of American-born white parentage." Most of the children came from families who were Italian, Black, Jewish, or Danish. For another study, she complained about racial mixing, which made it hard for her to separate "mulatoo" children from the "pure" Black children.

Goodenough included the artwork of eighty-one children in her book *Measurement of Intelligence by Drawings,* noting the race, age, and school grade of each child. One drawing shows a person with a giant Afro and a pair of pants that reaches their neck. I write *their* because the figure is, to me, genderqueer. The pants are simultaneously pants and a long skirt. The child bestowed the figure with tiny feet and ears that spring from the head in the shape of prehistoric bones. I would interpret it as a celebratory drawing except for one detail: the diagonal lines across the mouth. The child covered the mouth with wire. The child, the artist, the nena, was a nine-year-old Black girl.

"Drawing, to the child, is primarily a language," Goodenough wrote in her book.

It was a language she could not read. A language she refused to read. She told the children to draw a man, when she was, in fact, saying: Draw a college-educated white man, the kind of man I know, the kind of man I saw at Stanford, the kind of man I am trying to impress right now with these tests.

Still, researchers loved the Goodenough test. It was easy to administer ("Draw a man") and simple to score. Over the years, the test was deployed across the United States and also abroad in Egypt, Lebanon, and Bolivia. In 1941, one psychology professor used the Draw-a-Man test to measure the intelligence of more than a hundred children on the Hopi reservation in Arizona. The boys' IQs turned out higher than the girls and also than "for any white children." The researcher did not attribute this extraordinary intelligence to biology, as had been done with white children, but to community resources. The Hopi Tribe trained the boys in the visual arts so they could sell their intricately designed pottery to white tourists.

Faced with Indigenous boys who could draw better than white children, as well as the cultural shift after World War II to decouple race from biology, Goodenough conceded in 1950 that "the search for a culture-free test, whether of intelligence, artistic ability, personal-social characteristics, or any other measurable trait is illusory." She disclosed that her own study decades earlier had failed in this regard, and in what may be one of the more unusual racial apologies, she wrote, "The writer hereby apologizes for it!"

The admission and the apology were tucked into the eighth footnote of an article written by Goodenough. Today, when she is considered, which does not often happen, she is presented as someone who must be rescued from the archives. Two psychology professors and their undergraduate students included her in their online biography of "marginalized psychology pioneers." On the website of Psychology's Feminist Voices, a project run by a Canadian-based group of feminist psychologists, Goodenough is praised for creating a test of children's drawings that remained in use for four decades. In a biographical article, her anti-feminism is briefly noted. Goodenough did not want to be thought of as a woman psychologist, only a psychologist. About her racism, the article's authors remain silent.

Her test was popular enough, though, that word of it reached the Defense Department, and months after the attacks on Pearl Harbor, the U.S. Army contacted Goodenough. It wanted to test incoming female officers for the newly created Women's Army Auxiliary Corps. Could she come up with a way of screening these women for leadership qualities, as well as the degree to which the women were feminine or masculine? In short, could she find the chingonas?

Goodenough had already been at work on such an idea, and she adapted it for the Defense Department. In this test, women were presented with words whose spelling did not change even when multiple meanings did. Ring, for example, could mean an engagement ring or the shape of a circle or a boxing ring. After administering this test, the army and Goodenough learned that divorced women were the most masculine, las más chingonas, as they were more likely than other women to offer "rare responses."

In the 1960s, the psychologist Dale B. Harris revised the Draw-a-Man test. The norms on which the scoring had been created were changing. Post–World War II children drew more of the human body. They spent time adorning their men with hair and limbs and hands. They ignored the faces though, including the eyes, brows, and mouths. Harris conceded that one could speak of a "faceless generation" following that terrible war but added that he did not want to sound too dramatic.

Harris updated the scoring system, making it possible for children to earn more than seventy points. They could get credit if they drew a white man who had combed his hair. The way to create such a man was to give him a few black lines over his head. The children did not get the same recognition for producing on paper a man with an Afro or locs. Harris also developed the Draw-a-Woman test and found that Goodenough had been correct forty years earlier. "The female figure is more 'culture bound' than the male figure," he wrote. As if to underscore this, he did not give children a point for drawing a woman in what he called a "solid shoe." The footwear had to be feminine, and he provided a list of what qualified: "a pump, tie, open toe, wedgie, saddle shoe, etc." If there was a heel, it had to be a third of the shoe's total height.

There was another test too, one that Harris did not create but that clinical psychologists began to favor after World War II: the Draw-a-Person test. In this scenario, children and adults alike can draw the gender of their choice. Harris concluded, "The figure drawn was significant in indicating unconscious sex role identification." To use the language of those years: The test could signal "sexual deviation."

My parents did not save any of my childhood drawings. No one did it for them in Cuba and Colombia. Childhood was a time to be endured, not celebrated, documented, or analyzed. I wonder now if I would have had the courage to draw pointy heels, or if I would have sketched what I knew best: the shoes with a wide half-inch heel, the kind of shoes my mother wore to the factory.

La Tía Chingona

I love the photographs of my Tía Rosa. The one of her in a black dress surrounded by schoolchildren in the campos of Colombia. The one of her after she married her Puerto Rican husband in New Jersey. The one of her with my sister in our front yard, my sister in white baptismal attire and my auntie in a frilly red top. In all of these photographs, Tía Rosa never smiled. She wore a face from another century, a time when having your photograph taken was a serious undertaking. She had a stunning jawline, the kind you only see on actresses from old black-and-white films. In every photograph, she stares at the camera as if to say: Don't fuck with me.

For most of my life, I believed the women in my family had avoided la migra by flying into the United States on visas. They had gone to the U.S. consulate in Bogotá, application in hand, and a white man in a suit had reviewed their identification cards and asked them about their reasons for traveling to New York City. Maybe the white man at the consulate trusted that a woman like Tía Rosa would not lie to him. She had been a schoolteacher. Maybe the white man could not bear the notion of a schoolteacher, a spinster schoolteacher, lying to him. He looked kindly upon her and stamped the papers that turned into a tourist visa.

The same was not true for my uncles. I grew up hearing

that this tío and that tío had applied for a visa in Bogotá and been denied. The white men at the U.S. consulate apparently did not hold any of the men in my family in high regard. Or maybe it was that all my tíos had wives and children, and the officials wanted to avoid a slew of married men leaving their families. Either way, I grew up knowing that the U.S. consulate in Bogotá was a gamble, a puzzle, a game of chess or tic-tac-toe. It all depended on the man assigned to you that day.

In her book *Impossible Subjects,* the historian Mae M. Ngai chronicles how deportation "came of age" during the 1920s thanks to new immigration laws that instituted racial quotas, created the Border Patrol, and made it a crime to enter the country without certain papeles. But a difference also sprang up between those who came by sea and those who arrived by land. During those years, advocates for undocumented Italians and Irish called for compassion when it came to enforcing deportation orders. The Italian man didn't have his papers, his advocates conceded, but he had a job and young children. He had found love. He had found work. He had found a new life. He deserved to stay.

The same was not said of Mexicans during those years. Instead, federal officials enacted new policies to police the southern border. Starting in 1919, Mexicans had to apply for entry into the United States at designated ports of entry, and then the federal government began hiring cowboys and ranchers, some of whom were members of the Ku Klux Klan, to work as Border Patrol agents. Arriving in the United States without papers for a second time became a felony. One by one, federal policies began linking Mexicans to criminality, to the violation of laws about borders and maps, about the land itself.

Of course, the new immigration laws did not target all Mexicans. Those who could afford a first-class train ticket entered the country like Europeans. They did not have to strip naked in El Paso, Texas, and take chemical baths to rinse themselves of the possibility of contagious diseases like typhus. They did not have to present their armpits and the inside of their mouths for inspection. They did not have to prove that they could read and write. The Mexicans subjected to all this policing were mixed race, people who had come to work in the fields and in the laundromats. The implication was clear: If a Mexican had not been inspected and approved, if they had not been bestowed with papers to be in this country, they did not deserve to be here. They had done something wrong.

I suspect the obsession with migration at the southern border grew, in part, because it can be photographed. The woman crossing the highway, the woman wading through the river, the woman huddling with her child next to the Border Patrol truck—she can be photographed, documented, and turned into a story. Her body, or at least the story of it, can be shared with strangers, and because this visual language has circulated for at least a hundred years, a child now can be told: Draw a woman crossing the border, and the child can do it.

But how would anyone photograph the woman who overstayed a tourist visa? A photograph would show the most ordinary of lives: a woman boiling water in the morning, a woman washing her underwear in a bathroom sink, a woman cradling her son to sleep with a song. The photograph could show a date, a stamp, even a clock, but those objects are not mythologized in the American mind, not the way the land is.

For years, I thought the women in my family had nothing to do with the U.S.-Mexico border. One day, apropos of nothing, except that maybe in my thirties I was finally old enough to hear it, the aunties told me the truth about their oldest sister: Tía Rosa arrived in the United States in the early 1970s with a tourist visa. She stayed. She found an apartment. She found a boyfriend. But then the call came from Colombia. Her father, a tiny man with a stern face, had died. Tía packed her bags and ignored her sisters' pleas. Yes, her visa had expired. Yes, if she left the country, she would not be able to return, but her father had died and she had loved him and so her grief refused the tyranny of maps. She would fly home to him and to her mother, who was still very much alive. Also, she had ten brothers and sisters, and she wanted to get her name on the deed to her parents' house. She was chingona like that.

Months later, after my grandfather was buried and the house firmly in my auntie's name, our phone rang in Jersey. Tía Rosa had reached Mexico. Maybe she took a flight from Bogotá to Mexico City to Juárez—a flight because I refuse to imagine my auntie with the stunning jawline crammed into buses, trekking through Panama and all of Central America to reach Mexico. A flight because she never told me this story herself, and now with her Alzheimer's, she cannot tell me the story.

She called my mother from the border. She needed to cross over. My mother and her sisters phoned their brothers, their cousins. Someone found a priest. The priest agreed. At first, I pictured the priest with his clerical collar, his black shirt and pants, a pocket Bible on the dashboard, driving my tía across the border into El Paso with fake papers, even passing her off as a nun. But it's more likely that the priest found someone else to do the deed or, worse, that Tía crawled into the trunk of someone's car and prayed.

The part I cannot imagine is how she took buses across the United States. Maybe it was simple, and she boarded a Greyhound from El Paso to Penn Station. Maybe she only had to stay on one bus whose drivers changed. Her light skin surely helped. She carried herself with confidence, and people probably mistook her for an Italian or Portuguese woman. Still, Tía navigated a long stretch of this country with her limited English. It's a kind of intelligence, of chingona-ness, no test can measure.

She arrived in Jersey, where over the next twenty years she became the auntie who trekked to New York City every day, who learned the subway system as if she had grown up here, who found work in Manhattan cleaning up after white ladies. Tía became the chingona, the only woman in our family brave enough to venture into the city during the 1980s, when the headlines screamed of rapes and robberies at the Port Authority Bus Terminal. She married a Puerto Rican and fixed her papeles. She took trains and buses up and down Manhattan and into the Bronx, where people told her she could find a particularly good Catholic church, one with a devoted priest, one with a Mass in Spanish.

I have never been to the southern border, the border with Mexico, and so it is revealing of American life that people are often curious to know if I am from there. Are you Mexican? they ask because we are in Ohio and they have only met Mexicans. Are you Mexican? they inquire because they only read about Mexicans on social media and we are ordering at a local taquería.

The border with Mexico is less than 2,000 miles. The one with Canada? More than 5,000. In the American imagination, the border with Mexico might as well be 10,000 miles. I want to suggest that this obsession has to do with the guilt and fear of retribution that plague empires. The United States invaded Mexico in 1846 after it tried but failed to buy that country's land, and U.S. politicians invented the story of Manifest Destiny to assert that it was this country's divine right to slaughter Indigenous people and Mexicans and to take ownership of miles upon miles of red sandstone and Ponderosa pines. I want to suggest that guilt and fear reign in the American psyche over what was done. The fear is they (a great many theys) will return with a valid right to the land. I want to suggest that every time Americans talk about more policing of the border, it is because we understand the scale of our crimes, past and present.

But I prefer the stubborn facts, which are these: The border vanishes when the United States needs cheap labor. The racist quotas on migration in the early part of the twentieth century did not include Mexicans, since private businesses wanted them to work the farms. In the 1930s, during the Great Depression, the United States deported more than a million Mexicans and Mexican Americans, and the border closed. World War II produced more jobs than the United States had workers, and a 1942 executive order opened the border again with the Bracero Program, which brought more than four million Mexicans to labor on farms in the United States. The Immigration and Nationality Act of 1965 placed a quota system on those migrating from Mexico.

I grew up hearing that everyone in my family had flown to the United States: my father, my mother and her sisters, and my uncles. We were a family of birds. Everyone flocked to this country clutching too many papers: visas and passports, airline tickets and baggage claim numbers and declarations for customs. They flew over water and land, their flights my inheritance.

The only time my mother referred to el borde was when she spoke of fabric. A seamstress, she had to be practical about how to alter clothing to fit women. She could alter this plain button-down shirt but not that blouse with the border, the hand-stitched pattern. Or she could do it, but no one should be surprised by the results.

On a website for "fiber enthusiasts," a man named Tom shares "Some Thoughts About Borders." He laments that classic weaving books from the early twentieth century do not offer suggestions on working with borders. Many types of borders exist, he writes, including one named rosepath. He reminds us that a border brings our eyes to the interior. A border tells us to look at the center of the blanket or the placemat or the rug. He does issue a caution that could serve as public policy: "Not everything we weave requires a border."

The Faceless Generation

In Chicago, at the start of 2024, there were almost as many immigrants in the city's shelter system (about 14,500) as there were students at the university just north of the city where I had begun to teach. Immigrants had been bused from Texas at the behest of that state's governor, who had the National Guard take control of the southern border at a park along the Rio Grande. On January 12, while Chicago prepared for its first winter storm—opening warming centers, directing immigrants to the safety and heat of the main library—two sisters in Mexico, Monica and Virterma de la Sancha Cerros, stepped into the Rio Grande with their three children.

Like everyone who enters the river, Monica and Virterma must have prayed. They held hands, Monica clasping her son's while Virterma clutched those of her ten-year-old daughter, Yorlei, and eight-year-old son, Jonathan. They began to cross like that, all five of them together, mano a mano, intent on reaching the dry land on the other side. But the water was cold, much colder than they could have expected. The water began rising. It soon reached Virterma's hips. She shivered. So did her children and her sister. One of the children lost their grip. The women panicked. The river's current pulled at their legs. Virterma and her children began to sink. They screamed for help. Everyone screamed.

The Mexican government sent a distress call to the U.S. Border Patrol, whose agents arrived at the park by the river to find that the Texas National Guard would not let them enter. It is not clear if there was a standoff, if the Border Patrol agents wanted to save Virterma's life or her daughter's life or anyone's life; later reports gave the impression that no such standoff took place, that no agent went to the park, that the Border Patrol merely called the National Guard to request access. Nevertheless, the moment reminds me of accounts of federal troops in the 1950s enforcing the racial integration of public schools by overriding local police. The moment makes me think: This is not supposed to happen, not now, not here. Such face-to-face confrontations between federal troops and state soldiers are supposed to happen in other places, in other countries, not here.

What happened here is that Virterma and her sister and their children fought the river solitas. They tried to stay alive in all that cold water, which must have felt as if it were a terrible wall and not anything as porous as agua. They tried to keep each other and their children alive, but the night was cold and so was the river and the hypothermia crept into their bodies, making it harder to breathe, to move their legs, to carry their children. Monica and her son pushed on and reached dry land, shaken and needing medical care, but vivos. Virterma drowned with her two children, Yorlei and Jonathan, all three of them vanquished by the water, all three of them pulled from the river by the Mexican authorities—not because Virterma and her children had citizenship in that country but because their bodies had been easier for the Mexican men in uniforms to reach.

A week before their deaths, Texas governor Greg Abbott told a radio host that the state was doing everything it could to stop the arrival of immigrants. He added, "The only thing that we're not doing is we're not shooting people who come across the border, because of course, the Biden administration would charge us with murder."

He did not say: We don't shoot women and children since to do so would be evil, inhumane, barbaric, morally indefensible. No. He said: We don't murder women and children because another white man would bring murder charges against us, another white man might come and fuck us up.

Dale B. Harris had worried that World War II produced

children who would not draw the human face. He called these children the "faceless generation," which makes me wonder about the boy who survived the river, the boy who watched his cousins and tía die. What will we call a generation that draws the faces of dead children?

Size 6

The Chicago community organizer told me she had something like a hundred shoes that local residents had donated for immigrant families. I did not believe her until I showed up at her house and found piles of children's rain boots and snow boots, mounds of lace-up boots for women and sneakers for men. There was a pair of women's cowboy boots and more pink toddler boots than I could have imagined possible. The organizer said, I want to ban all pink shoes. I had one boy who saw pink on a pair of sneakers and refused to wear them. The mom didn't care. But he wouldn't put them on.

I could not help but think that if given the Draw-a-Man test, the boy would have scored points for knowing so much about the rigidity of gender lines. He would probably draw a woman's shoe in pink with a spike heel. He would give her a wide skirt and long earrings. Maybe he would gift her a necklace, the one he wanted for his mother.

My task at the organizer's house was to pair the donated shoes with sheets of paper that listed the members of immigrant families and their shoe sizes. The women mostly needed a size 6, sometimes a 5, but most of the donated shoes were a 9 or 10, and they were name-brand shoes. Several shoes were so worn that the sizes had blurred, and so I stuck my own size 7 foot in to see if it might be a good fit. After all, a woman with a size 6 might be able to do what my mom and I used to do when we found shoes on sale that were too big for us: We shoved cotton balls into the toe to make a larger size the right size.

I managed to match several families with the shoes they needed. In other cases, I could only match the children's and the father's. I learned that the organizer was right: The pink boots outnumbered the girls at the shelter.

Overall, the situation was an absurd metaphor for immigration policy in the United States. There were so many shoes, piles of them, and it was a matter of matching the right shoe to the right person, of finding the places in the city where women who wore size 6 shoes had ones to give away. Similarly, there was so much housing, so many single-family houses and apartment units and old hotels where no one lived, and for the city, it was a matter of finding the places that could be donated, refurbished, and matched to those who needed homes.

After I hauled the shoes with another volunteer to a shelter that was housing about a hundred immigrants, I sat in the car, stunned by the sheer volume of the donated shoes. The idea that the United States is a rich country, a country of plenty, a country of excess, never felt so tangible as when I held that many used shoes in my hands. I wanted to show these shoes to all the people demanding that the border be shut down. I wanted to say: We have so much that we can give it away. What are you afraid of?

I was not asking that question, though, because I already knew the answer. My father voted for Trump and my Cuban American cousins who could vote for him probably did too, and I understood that they carried within them a different story than I did. In their story, we only had an excess of shoes in the United States because we had kept the borders closed, because we had kept citizenship as a coveted status, because we had kept citizenship limited to only whites for more than a century. We were in this position of wealth precisely because we had not let everyone in.

They did not want to hear that maybe we were in this privileged position because we had taken so much, because we had forced so many generations of Mexican families into low-wage farm jobs, because we had insisted that our private companies win the best financial deals in Central America, because we had supported so many dictators in so many Latin American countries when it suited our political agendas, and because more recently we had forced Central American countries to open and close their borders to suit our needs. They did not want to hear that the United States was still an empire and that, as the legal scholar E. Tendayi Achiume has proposed, migration might be a form of reparations.

That day when I dropped off the shoes at the immigrant shelter, the air was cold, and the sky blue and bright. Two women pushed strollers, side by side. I eyed their sneakers and wondered if they could be a size 6, if they were walking far or just to the corner. Later I realized I had not thought about shiny red pumps or pink patent stilettos or leather boots. I had not considered the possibility that the two women, like me, would want to wear shoes that made them think, however briefly, of another life.

THE PEOPLE

THE COLOMBIAN CONSULATE was tucked away among palm trees and restaurants with terra-cotta roofs and Mediterranean-inspired archways. No one had hoisted a flag at the entrance, making it easy to walk by and mistake the consulate for another pretty office building in Coral Gables, a wealthy city next door to Miami. I knew the location, though, so I marched past the men ordering brunch, past the bookstore and the new coffee shop, to the consulate, my mother and auntie trailing behind me.

It was a few months before the 2024 presidential election, and I was at the front steps of the consulate to ask about becoming a citizen of Colombia. A 1993 law in my mother's home country made dual citizenship a legal possibility, and by being her daughter, I was eligible even though I had been born and raised in the United States and had probably spent, over the course of my lifetime, less than nine months in Colombia.

The idea of dual citizenship had never occurred to me before the fall of 2016. I had grown up with immigrants who only wanted one citizenship—that of the United States. Always, I had been told that the papers I acquired by being born on this land were the only papers I would ever want. This was true until Trump won the presidency the first time. Then, in the months that followed, a friend told me she was applying for Canadian citizenship through her parents in case political life became unbearable here, and other friends revealed they already had second citizenships and the political escape routes these offered.

My friends were not anomalies. Dual citizenship is a phenomenon of the twenty-first century. Only about 25 percent of the countries in the Americas and Europe permitted people to claim dual citizenship in 1990, according to the sociologist Yossi Harpaz. By 2016, that number had shot up to more than 80 percent thanks to globalization, which made it cheaper to fly back to the motherland and also to call home. In New Jersey, shops opened in the late 1990s devoted to nothing other than "selling minutes" so immigrants, new and old, could make inexpensive phone calls to Colombia, Guatemala, and Mexico. Those who became naturalized citizens of the United States began urging the political leaders of their home countries to grant them the right to vote back where they still had family and were building their casitas.

I stood at the front door to the Colombian consulate inquiring about citizenship almost five decades after my mother walked into the United States consulate, pregnant with me and seeking U.S. citizenship. Our circumstances could not have been more different. She worked in factories and made minimum wage. She was pregnant and married to a political refugee. In contrast, I strode in childless and unmarried, earning six figures, my pocketbook jammed with all the documentation of a typical middle-class citizen's life: a Real ID driver's license, a health insurance card, two credit cards, a bank debit card, and an identification card for my job.

The security guard at the Colombian consulate did not

care about any of the papers I carried. He was tall, much taller than any of my primos or tíos, and it was clear from his sour face that he had been tasked with making the same statements to god knows how many people for many hours. He handed me a brochure, and, looking over my head to the people lining up behind me, he said, Come back tomorrow at eight-thirty. There will be a line at the door.

The brochure, a single page, covered many aspects of Colombian citizenship, from applying for a national identity card and a passport to renouncing your citizenship (you were to email in this case). If I wanted to become a Colombian citizen, there was nothing emotional or even political about the matter. For an initial appointment, I had to show up with my U.S. passport, my original birth certificate, an official consulate-approved translation of my birth certificate, my mother's Colombian passport or national identity card, and knowledge of my blood type. It was not clear if I would be required to live in the country or know its laws and political culture.

I left the consulate clutching that sheet of paper, acutely aware that I was part of a new generation for whom U.S. citizenship might no longer be the answer.

The act of acquiring a new citizenship is often the last chapter in narratives about migration to the United States. Every American is familiar with this story, even people who have no connection to immigrant communities. It is the tale depicted in films and novels, in documentaries about the famous and the talented and the persecuted. It is the story that opens with departure from a homeland, then moves through a series of obstacles, and triumphs in the United States. Each victory measures the degree to which the pre-citizen can manage the behavior of the good citizen: She marries, she lands a job or two or three, she opens her own business, she gives birth, she sends her children to college. In the final scene, she does not study for the citizenship test. She does not feel anxious about her mastery of the English language. She heroically raises her right hand and vows to defend the government of the United States of America. There is a finality to the gesture: the hand lifted, the vow made. It is a marriage. A political marriage. A marriage for life. Except it's not. Citizenship is no longer the final act. It is no longer the end of the story.

In 2008, the federal government began digitizing more than three hundred thousand immigration files—paper cards bearing the fingerprints of people who had come into contact with the federal government because of their immigration status. These were people who had applied for legal residency or had been ordered to leave the country or who had been approved for citizenship. The government turned their fingerprints into square pixels, and in this way, the government began matching records and finding people who had become citizens after an order had been issued for their deportation. It also discovered people who had become citizens despite having multiple names in the system. It did not matter if the person had never received the deportation order or if government employees had misspelled their name multiple times. It did not matter if the naturalized citizen had hired a friend of a friend to submit their application for asylum and then that person had used their fingerprints to submit someone else's application too. According to the government, the person had lied when they applied for citizenship.

Immigration and Customs Enforcement agents began showing up at people's homes. The Justice Department began sending letters. Sometimes the person faced criminal charges. Sometimes it was only a civil matter. The point was the same: the United States government would be revoking their citizenship. While this had happened before, the new digital files made it easier. On average, about forty-six people faced the prospect of losing their citizenship every year between 2004 and 2016. Then Trump won the 2016 election, and in the first two years of his administration, the numbers doubled. The Justice Department even tried to terminate the citizenship of a grandmother.

Norma Borgoño arrived in the United States from Perú in 1989. In Miami, she raised her children and found a secretarial job and volunteered at her church. In 2007, she took the oath of U.S. citizenship. She became a grandmother. The government showed up in 2018, almost thirty years after she first set foot in this country, alleging she had lied on her citizenship application because she did not report a crime of which she had been convicted—except the conviction had occurred four years after she became a citizen. The Justice Department maintained that this did not matter because the crime had been committed while Norma had a green card and worked as a secretary for an export company, where her boss stole about $24 million from a federal government agency. Norma had cooperated with authorities, making it possible for them to bring charges against her boss. She had also spent a year under house arrest and paid $5,000 in restitution. None of the lawyers involved in the fraud case told her that she could jeopardize her citizenship by pleading guilty for secretarial work tied to a crime. After all, when they were in court, she was already a citizen.

Faced with the threat of losing her citizenship, Norma became the subject of a slew of news reports, and her lawyer told me that while it took time, the Justice Department eventually dropped the denaturalization case against her.

Trump's Justice Department announced in 2020 a new unit in its Office of Immigration Litigation called the Denaturalization Section. In April of that year, as the world burrowed in for the Covid-19 lockdown and more than a million people began dying from the virus in this country, multiple federal agencies busied themselves by sending the Denaturalization Section the names of more than five hundred people who were to be investigated and their citizenship possibly revoked.

Two years later, Biden's Justice Department renamed the Denaturalization Section the Enforcement Unit and announced it would be pursuing citizens "who pose a potential danger to national security" and people who had engaged in war crimes and people who had committed "very serious felonies." The phrases sounded reasonable. Few people want the war criminal to live in their apartment building, and few want to stand in line at the grocery store next to the sex trafficker. But then I remembered how language can ruin us, how nouns and verbs, even adjectives, can be used to sell brutality. In the aftermath of the September 11 terrorist attacks, the United States tortured men and detained teenagers at Guantánamo Bay on the grounds that they endangered national security. The countries marked as dangerous by federal authorities back then, like now, were majority-Muslim countries. The journalist Seth Freed Wessler found that people from Yemen, Somalia, and Iran made up only about 1 percent of the foreign-born population of the United States, but they were an estimated 10 percent of the citizens the Trump administration moved to denaturalize in 2017 and 2018.

Naturalized citizens can be children. They can be teenagers. And they can lose their citizenship if it came by way of a parent whose legal status is revoked. When members of the Trump administration created the Denaturalization Section, they knew this. They were stripping citizenship not only from grown people but also from their children. They were trying to deport entire families. What the department advertised in its press releases, however, were the war criminals and sex offenders whose citizenship was being taken away. They did not talk about grandparents like Norma.

Supreme Court justice Hugo Black observed in a 1967 ruling: "The very nature of our free government makes it completely incongruous to have a rule of law under which a group of citizens temporarily in office can deprive another group of citizens of their citizenship." But this is exactly what happens now. In the summer of 2024, each time the Justice Department decided to revoke someone's naturalized citizenship, a white man with a friendly face and glasses approved the decision. He was a lawyer and a Biden appointee. He probably woke early to jog, then sliced apples for his three children while his wife boiled water for the instant oatmeal. He brewed a pot of coffee and hopped on his government-issued laptop, sifting through digital papers, through dates and accusations, to ultimately decide whether or not a person would lose political and legal and social and familial membership in this country.

His name does not matter. He was one citizen "temporarily in office."

I found a copy online of the Constitution of the Republic of Colombia. I tried reading it in Spanish. The words—el conocimiento, la libertad y la paz, un orden politico—were familiar but stiff in my ears. They were not my mother's Spanish. I attempted reading it in English, which made the task easier, and I liked what I found. Of course, I already knew that Colombia's government had been a democracy since the late nineteenth century and that two political parties essentially traded power through national elections. Its constitution, though, had been rewritten in 1991, and it promised a new way forward for the country. The government would protect ethnic and cultural diversity, and people would have the right to healthcare. The constitution outlawed the death penalty. It acknowledged that Indigenous communities have their own justice systems and granted these communities two seats in the Senate. Spanish remained the country's official language, but "languages and dialects of ethnic groups are also official in their territories."

The Colombian Constitution is long. It has a total of 380 articles, and it mentions Afro-Colombians only twice. It completely ignores abortion, which had been a crime until 2022, when activists took what was on paper—the constitutional right to healthcare—and argued that this included abortion. The country legalized the procedure in the first twenty-four weeks of pregnancy, making Colombia the second most progressive country on abortion in the Americas, after Canada. Two years after it adopted the constitution, Colombia's Congress passed a law ensuring that Afro-Colombians received two seats in the House of Representatives. The law also recognized that Black people in Colombia have their own culture and ethnic identities and that those living in certain regions have a collective ownership of the land, though not of anything found underground, like oil. The results have been complicated, since by granting land to Black communities, the law has contributed to their being the targets of violence by local armed groups. Black and Indigenous Colombians account for more than 60 percent of the people displaced from the Pacific region of the country, where gangs of men still control who can enter and who can leave an area and when and how drugs move out of the country.

The act of reading the constitution of another country felt intimate, as if I were making my way through the memoir of someone I had known all of my life. Here was page after page of what this person expected of the world, of what they valued, of what they wanted. And I was thinking of marrying this person. Perhaps this explained the cold feet. I began to worry. My Spanish was still that of someone who had learned the language at home. There were so many words in English that I did not know in Spanish. If I had dual citizenship and a police officer stopped me in Bogotá or Cali or Tunja, I would no longer be a clueless American tourist on paper who could retreat to English. I would be treated as a Colombian woman, a queer Colombian woman with citizenship who had no recourse to a United States consulate, where I would be, if not safe, at least on familiar linguistic ground.

What did it mean to be safe? I had grown up in a family

where papeles translated into a modicum of safety. But what did that mean now?

I thought about safety often in 2024. For the first time, I watched people in my life—people with U.S. citizenship, people with hefty bank accounts, people with all the coveted privileges—experience political fear. They were afraid to talk publicly about the genocide of Palestinians. They were scared of losing their jobs, of having their families targeted, of having their faces and names scorned on social media. They were scared to be accused of antisemitism. They told me they knew two women who had already lost their jobs when they tried to move their organizations into making a public statement opposing the slaughter of Palestinian families. They confided their political confusion to me over the phone in the simplest of terms: It's wrong to kill people like this. How is that not clear to everyone?

I listened and watched and advised, and most of the time, I was utterly dumbfounded, not by the people around me, but by myself: I had thought this would never happen again in the United States. I had thought of McCarthyism as a historical event. Now a Congress member spent hours interrogating the president of the university where I taught, demanding he disavow one of my colleagues and also our students. Our campus police charged four colleagues with misdemeanors for standing between them and students protesting the genocide. While the county prosecutor refused to pursue the charges, the point was made. Where people had once feared losing their jobs over an accusation that they were Communists, now they feared losing their jobs or college degrees for opposing war crimes against humanity.

The week I began reading Colombia's constitution, the

Israeli military killed an eight-year-old boy in Gaza. Its weapons amputated the feet of another boy and catapulted a two-year-old child into the air. The Associated Press did not name the children. Three days later, Israel bombed a school run by the United Nations, murdering the journalist Mohammad Meshmesh. The death count that week in 2024 stood at more than thirty-eight thousand people, half of them thought to be children and 160 known to be journalists.

Unlike the United States, Colombia broke diplomatic ties with Israel and began banning the export of its coal to that country. I found myself wondering: How would it feel to be a citizen of a country protesting this genocide? How would it feel to be a citizen of a country where friends and co-workers were not terrified of losing their jobs for protesting Israel's relentless massacres of children from an ethnic and religious community?

I was old enough to appreciate that with another election, Colombia's president could be voted out of office, and by the time my citizenship application was processed, his administration could be replaced by one aligned with the authoritarianism sweeping the globe. Still, I wondered how it would feel to be a citizen of a country that, when children and entire families were being murdered every day, took a moral stand against such crimes. My friend the peace activist Vijaya Priyadarshini Thakur observed the irony of the situation: "Solidarity for a stateless people is attracting you to another state."

My mother did not understand my attraction. That afternoon, outside the Colombian consulate, she looked at me with her usual worried face: eyebrows knitted, thin lips downturned. She did not know why I would want to be a citizen of a country she had left decades earlier. Her homeland still had about 5.1 million people displaced by violence—the fourth-highest number in the world, after Sudan, Syria, and the Democratic Republic of Congo. It did not change my mother's mind that the Colombian government, after six decades of war with the guerrilla group the FARC, had signed a peace accord, or that, in the same year it broadly legalized abortion, Colombia joined a number of Latin American and European countries in offering visas to digital nomads—people whose jobs allow them to work beyond the borders of their own homelands.

I was not my mother. I wanted to talk to the digital nomads, the people who had chosen a new kind of citizenship.

The day Kamala Harris picked her vice presidential candidate for the Democratic ticket, I talked with a digital nomad for the first time. I'll call her Paloma. A queer Black woman in her fifties, Paloma felt that she could not breathe when she walked on the streets in this country. She found the United States antithetical to Black life. Then came Trump in 2016, and the pandemic, and the murder of George Floyd and many other Black Americans. Paloma packed her bags. She knew from her trips to Latin America that the region offered a refuge for Black Americans, and that is what she found. She worked remotely in several Latin American countries before landing in Colombia, where a digital nomad visa in 2024 permitted remote workers to live in the country for at least a year. A person only had to show that they did, in fact, work for a company long-distance or that they had a freelance contract and an income of at least a thousand dollars a month. Colombia accepted digital nomads with citizenship from a hundred countries, most in Latin America, the Caribbean, and Europe. The United States did not offer these visas.

Most countries wanted the same kind of digital nomad, the same kind of temporary citizen: a person with high earnings, which, given the correlation between race and income, generally meant a white person. Except for Turkey. That country, which only started its program in 2024, sought people who were well off, European or American, and youngish. They would not issue digital nomad visas to people over the age of fifty-five.

The day I spoke to Paloma, I was, like all of my friends, high on Kamala Harris, or maybe it would be more accurate to say I was high on what a Harris presidency could mean for social citizenship. At the very least, the Affordable Care Act and Medicaid would be protected, and presumably she would not direct the Border Patrol to separate newborns from their parents. Harris did not want to stop sending weapons to Israel, but I believed she would, over time, become open to hearing from people opposed to the genocide.

If I am being honest, I was more high on possibility than reality. In Colombia, Paloma stood in reality. Over a video call, she said, The Democrats have done nothing to stop the slaughter of Black lives. She pointed out that the party was not even stopping fascism, only slowing it down. I nodded. I could not disagree with her. She was the one living in a country where women had a universal right to abortion. I was in a country where women in the South were dying after being denied abortions and governors were shuttling immigrants to Chicago in the middle of winter.

Paloma paused. Her curls stopped moving in and out of the blurred virtual background. She acknowledged, "If Kamala wins, I might be interested in going back and forth."

But, of course, that is not what happened. Paloma hoped to be granted a second year in Colombia, but if not, she would move to another country in Latin America. She was unusual in that Latin America had been an escape for her from the racism of the United States. The digital nomad community at large is predominantly white and primarily, it appears, interested in keeping overhead costs low while traveling the world. They often move from country to country, one visa to another, year after year, making their dollars stretch in countries where a sumptuous dinner might cost a few dollars. If political life soured in a country, if a military coup took over the presidential palace, if the government stopped issuing visas for remote workers, the digital nomads would not need to worry. They could simply leave for the refuge of their first citizenship in the United States or Western Europe.

The public radio program *Marketplace* reported that about 8,300 digital nomads descended on the city of Medellín every month in 2024, driving rent prices up in some cases by 80 percent, and that same year, an investigation by one of the country's leading newspapers, *El Tiempo,* showed that 1,244 people had been flying out of Colombia every single day for the past two years without returning. The country's journalists and migration experts speculated that people were leaving because they couldn't find work (unemployment was close to 10 percent, and in 2020 it had reached 18 percent) or because inflation was high or because, despite the peace accords, violence continued in the country. Others blamed social media, claiming it made people covet the earnings possible in other countries. My tía held the leftist president responsible. She suspected people were fleeing out of fear that Colombia would follow in the economic and political footsteps of Venezuela's dictatorship. In 2023 alone, 170,000 Colombians were apprehended at the U.S.–Mexico border.

Colombians left Colombia, and the digital nomads arrived and so did the immigrants. *El Tiempo* noted that between 2021 and 2023, when 1,244 people emigrated from the country on a daily basis, it was still less than the number of people arriving in the country every day from Venezuela.

My first year after moving to Chicago, I had coffee with Veronica Arreola, a feminist activist. She struck me as pragmatic. At the University of Illinois Chicago, she worked to increase the number of Latinx students getting STEM degrees, and she had recently been elected to serve on one of the city's new police district councils, created to reimagine policing in the city. I was contemplating the political obsession in the news with citizens and noncitizens, so I asked Veronica, What word can we use that's not citizen? She nodded and said, We talk about residents. We talk about neighbors.

Indeed, a few miles away, local volunteers had opened a clothing distribution center for immigrants and named it Nuevos Vecinos. New Neighbors.

Neighbor had none of the intensity or historicity of citizen. It evoked instead the wispy and whimsical voice of Mister Rogers. It hinted at a person we could see across the street or at the mailbox in our apartment building. In a world of online interactions, neighbor suggested a person whose body could be found in close proximity to ours.

In 2024, a Louisiana banker decided he no longer wanted to have anything to do with the word *citizen.* Jason Smith, the chief executive officer of Citizens National Bank, told a local paper: "When we would go to chamber of commerce or other events, our name would always get shortened to 'Citizens Bank' and so to try to tell somebody, 'Well, we're Citizens National Bank and they're Citizens Bank and Trust, or they're Citizens Trust Savings,' it just got confusing." He hired a branding company, and after forty years in business, the bank returned to the state's French colonizer roots, renaming the bank Bonvenu, or "Welcome."

One media outlet reported that the United States had 177 banks with citizen in their names. I doubted this, but with an online search I found: First Citizens, Citizens State Bank, Citizens Community Bank, Citizens Savings Bank, Citizens Bank & Trust, Citizens Bank of Kansas, and so on. In some cases, using the name signaled the ambitions of the company. Citizens Business Bank, which started in California in 1974, was originally the Chino Valley Bank. In other cases, the designation suggested the weight of history. Florida's Citizens Bank & Trust was formed in the wake of the First World War.

Writing for *The New York Times* in 2023, the reporter Karen Loew observed that more restaurants, hotels, and even tattoo shops were branding themselves with the word *citizen.* I hopped on Tripadvisor and saw that this was true. I could drink a cappuccino at Citizen Collective in Seattle and also at Good Citizen Coffee in Nashville. I could enjoy an evening at Citizen Cider in Vermont and then make my way south to Charlottesville to dine at Citizen Burger Bar. Across the country, at Citizen Public House in Scottsdale, I could feast on "fair trade short ribs." Citizenship becoming the theme for a food show was, I suspected, only a matter of time.

For these restaurants and coffee shops, the citizen brand tapped into a language familiar to anyone who had attended elementary school in the United States or binged on Hollywood blockbusters. The restaurants boasted on their websites that they produced "cider for the people" or "pizza for the people." One venue declared that enjoying a burger was a right and a responsibility, while two eateries held that grilling meat over a wood fire, a type of cooking that has presumably been done for thousands of years, was essential to American culture. Yes, the restaurant sold food and drinks, and also one particular idea of what it meant to be an American citizen: a man who preferred eating dead animals cooked outdoors.

None of this was limited to the United States. If I were a different person, one with different political inclinations, I could travel the world with the sole intention of drinking and dining my way through citizenship. I could enjoy an espresso at the Citizen Café in Spain and also at the Citizen Cafe & Bar in Shanghai. In Romania, I could watch people feast on chicken wings at CitiZen Bistro & Lounge, and in Dubai, I could indulge in South Indian cuisine at an eatery simply named Citizen Restaurant.

I would not, however, find in other countries the same meaning of citizen. A Canadian coffee shop wanted to "do good in our city," while the Romanian restaurant had picked CitiZen for the Buddhist reference embedded in it, hoping customers would "escape" to their eatery. The Citizen in Glasgow looked toward the past: Its kitchen and dining area occupied what had once been the office and printing rooms of the *Evening Citizen,* a city newspaper. The hotel chain CitizenM careened toward the future, focused on a single demographic: "mobile citizens" who "cross countries as easily as others cross streets." The company had hotels in Taiwan, Zurich, and Boston.

One branding expert summed it up for *The New York Times* this way: "It's aspirational. 'Citizen' invokes: I'm a member and I'm important. I'm a citizen, not a customer. It's about a contribution, not a transaction."

This explanation amused me. If I am giving you money and you are giving me a sense of belonging, that is a transaction, not a community. I suspected that the new pervasiveness of the word in the United States and around the world, if it was new, suggested instead a longing to connect with a place when so many of us spend so much time online and unrooted. Maybe citizen signaled not "I am important" but rather "I want to be important to others; I want to belong to a group of people who know me, who see me, who hear me."

The fact also remains that citizenship today is more than a metaphorical commodity. It is an actual commodity. Its value can be described in dollars.

The chairman of the firm Henley & Partners has dual citizenship. So does his CEO. Together they are citizens of the United Kingdom, Malta, and the United Arab Emirates. Every year, their company publishes a guide to the best passports, the ones permitting you to travel without the hassles of submitting visa applications. In 2024, the Henley Passport Index ranked the U.S. passport in seventh place since it only opened the door visa-free to 188 countries. Passports from Japan, France, and Singapore topped the list, making it possible to see 194 countries without a visa. At the bottom of the list? Muslim-majority countries including Afghanistan, Iraq, Yemen, and Pakistan.

The Henley Passport Index underscores the inequities of citizenship. By virtue of having first opened my eyes on land called the United States, I can travel without worry or a visa to more countries than I can name, while a woman born in Haiti or Egypt or Jordan cannot. Yet the index serves another purpose, which is presumably its actual point: It clarifies for the wealthy which citizenships they should purchase if they want to travel freely and easily. The practice is known as citizenship by investment, and the applicants are called investor citizens, though they could just as well be named millionaire migrants.

Purchasing citizenship usually involves buying real estate in the chosen country. In exchange for the investment, the country grants papers: residency and a passport. The person is not necessarily required to live in the country, or they are but only for a short time. Some governments can take a year or longer to process these investor citizen applications, but Vanuatu, a country of more than eighty islands in the South Pacific with a population similar to that of Orlando, Florida, handled applications in only a month or two, giving well-off migrants visa-free access to ninety-four countries, including most of the European Union. Its program came to a halt in 2022, when the EU suspended its visa waiver agreement with Vanuatu, citing the low rejection rates and the short processing time for applications.

Life, of course, is not only about travel, not even for the wealthy. Henley & Partners also publishes an index that serves as a more holistic consumer guide to buying citizenship. This one considers the reputation of the country, its residency requirements, and the quality of life as measured by life expectancy and how free you are to do what you want with your money there. Austria and Malta, both members of the European Union, topped the list for quality of life in 2024, but Cambodia came in high if you wanted a citizenship that did not require you to live in the country. Citizenship to Antigua and Barbuda, where English is the official language, only requires a millionaire migrant to live there for five days during the first five years of citizenship. And even millionaire migrants have to take cost into account. At $100,000, Antigua and Barbuda offered the cheapest option, though in 2024 the country hiked its price to $230,000.

This is the migration of elites, then, the migration that never makes the nightly news or the presidential debates, and it can generate a great deal of income for cash-starved countries. The journalist Atossa Araxia Abrahamian found that the profit from selling citizenship made up a quarter of St. Kitts and Nevis's gross domestic product in 2014. The BBC reported in 2019 that as much as 30 percent of Vanuatu's revenue might have been from the sale of citizenship—money local advocates said never reached ordinary people, though government officials were sighted driving luxury cars. Kristin Surak, a sociology professor at the London School of Economics, found that selling citizenship has generated €21.4 billion for the European Union.

In the United States, citizenship is discussed as if it were so valuable it could never have a price tag. The images from the southern border—discarded water bottles in the desert and people's heads bobbing in the river—emphasize the message that people are dying in the heat and in the water precisely because there is no other way to obtain citizenship to this country. But that is not true. In early 2025, the price tag on U.S. citizenship started at $800,000.

A lot of paper is involved in buying citizenship to the United States. And emails. And phone calls. The U.S. government technically calls the sale of citizenship the EB-5 Immigrant Investor Program. On paper, a person is spending $800,000 on a business project in a rural or a high-unemployment area. If they want to invest in other areas, the price tag tips over a million dollars. The investor citizen may pour their money into their own project or apply through one of the more than nine hundred regional centers approved by the government. There are more details, but this is the gist of it: The EB-5 visa covers the investor, as well as their spouse and their children under the age of twenty-one. They do not have to live in the town or city where they have placed their money, which means that an EB-5 investor can buy American citizenship by spending cash on a project in Nebraska while they purchase a family home in San Francisco.

In Philadelphia, millionaire migrants have funded the construction of public train stations, hotels, and the city's convention center. In Manhattan, they invested in the construction of Hudson Yards, where luxury one-bedrooms can start at $6,000 a month. Austin devoted a page on its city's website to welcoming EB-5 investors by underscoring that nine census tracts there qualify as "targeted employment areas," places a millionaire migrant can spend under a million dollars to buy U.S. citizenship.

The sale of this citizenship happens on a first-come, first-served basis. The federal agency responsible for it, Citizenship and Immigration Services, issues fewer than ten thousand of these EB-5 visas every year, and it hit that max for the first time in 2014, even though the government started the program in the 1990s. Today millionaire migrants account for about 1 percent of all new green card holders, according to the Migration Policy Institute, and like ordinary immigrants, they too face the backlog of the U.S. immigration system. One EB-5 investor told *The Wall Street Journal* she was still waiting on her green card seven years after her initial investment.

Not every investor citizen is a millionaire. Some arrive in the United States on student or work visas. They might be physicians or people working in tech. They tire of the slow process of traditional applications for legal residency, usually by way of a work visa, and try the investment route, some taking loans against the equity in their houses to make the investment. The gamble does not necessarily pay off, since Congress has to renew the program every five years, and applications get stalled, as they do for all immigrants.

Still, it is worth considering that a person can buy American citizenship. Some people pay for this citizenship with cash from their home countries or with the equity they have in their homes here; other people pay for it with their lives and the lives of their children. Of course, this is not how we talk about the arrival of people to the United States. Elected officials and media pundits and ordinary Americans speak instead of a migrant crisis, a crisis at the border, even an invasion, though it would be just as fair to say that there is no crisis. It is simply that the families showing up at the U.S.-Mexico border do not have a million dollars each, and that is what we have decided we want—a million dollars for citizenship to this country.

A month after his 2025 inauguration, Trump declared that his administration would replace the EB-5 visa program with a "gold card." He was raising the price fivefold, to $5 million, for U.S. citizenship.

Some people do not want to buy citizenship in the United States, just a condo or a bungalow. They dream of pendant light fixtures, magnets of kittens on the fridge, and plastic flamingos with rainbow hats in the front yard. They are thinking about the American Dream, or they are thinking about the here and now. They came to the United States on a student visa and now they have a career and some savings, and they want to settle down and make a good investment. But in July 2023, people who had come to the United States from China and lived in Florida without citizenship woke up to the news that a state law was barring them, in essence, from buying a home.

The law, known as SB 264, mandates that a person from China without U.S. citizenship cannot purchase a residential property in the state unless they have a work visa or asylum, and even then the person has to find a home that is not within five miles of a military installation. Since most of Florida's military sites are located near major cities, the law severely limits the options. The law also applies to noncitizens from Cuba, Venezuela, Syria, Iran, Russia, and North Korea, but the prohibitions and punishments are worse for people from China, who face felony charges and up to five years in prison if they break this law. Anyone who participates in the transaction would also be charged. The person who sold the home to an ineligible buyer could spend a year in prison.

SB 264 also targeted people who already owned their Florida homes, requiring Chinese homeowners without green cards or citizenship to register their property with the state if they bought it before the law went into effect. This was true for noncitizens from the other designated countries, too, which led Spanish-language television news programs to feature lawyers warning Cubans and Venezuelans to register their home with the state or face a daily penalty of a thousand dollars.

The federal district judge who refused to temporarily block Florida's law asserted that it was not racist. According to Judge Allen Winsor, the law did not single out Chinese people. It pertained to anyone who had a "domicile" in China, and so, employing a perverse racist logic, he wrote that since a person of any race could live in China, the law did not discriminate against the Chinese. In 2024, the U.S. Court of Appeals for the Eleventh Circuit temporarily blocked parts of the law while a lawsuit against the state made its way through the courts.

The irony is that if Florida wanted to ban foreigners from purchasing property, it would have gone after Canadians. In 2022, they made up the largest share of foreign owners in the state, accounting for 21 percent of all transactions, followed in smaller numbers by Colombians, Argentines, and Brazilians.

Other states have passed less punitive versions of the Florida law. In Georgia, a Chinese person without a green card could still buy a home in 2024 but not farmland near a military base if they were an "agent" of the Chinese government. Texas tried to pass a closer copycat of the Florida law in 2023, and Governor Greg Abbott promised to sign it, but protests broke out in Austin and Dallas, and Asian Americans organized and lobbied state legislators, making it so the bill was dead on arrival. Oklahoma's governor suggested the Chinese were to blame for the 300 percent jump in foreign ownership of land in the state between 2015 and 2021, but the reporter Ben Felder uncovered that the foreigners driving those statistics were actually Canadians and Europeans.

All of this meant that for several months starting in 2023, a woman from China, regardless of citizenship, could buy a condo in Chicago near me but not in Miami near my mother. The same woman could have an abortion in Illinois but not next door in Indiana unless her father or uncle or a stranger had raped her. If she lived in Arkansas, her transgender daughter would be banned from competing on girls' teams in sports competitions, even in college, while in Massachusetts, schools would permit her to play on the girls' team.

A year after the Florida law was signed, a real estate agent told *The New York Times* that when sellers saw a Chinese name on an offer to purchase a home, they now inquired if the person could legally buy a home. Sellers did not think that those barred from buying homes were Chinese people without papeles. They thought it was anyone who was Chinese. They could no longer imagine a Chinese person with U.S. citizenship.

A Chinese American woman in Florida with a green card, Susan Li had planned to buy a home, but she put her search on hold, telling CNN, "No matter if I have a green card or I'm a citizen, I still have a Chinese face."

The same summer that I walked into the Colombian consulate, I showed up at a church gymnasium in Chicago's Little Village neighborhood to assist people with their applications for U.S. citizenship. Local community organizers had placed folding chairs into rows where people could fill out their forms. They had assigned the tables on one side of the room to the lawyers and interpreters who determined if the person was eligible to apply. If they were, volunteers ferried the person across the aisle to lawyers and interpreters who would complete the forms.

I was one of the interpreters across the aisle. The work was straightforward. How long have you lived at this address? How long have you been married? Do you have disabled children who depend on you? The women who came to us, one by one, turned out to be versions of my mother: elderly women in modest, thin tops designed for the heat, women who wore little makeup, who smiled politely, who startled when I asked if they had ever been married to anyone other than their current husband. They had all lived in the United States for decades. One of them had bought her home in the neighborhood with her husband almost forty years earlier. Just like Mami. Another told me she had failed her citizenship test the last time she took it. Another brought her grown daughter and confided, You're not supposed to have favorites, but she's my favorite.

Each one of them had built an entire life in Chicago, in the United States. They were now in their sixties and seventies. They had children and grandchildren who had been born on this land. They had spent decades as legal residents. I wondered if they were finally applying for citizenship because of the rising vile public rhetoric about immigrants, but no, that was not motivating them. They had aged and so had their family members in Mexico. The people they loved across the border were having health issues. The women wanted to travel more easily between the two countries. Of critical importance, they no longer had to take the naturalization test in English. Their advanced age and their decades as legal permanent residents qualified them for testing in Spanish or with interpreters. This is what had stopped them before: a policy prohibiting them from speaking about political life in their mother tongue.

One of the women had applied for citizenship previously, but when she showed up to take the naturalization test, the immigration official posed unexpected questions. She asked me about a yellow river and a guerra fría, she told me, her eyes still alarmed. I inquired more about the yellow river but had to admit that I did not know what the question might have been. The Guerra Fría I knew. I summarized the Cold War as the United States and Soviet Union battling over political ideologies, but when I looked up the question later, I saw my tip would not have helped the woman, since the actual question is "During the Cold War, what was the main concern of the United States?" The answer: communism.

I did not know if I would have to take a naturalization test for Colombian citizenship, and what would it reveal about political membership except that I could study a country's history and provide the answers officials wanted to hear?

In 2023, 15.2 percent of Americans had been born in another country—the highest percentage in United States history. This included people like my mother and auntie and best friend and the women in the church gymnasium, all of whom have been in the United States for decades. It also included the women who arrived last week. And the children. And the nonbinary. And the men.

That day, surrounded by legal documents and passports, file folders and women's anxious faces, I did not need a piece of paper to tell me who belonged in this country. They were here now. They were sitting next to me. They were loving and bickering and making home here. None of them, not these women-about-to-be-citizens or the ones who arrived last week, none of them had papeles telling the truth, which was this: No matter how long they had been living in this country, the United States, as an economic and military power, had been in their lives before they ever set foot on this land.

In South Florida, when I left the Colombian consulate with my mother and auntie, minimal instructions on dual citizenship in hand, we made our way down the street to the new coffee shop. Quietly we slipped into the delicious air-conditioning, past a smattering of twentysomethings, each at their own table, each silently facing a laptop, headsets firmly in place. My tía ordered a regular coffee and so did Mami. We admired the coffee shop's sunflower-yellow walls and the bookcase with its oddly shaped shelves and the small portrait of the novelist Gabriel García Márquez laughing. The waiter, a very young man, lithe and pale, told us that he was from Colombia, from Medellín, and he spoke to my mother in the deferential way of young people raised in that country. It was nothing my mother had ever been able to persuade me to do. I had turned out too crass, too loud, too American.

The coffee shop had been named Macondo after the fictional town in García Márquez's novel *One Hundred Years of Solitude.* It occurred to me that my study of citizenship, its fictions and its facts, had brought me here to this place named for a town that existed only in the imagination. Citizenship did require imagination. The historian Benedict Anderson described nations as "imagined communities," positing that before a person can become a member of a country, they must be able to envision themselves as part of such a community—a process that historically came about through printed stories in a shared language. By the summer of 2024, it was clear to me and probably to everyone else, too, that many of us were no longer imagining the same country when we spoke of the United States. Perhaps we never had.

We still discussed citizenship though, and we did this often. When ICE raids spread across the country at the start of 2025, federal authorities questioned and detained members of the Diné (Navajo) Nation, not officially because of their race (that would have been illegal) but because they suspected the Diné of not having citizenship. When Florida banned many Chinese nationals from homeownership, a federal judge concluded this exclusion was about citizenship, not race. When parents sought medical care for their transgender children, they found themselves on social media designated as "bad citizens." When the Supreme Court's *Dobbs* decision overturned the federal right to an abortion, Justice Samuel Alito, writing for the majority, did not talk about the state controlling the bodies of women and pregnant people; he only maintained that the Constitution never mentioned citizens having the right to terminate a pregnancy. And when Trump signed an executive order in 2025 attempting to eliminate birthright citizenship, the document said nothing about robbing Latinx of political membership in the United States. It only argued that undocumented parents and their children were not subject to the jurisdiction of this country as required by the Fourteenth Amendment. The newborns were citizens of elsewhere and nowhere.

Citizenship has become a political dog whistle, a proxy for race, a way to talk about white supremacy while avoiding accusations of racism—or of xenophobia, sexism, or transphobia. It is presented to us as a neutral term, when in fact citizenship has been and continues to be thoroughly immersed in our national ideas about race and gender, sexuality and economics. It is a story, and a story can be reconsidered, revised, and retold. I know this because when I was a child, no one spoke of being undocumented. Now families and poets and entire organizations embrace the term. Churches that once offered sanctuary to those fleeing the wars in Central America provide sanctuary now to those fleeing deportation orders. College classrooms filled almost exclusively by white students when I was an undergraduate are now multiracial, and the white man's literary canon is not dead but in its rightful place alongside the works of James Baldwin, Gloria Anzaldúa, and Piri Thomas. Reparations for Black

America, an idea once openly mocked, are under way these days in some cities and institutions.

Papers did not make any of this happen. People did. Everything I learned about being a member of a political community has come from people. There were the journalists documenting the deaths at the border; the Chicago neighbors organizing lawyers and interpreters; the girl in elementary school who showed me how to be an artist in defiance of authority. Over and over again, I have seen people change how we understand citizenship, and so whether or not I became a citizen of another country, I still wanted to be here in this country. I wanted to be part of a movement that would rewrite how we talked and thought about citizenship.

I finished writing this book when the president of the United States had fired the country's top general, the vice chief of the air force, the chief of the navy, and the military's top lawyers. Congress members were talking about removing federal judges opposed to the president's agenda, and administrators at my university temporarily took down the websites for the Gender and Sexuality Resource Center and Multicultural Student Affairs in response to a threat of losing federal funding. Around the country, ICE agents grabbed international students outside their homes and shipped them to detention centers hundreds of miles away. I was writing, and the country was unraveling.

A very dear friend asked me if it was still safe to produce a book about citizenship. Maybe I needed to think it over. She still had her job in the federal government, but now she had to email the Department of Government Efficiency every week with five things she had done at her job. Her work had become a work of fiction.

I continued writing despite her warning and even my own fears. I could not bear the thought of allowing someone else to write the story of our lives. We are citizens of the stories we tell. We belong to the stories we scribe about democracy and authoritarianism, about borders and neighbors, about love and grief and one another. In the end, we only truly belong to one another, and this is worth sharing and celebrating, no matter the cost.

GRACIAS

A MI FAMILIA. Le doy gracias a mi mami, Alicia, por tu amor a traves de tantos años, y a mi tía María de Jesus por tu apoyo y tu curiosidad con todo lo que escribo.

A mi hermana, Liliana, for being my best friend and reading an early draft.

A mi Tía Rosa Elena, who passed away while I was finishing this book and who taught me so much about devotion.

Frankie Clark for your love and the many nutritious meals while I worked on this book. Thank you for taking care of me, our little sweethearts, and our home.

Lula por su cariño and for giving me a good reason to leave my desk.

Sarah Schulman for your honest feedback on the early draft, your own thought-provoking, life-changing books, and, most of all, your friendship.

Vijaya Priyadarshini Thakur for your brilliance and your light and your insights into the book.

Sonia Guiñansaca for your fierceness and compassion in equal doses and for reading and talking with me about this book when it was still in manuscript form.

Laura Halperin, N.C. Happe, Melissa Rivero, and Hannah Wilson-Black for dedicated research assistance.

Aleah Vega for formatting and fact-checking the notes and being so patient.

Christian Vasquez Infante, Mariam Xirsi, and S. Yarberry for fact-checking and researching. Your efforts were essential to this project.

Alice Elliott-Sowaal for your spiritual guidance and deep friendship over the course now of three books, and to Owain and Grace for offering me a home away from home.

Kim D. Brandon and Minal Hajratwala for the weekly phone calls that kept me grounded.

Audrey Silvestre and Mérida M. Rúa for your friendship and scholarly commitments.

Mariajosé Rodríguez Pliego for introducing me to the work of Yásnaya Elena Aguilar Gil.

The team at Hogarth Press, including Evan Camfield, Amy Schroeder, and Maddie Woda, for their essential work behind the scenes.

David Ebershoff, my editor at Hogarth Press, for his intellectual curiosity and insightful editorial feedback. Thank you for encouraging me to write more deeply.

Rayhané Sanders, my agent, for seeing this book's potential and being an ally of the book and me.

The community organizers, poets, historians, sociologists, legal scholars, and journalists whose work made this book possible.

NOTES

THIS BOOK IS a work of creative nonfiction. Nothing is fabricated. Everything I wrote is based on the work of historians, sociologists, legal scholars, policymakers, classics professors, and journalists and also on formal and informal interviews I conducted. Quotation marks signal formal interviews, and their absence indicates that I am writing from memory.

Throughout the manuscript, I primarily used the term Latinx to be expansive about gender, and I kept Latino when writing about the census and when quoting the work of others or referring to those who had made their preference clear.

I debated whether to call people immigrants or migrants. The latter is historically more common in Europe, and journalists in the United States started using it more frequently in 2015, when close to a million refugees arrived in Europe. In this country, immigrant is a legal term for people who have a green card, though, of course, we use it more broadly in the news and in conversations. The political theorist Cristina Beltrán has observed that "*migrant* is a broader term that refers to anyone who is in the process of relocating to another country as well as someone who has already moved." Latinx communities have also had a different migration pattern from others arriving in the United States—often moving back and forth between here and Latin America—and so perhaps the designation of migrant is more fitting. However, I suspect that far-right political leaders in the United States are calling the new arrivals migrants to mark them as different from (and less deserving than) previous waves of immigrants, and so when I use the term *immigrants* in this book, I am resisting that xenophobic language.

Invitations

The work of the legal scholar E. Tendayi Achiume offers a radical understanding of citizenship, colonialism, and migration. Two of her articles informed my thinking for this essay and the entire book: "Racial Borders" in *The Georgetown Law Journal* and "Migration as Decolonization" in the *Stanford Law Review.*

The quote from the 1930s Los Angeles city manager comes from Marla Andrea Ramírez's article "The Making of Mexican Illegality: Immigration Exclusions Based on Race, Class Status, and Gender" in *New Political Science.* For more about the use and abuse of water-related metaphors in describing immigration, see Otto Santa Ana's *Brown Tide Rising: Metaphors of Latinos in Contemporary American Public Discourse.*

The reference to the stolen ten-dollar video game comes from *United States v. Pacheco,* a case from 2000 decided by the U.S. Court of Appeals for the Second Circuit.

The federal government does not regularly track the number of arrests under the 287(g) program. The figures I used are from *287(g) End-of-Year Report: Fiscal Year 2022 Report to Congress,* issued on February 21, 2023, by U.S. Immigration and Customs Enforcement.

When I interviewed the legal scholar Dimitry Kochenov,

he was teaching at Central European University in Vienna after Hungary's government refused to allow the school to run its U.S.-accredited academic programs in Budapest. Elizabeth Redden wrote about this for *Inside Higher Ed* on December 3, 2018: "Central European U Forced Out of Hungary."

The family stories in this essay come from my mother, but my description of the tax man's office comes from my own memory. Every year, I accompanied her into that basement office when it was time for her and my father to file their tax return, until one day, when I was fifteen, it was my turn to do that duty of citizenship.

Books

Balderrama, Francisco E., and Raymond Rodríguez. *Decade of Betrayal: Mexican Repatriation in the 1930s.* Rev. ed. University of New Mexico Press, 2006.

Beltrán, Cristina. *Cruelty as Citizenship: How Migrant Suffering Sustains White Democracy.* University of Minnesota Press, 2020.

Dunbar-Ortiz, Roxanne. *Not "a Nation of Immigrants": Settler Colonialism, White Supremacy, and a History of Erasure and Exclusion.* Beacon Press, 2021.

García, María Cristina. *Seeking Refuge: Central American Migration to Mexico, the United States, and Canada.* University of California Press, 2006.

Gómez, Laura E. *Inventing Latinos: A New Story of American Racism.* New Press, 2020.

Jones, Martha S. *Birthright Citizens: A History of Race and Rights in Antebellum America.* Cambridge University Press, 2018.

Kochenov, Dimitry. *Citizenship.* MIT Press, 2019.

Lalami, Laila. *Conditional Citizens: On Belonging in America.* Vintage Books, 2021.

Levin, Josh. *The Queen: The Forgotten Life Behind an American Myth*. Little, Brown and Company, 2019.

Ngai, Mae M. *Impossible Subjects: Illegal Aliens and the Making of Modern America*. Rev. ed. Princeton University Press, 2014.

Prieto, Yolanda. *The Cubans of Union City: Immigrants and Exiles in a New Jersey Community*. Temple University Press, 2009.

Shachar, Ayelet, Rainer Bauböck, Irene Bloemraad, and Maarten Vink, eds. *The Oxford Handbook of Citizenship*. Oxford University Press, 2017.

Spiro, Peter J. *Citizenship: What Everyone Needs to Know*. Oxford University Press, 2019.

Articles on the "Renaissance" of Citizenship in the 1990s

Heater, Derek. "Citizenship: A Remarkable Case of Sudden Interest." *Parliamentary Affairs* 44, no. 2 (April 1991).

Held, David. "Between State and Civil Society: Citizenship." In *Citizenship*, edited by Geoff Andrews. Lawrence and Wishart, 1991.

Kymlicka, Will, and Wayne Norman. "Return of the Citizen: A Survey of Recent Work on Citizenship Theory." *Ethics* 104, no. 2 (1994).

Scobey, David. "The Specter of Citizenship." *Citizenship Studies* 5, no. 1 (February 2001).

Articles on the Latino Exclusion Act

Abrego, Leisy, Mat Coleman, Daniel E. Martínez, Cecilia Menjívar, and Jeremy Slack. "Making Immigrants into Criminals: Legal Processes of Criminalization in the Post-IIRIRA Era." *Journal on Migration and Human Security* 5, no. 3 (September 2017).

American Civil Liberties Union. *License to Abuse: How ICE's 287(g) Program Empowers Racist Sheriffs and Civil Rights Violations.* April 26, 2022.

Johnson, Dawn Marie. "AEDPA and the IIRIRA: Treating Misdemeanors as Felonies for Immigration Purposes." *Journal of Legislation* 27, no. 2 (2001).

Kerwin, Donald. "From IIRIRA to Trump: Connecting the Dots to the Current US Immigration Policy Crisis." *Journal on Migration and Human Security* 6, no. 3 (July 2018).

Lind, Dara. "The Disastrous, Forgotten 1996 Law That Created Today's Immigration Problem." *Vox,* April 28, 2016.

López, Jane Lilly. "Redefining American Families: The Disparate Effects of IIRIRA's Automatic Bars to Reentry and Sponsorship Requirements on Mixed-Citizenship Couples." *Journal on Migration and Human Security* 5, no. 2 (June 2017).

Misra, Tanvi. "Inside the Massive U.S. 'Border Zone.'" *Bloomberg CityLab,* May 14, 2018.

Rannik, Julie K. "The Anti-Terrorism and Effective Death Penalty Act of 1996: A Death Sentence for the 212(c) Waiver." *University of Miami Inter-American Law Review* 28, no. 1 (October 1996).

Articles on Birthright Citizenship

Anton, Michael. "Citizenship Shouldn't Be a Birthright." *Washington Post,* July 19, 2018.

Blackman, Josh. "An Interview with Judge James C. Ho." *Reason,* November 11, 2024.

Dias, Isabela. "The Plot Against Birthright Citizenship." *Mother Jones,* November 26, 2024.

Janetsky, Megan. "No Country to Call Home? Some Babies Born in Colombia to Venezuelan Parents Lack Birthright Citizenship." *USA Today,* August 11, 2019.

Karni, Annie, and Eliana Johnson. "How Trump's 'Birthright' Idea Went from the Fringe to the Oval Office." *Politico,* October 30, 2018.

People for the American Way. *Citizenship in the Balance: How Anti-Immigrant Activists Twist the Facts, Ignore History, and Flout the Constitution.* 2010.

Román, Ediberto, and Ernesto Sagás. "Birthright Citizenship Under Attack: How Dominican Nationality Laws May Be the Future of U.S. Exclusion." *American University Law Review* 66 (2017).

Other Articles

González, Juan. *The Current Migrant Crisis: How U.S. Policy Toward Latin America Has Fueled Historic Numbers of Asylum Seekers.* Great Cities Institute, University of Illinois at Chicago, October 20, 2023.

Massey, Douglas S., and Karen A. Pren. "Unintended Consequences of US Immigration Policy: Explaining the Post-1965 Surge from Latin America." *Population and Development Review* 38, no. 1 (March 2012).

Migration Policy Institute. *Regions of Birth for Immigrants in the United States, 1960–Present.* 2019.

Reagan, Ronald. "Radio Address to the Nation on Welfare Reform," February 15, 1986. Ronald Reagan Presidential Library & Museum.

Rodriguez, Nestor P., and Cecilia Menjívar. "Central American Immigrants and Racialization in a Post–Civil Rights Era." In *How the United States Racializes Latinos: White Hegemony and Its Consequences,* edited by José A. Cobas, Jorge Duany, and Joe R. Feagin. Routledge, 2009.

Rosaldo, Renato. "Cultural Citizenship, Inequality, and Multiculturalism." In *Latino Cultural Citizenship: Claiming Identity, Space, and Rights,* edited by William V. Flores and Rina Benmayor. Beacon Press, 1997.

Ajedrez

Once upon a time, freelance reporters who gathered quotes and details on a breaking story and phoned this information to newsrooms were called stringers. The *Oxford English Dictionary* suggests that this originated with the reporters being paid for a string of words. The end result was that when a reporter collected facts, quotes, and observations for a future story, they were said to be "gathering string."

This essay began as string, as a file of quotes and facts and observations about citizenship that I started to keep for this book project. Bra Willie's quote is from his poem "No Serenity Here." Bryan Turner suggested the use of denizen in his 2016 article "We Are All Denizens Now: On the Erosion of Citizenship" in *Citizenship Studies,* and Catherine Dauvergne's quote is from her 2007 article "Citizenship with a Vengeance" in *Theoretical Inquiries in Law.* The information on the voting rights of Black men and women in New Jersey can be found in the 2017 article "For a Few Decades in the 18th Century, Women and African-Americans Could Vote in New Jersey" by Kat Eschner for *Smithsonian* magazine.

In addition to Josine Blok's book *Citizenship in Classical Athens* and Jennifer Tolbert Roberts's *Athens on Trial: The Antidemocratic Tradition in Western Thought,* I relied on David Whitehead's 1975 article "Aristotle the Metic" in *The Cambridge Classical Journal* and John K. Davies's 1997 essay "The 'Origins of the Greek *Polis*': Where Should We Be Looking?" in *The Development of the Polis in Archaic Greece.*

Carrie Hyde's book *Civic Longing: The Speculative Origins of U.S. Citizenship* helped me to appreciate Christian engagements with this topic, and for details about the life of the apostle Paul, I turned to N. T. Wright's colorful work *Paul: A Biography.* I used online editions of the Bible to see how over time translations of the words ascribed to Paul had changed, and the information on Luke's remains can be found in Nicholas Wade's *New York Times* article from October 16, 2001: "'Body of St. Luke' Gains Credibility."

Tom Torlino's photographs were located on the website for the Carlisle Indian School Digital Resource Center, and for an introduction to the topic of citizenship and Indigenous peoples, I recommend the historian Daniel Mandell's October 14, 2024, article from *Time:* "The Ambivalent History of Indigenous People and U.S. Citizenship." Richard Henry Pratt's comments are from his speech at the 1892 National Conference on Charities and Correction and can be found in the 1973 book *Americanizing the American Indians,* edited by Francis Paul Prucha. Details about Indigenous nations and U.S. citizenship and also the quote from Chief Clinton Rickard are from Robert B. Porter's 1999 article "The Demise of the Ongwehoweh and the Rise of the Native Americans: Redressing the Genocidal Act of Forcing American Citizenship upon Indigenous Peoples" in *Harvard Blackletter Law Journal.*

Warsan Shire's poem "Home" influenced my writing toward the end of this piece, and the phrase "single, uncomplicated story" alludes to the novelist Chimamanda Ngozi Adichie's talk "The Danger of a Single Story."

An earlier version of the section on the immigrant children and the foster care agency was published by *CultureStrike.*

A Place Called Negro

This essay began for me more than fifteen years ago when I first read the 2001 article "Making Blacks Foreigners: The Legal Construction of Former Slaves in Post-Revolutionary Massachusetts," written by the legal scholar Kunal M. Parker and published in the *Utah Law Review.*

To carry out research about healthcare access in the United States for those without citizenship, I turned to many resources, including the website of New Jersey's Department of Human Services, a letter about emergency dialysis to state Medicaid directors from the American Society of Nephrology and similar organizations, and media coverage by reporters on the ground in Delaware, Illinois, and other states. I was able to write about Iowa's prenatal care programs thanks to the work of Rebecca Feldhaus Adams and Natalie Krebs and their piece "Barred from Medicaid, Some Pregnant Immigrants Have Few Options for Care," which aired on October 25, 2022, and was funded by Iowa Public Radio and Side Effects Public Media. The data about poverty designations in Texas and New York comes from the 2023 Poverty Guidelines Computations published by the Office of the Assistant Secretary for Planning and Evaluation at the Department of Health and Human Services.

The 2018 study comparing access to dialysis among the undocumented in multiple cities is by Dr. Lilia Cervantes and her colleagues and was published in *JAMA Internal Medicine:* "Association of Emergency-Only vs. Standard Hemodialysis with Mortality and Health Care Use Among Undocumented Immigrants with End-Stage Renal Disease." The work of

Dr. Cervantes led Colorado to expand Medicaid coverage to undocumented patients for lifesaving kidney failure treatment.

To imagine the deportation of the blind man named John Skyrme, I turned to Google Maps since many highways were once well-used walking trails. I researched the birds that populate the region and that he and the constables might have heard on their walk from New York to Rhode Island.

The reference to a "citizen in waiting" is from Hiroshi Motomura's book *Americans in Waiting: The Lost Story of Immigration and Citizenship in the United States.*

In 2025, the National Immigration Law Center updated its map of healthcare coverage for immigrant children, undocumented people, and pregnant immigrants. It can be found at nilc.org/resources/healthcoveragemaps.

Books

Chavez, Leo R. *The Latino Threat: Constructing Immigrants, Citizens, and the Nation.* 2nd ed. Stanford University Press, 2013.

Herndon, Ruth Wallis. *Unwelcome Americans: Living on the Margin in Early New England.* University of Pennsylvania Press, 2001.

Parker, Kunal M. *Making Foreigners: Immigration and Citizenship Law in America, 1600–2000.* Cambridge University Press, 2015.

Villarosa, Linda. *Under the Skin: The Hidden Toll of Racism on American Lives and on the Health of Our Nation.* Doubleday, 2022.

Articles

Agrawal, Shantanu. "Immigrant Exclusion from Welfare: An Analysis of the 1996 Welfare Reform Legislative Process." *Politics & Policy* 36, no. 4 (2008).

Fox, Cybelle. "'The Line Must Be Drawn Somewhere': The Rise of Legal Status Restrictions in State Welfare Policy in the 1970s." *Studies in American Political Development* 33, no. 2 (2019).

Fox, Cybelle. "Unauthorized Welfare: The Origins of Immigrant Status Restrictions in American Social Policy." *Journal of American History* 102, no. 4 (March 2016).

Johnson, Kevin R. "Proposition 187 and Its Political Aftermath: Lessons for U.S. Immigration Politics After Trump." *UC Davis Law Review* 53, no. 4 (April 2020).

Lacarte, Valerie. *Immigrant Children's Medicaid and CHIP Access and Participation: A Data Profile.* Migration Policy Institute, June 2022.

Pillai, Drishti, and Samantha Artiga. *Potential Impacts of New Requirements in Florida and Texas for Hospitals to Request Patient Immigration Status.* KFF, August 26, 2024.

The White Man Who Loved Me

Research for this book led me to the organization Refusing to Forget, founded by Chicana and Chicano studies professors to document and raise awareness about state-sanctioned violence, including lynchings, against Mexicans on the Texas-Mexico border.

Making Hispanics: How Activists, Bureaucrats, and Media Constructed a New American by G. Cristina Mora assisted me greatly in writing this essay and also made me aware of how some respondents from the Midwest and the South identified themselves as Central or South American on the 1970 census. I also reviewed instructions and census forms on the website of IPUMS USA.

The 2004 survey of Dominican immigrants is from Rubén G. Rumbaut's article "Pigments of Our Imagination:

On the Racialization and Racial Identities of 'Hispanics' and 'Latinos,'" in *How the United States Racializes Latinos: White Hegemony and Its Consequences,* edited by José A. Cobas, Jorge Duany, and Joe R. Feagin.

Books

Hernández, Tanya Katerí. *Racial Innocence: Unmasking Latino Anti-Black Bias and the Struggle for Equality.* Beacon Press, 2022.

Lukens, Patrick D. *A Quiet Victory for Latino Rights: FDR and the Controversy over "Whiteness."* The University of Arizona Press, 2017.

Rodríguez, Clara E. *Changing Race: Latinos, the Census, and the History of Ethnicity in the United States.* NYU Press, 2000.

Rodríguez-Muñiz, Michael. *Figures of the Future: Latino Civil Rights and the Politics of Demographic Change.* Princeton University Press, 2021.

Articles

Barbero, Luis. "The Changing Faces of Miami's Cuban Community." *El País,* April 22, 2016.

Bhatnagar, Manav. "Identifying the Identified: The Census, Race, and the Myth of Self-Classification." *Texas Journal on Civil Liberties & Civil Rights* 13, no. 1 (2007).

Brown, J. David, Misty L. Heggeness, Suzanne M. Dorinski, Lawrence Warren, and Moises Yi. "Understanding the Quality of Alternative Citizenship Data Sources for the 2020 Census." Center for Economic Studies Working Paper 18–38. U.S. Census Bureau, August 1, 2018.

Cadava, Geraldo. "Should Latinos Be Considered a Race?" *New Yorker,* March 25, 2023.

Cohn, D'Vera, and Jeffrey S. Passel. "Key Facts About the Quality of the 2020 Census." Pew Research Center, June 8, 2022.

Contreras, Russell. "The Latino Burglars of Watergate." *Axios,* June 16, 2022.

García, Mario T. "Mexican Americans and the Politics of Citizenship: The Case of El Paso, 1936." *New Mexico Historical Review* 59, no. 2 (April 1, 1984).

Gratton, Brian, and Myron P. Gutmann. "Hispanics in the United States, 1850–1990: Estimates of Population Size and National Origin." *Historical Methods: A Journal of Quantitative and Interdisciplinary History* 33, no. 3 (January 1, 2000).

Gratton, Brian, and Emily Klancher Merchant. "La Raza: Mexicans in the United States Census." *Journal of Policy History* 28, no. 4 (October 2016).

Grunebaum, Amos, Laurence McCullough, Eran Bornstein, and Frank Chervenak. "253 Current US Birth Data Mask Significant Racial Disparities in Pregnancy Outcomes." *American Journal of Obstetrics & Gynecology* 224, no. 2, suppl. S167–S168 (February 2021).

Hernández, Tanya Katerí. "The Latinx Census Racial Category Debate and How to Unite Latinx Across Racial Differences." *Intervenxions,* April 6, 2023.

Hernández, Tanya Katerí. "The New Census Racial Categories 'Erase' Afro Latinos." *The Hill,* April 3, 2024.

Hochschild, Jennifer L., and Brenna Marea Powell. "Racial Reorganization and the United States Census 1850–1930: Mulattoes, Half-Breeds, Mixed Parentage, Hindoos, and the Mexican Race." *Studies in American Political Development* 22, no. 1 (2008).

Lee, Sharon M. "Racial Classifications in the US Census: 1890–1990." *Ethnic and Racial Studies* 16, no. 1 (January 1, 1993).

Levitt, Justin. "Citizenship and the Census." *Columbia Law Review* 119, no. 5 (2019).

López, Nancy. "Killing Two Birds with One Stone? Why We Need Two Separate Questions on Race and Ethnicity in the 2020 Census and Beyond." *Latino Studies* 11, no. 3 (September 12, 2013).

Macagnone, Michael. "2020 Census Undercounted Black People, Latinos, Native Americans." *Roll Call,* March 10, 2022.

National Archives and Records Administration. "African Americans and the Federal Census, 1790–1930." July 2012.

Noe-Bustamante, Luis, Ana Gonzalez-Barrera, Khadijah Edwards, Lauren Mora, and Mark Hugo Lopez. "Majority of Latinos Say Skin Color Impacts Opportunity in America and Shapes Daily Life." Hispanic Trends Project, Pew Research Center, November 4, 2021.

Peña, Jessica E. "Racial Identification for the Self-Reported Hispanic or Latino Population: 2010 and 2020 Census." U.S. Census Bureau, March 2023.

Pratt, Beverly M., Lindsay Hixson, and Nicholas A. Jones. "Measuring Race and Ethnicity Across the Decades: 1790–2010." *Random Samplings* (blog). U.S. Census Bureau, November 2, 2015.

Smith, Marian L. "The INS and the Singular Status of North American Indians." *American Indian Culture and Research Journal* 21, no. 1 (January 1, 1997).

Steinhauer, Jason. "The History of Mexican Immigration to the U.S. in the Early 20th Century." *Insights: Scholarly Work at the Kluge Center* (blog). Library of Congress, March 11, 2015.

United States Census Bureau. *1970 Census of Population, Subject Reports: Persons of Spanish Origin*. June 1973.

Queer Kin

While East Los Angeles has population rates of Latinx similar to Hialeah and Laredo, it is not, at the present moment, its own city. To read more about these Latinx-majority areas, I recommend the journalist Russell Contreras's *Axios* article "Analysis: Poverty Rates Much Higher in Nation's Most Latino Cities," published on July 16, 2024.

For this essay, I rephrased this wording by Diane Richardson: "Lesbian and gay politics over the last 30 years have been less about the right to privacy than about claims for the right not to have to be private." It's from her 2000 article "Constructing Sexual Citizenship: Theorizing Sexual Rights" in *Critical Social Policy.*

Books

Cossman, Brenda. *Sexual Citizens: The Legal and Cultural Regulation of Sex and Belonging.* Stanford University Press, 2007.

Evans, David T. *Sexual Citizenship: The Material Construction of Sexualities.* Routledge, 1993.

Ghaziani, Amin. *There Goes the Gayborhood?* Princeton University Press, 2014.

Articles

Bell, David. "Pleasure and Danger: The Paradoxical Spaces of Sexual Citizenship." *Political Geography* 14, no. 2 (February 1995).

Boyle, Colin, and Madison Savedra. "Alderwoman Attacked at Protest Over Brighton Park Migrant Tent Camp." *Block Club Chicago,* October 19, 2023.

Brandzel, Amy L. "Queering Citizenship?" *GLQ: A Journal of Lesbian and Gay Studies* 11, no. 2 (April 1, 2005).

Garcia, Regina, and Gisela Salomon. "After a Stint in Guantanamo Bay, a Venezuelan Deported from the US Adjusts to His Homeland." AP News, March 17, 2025.

Hall, Stuart. "The Great Moving Right Show." *Marxism Today,* January 1979.

Isikoff, Michael. "Report: Detainees to Be Treated Like Animals." *Newsweek,* April 20, 2009.

Issenberg, Sasha. "The Surprising Honolulu Origins of the National Fight Over Same-Sex Marriage." *Politico,* May 31, 2021.

Lefferts, Daniel. "My Afternoon with the 'Normal Gay Guys' Who Voted for Trump." *GQ,* February 10, 2025.

Lithwick, Dahlia. "Extreme Makeover." *New Yorker,* March 4, 2012.

Martínez-Beltrán, S. "Venezuelan Men Allege Mistreatment While in Detention in Guantánamo Bay." NPR, February 25, 2025.

McGhee, Josh. "Saying Goodbye to 'Girlstown': Andersonville's Lesbian Population Shrinks." *DNAinfo Chicago,* August 22, 2016.

O'Sullivan, Feargus. "The 'Gaytrification' Effect: Why Gay Neighbourhoods Are Being Priced Out." *Guardian,* January 13, 2016.

Pilkington, Ed. "The CIA Tortured Him After 9/11. Then They Lied. Will the Truth Ever Come Out?" *Guardian,* January 29, 2022.

Plummer, Kenneth. Review of *The Sexual Citizen: Queer Politics and Beyond* by David Bell and Jon Binnie. *American Journal of Sociology* 107, no. 4 (January 2002).

Richardson, Diane. "Rethinking Sexual Citizenship." *Sociology* 51, no. 2 (April 2017).

Rosenberg, Carol, and Charlie Savage. "ICE Returns All Migrants from Guantánamo to Stateside Facilities." *New York Times,* March 12, 2025.

Rosenberg, Jacob. "'It's the Economy, Stupid' Is Never Just About the Economy." *Mother Jones,* December 12, 2024.

Shoop, Lyn G. "Health Based Exclusion Grounds in United States Immigration Policy: Homosexuals, HIV Infection and the Medical Examination of Aliens." *Journal of Contemporary Health Law and Policy* 9, no. 1 (1993).

Taylor, Keeanga-Yamahtta. "The Pain Creating a New Coalition for Trump." *New Yorker,* November 22, 2024.

Volpp, Leti. "Feminist, Sexual, and Queer Citizenship." In *The Oxford Handbook of Citizenship,* edited by Ayelet Shachar, Rainer Bauböck, Irene Bloemraad, and Maarten Vink. Oxford University Press, 2017.

Wormer, Rachel. *Mapping Deception: A Closer Look at How States' Anti-Abortion Center Programs Operate.* Equity Forward, June 4, 2021.

Chingona Citizenship

One starting point to learn about Malintzin is "Life Story: Malintzin (La Malinche) (ca. 1500–1529)," published online by Women & the American Story, an educational initiative of the New York Historical's Center for Women's History. A scholarly account can be found in the historian Camilla Townsend's book *Malintzin's Choices: An Indian Woman in the Conquest of Mexico.* The full title of Yásnaya Elena Aguilar Gil's book is *Tres Veces Tres. En Clave Malintzin: Nueve Aproximaciones a Su Figura.* For an analysis of Aguilar Gil's work, see Mariajosé Rodríguez Pliego's 2023 article "The Many Forms of Malintzin: Remembering the Colonial-Era Interpreter Through Indigenous Storytelling" in *Revista de Estudios Hispánicos.*

The detail about the origins of *chola* in Mochica is from José Antonio Salas García's book *Historias de las Lenguas del Antiguo Obispado de Trujillo.*

My thinking for this essay was informed by Jillian Hernandez's book *Aesthetics of Excess: The Art and Politics of Black and Latina Embodiment.*

Texas governor Greg Abbott's quote is from a 2024 interview he gave on *The Dana Show* with Dana Loesch.

Articles on Cholas, Chongas, and Cholitas

Agence France-Presse, La Paz. "The Pollera, an Indigenous and Discriminatory Feminist Symbol in Bolivia." France 24, September 20, 2019.

Añaños Bedriñana, Karen Giovanna, Bernardo Alfredo Hernández Umaña, and José Antonio Rodríguez Martín. "'Living Well' in the Constitution of Bolivia and the American Declaration on the Rights of Indigenous Peoples: Reflections on Well-Being and the Right to Development." *International Journal of Environmental Research and Public Health* 17, no. 8 (2020).

Arellano, Gustavo. "Ask a Mexican: What Does the Word 'Cholo' Mean?" *Coachella Valley Independent,* July 27, 2016.

Bruguera, Tania. "Culture as a Strategy to Survive." Delivered as part of a performance at the art center Jeu de Paume, March 6, 2009. Available at taniabruguera.com/culture-as-a-strategy-to-survive.

Dear, Paula. "The Rise of the 'Cholitas.'" BBC News, February 20, 2014.

Gill, L. "'Proper Women' and City Pleasures: Gender, Class, and Contested Meanings in La Paz." *American Ethnologist* 20 (1993).

Leal, Eduardo. "The Rise of Bolivia's Indigenous 'Cholitas'—in Pictures." *Guardian,* February 22, 2018.

Lush, Tamara. "Chongas!" *Miami New Times,* June 14, 2007.

Reichard, Raquel. "14 Things That Defined the Life of a Chonga in the Early 2000s." *Remezcla,* November 29, 2017.

Articles on Goodenough and Measuring Intelligence

Capshew, James H., and Alejandra C. Laszlo. "'We Would Not Take No for an Answer': Women Psychologists and Gender

Politics During World War II." *Journal of Social Issues* 42, no. 1 (April 1986).

Dennis, Wayne. "The Performance of Hopi Children on the Goodenough Draw-a-Man Test." *Journal of Comparative Psychology* 34, no. 3 (1942).

Goodenough, Florence L. "Racial Differences in the Intelligence of School Children." *Journal of Experimental Psychology* 9, no. 5 (October 1926).

Goodenough, Florence L. "The Selection of Candidates for the Officer Candidate School at the Women's Army Auxiliary Corps Training Center." *Psychological Bulletin* 39, no. 8 (October 1942).

Harris, Dale B., and Glenn D. Pinder. *The Goodenough-Harris Drawing Test as a Measure of Intellectual Maturity of Youths 12–17 Years, United States.* DHEW Publication No. (HRA) 74-1620. U.S. Department of Health, Education and Welfare. *Vital and Health Statistics, National Health Survey,* Series 11, no. 138 (May 1974).

Imuta, Kana, et al. "Drawing a Close to the Use of Human Figure Drawings as a Projective Measure of Intelligence." *PLOS One* 8, no. 3 (March 14, 2013).

Jolly, Jennifer L. "Florence L. Goodenough: Portrait of a Psychologist." *Roeper Review,* 32 (2010).

Articles on Virterma and Her Children, Yorlei and Jonathan

Agren, David. "Migrant Drownings Stoke Cross-Border Tensions, Questions of Jurisdiction." OSV News, January 18, 2024.

Goodson, H. Nelson. "LULAC National Calls for Federal Criminal Investigation Against Texas Governor Abbott (R) in Connection with the Río Grande Drownings of Undocumented Mother and Her Two Children Ages 8 and 10 in Eagle Pass." Hispanic News Network U.S.A., January 14, 2024.

Katz, Dan. "Did Texas Block Border Agents from Rescuing a

Mother and Her Two Children Who Drowned in the Rio Grande?" Texas Public Radio, January 13, 2024.

The People

The journalist Atossa Araxia Abrahamian's book *The Cosmopolites: The Coming of the Global Citizen* introduced me to the industry of selling and buying citizenship. BBC reporters Sarah Treanor and Vivienne Nunis covered the topic in their 2019 story "How Selling Citizenship Is Now Big Business."

Articles on Losing Naturalized Citizenship

Biddle, Sam, and Maryam Saleh. "Little-Known Federal Software Can Trigger Revocation of Citizenship." *Intercept,* August 25, 2021.

Immigrant Legal Resource Center. "Denaturalization and Revocation of Naturalization." February 2020.

Mazzei, Patricia. "Congratulations, You Are Now a U.S. Citizen. Unless Someone Decides Later You're Not." *New York Times,* July 23, 2018.

Wessler, Seth Freed. "Denaturalized." *New York Times Magazine,* December 23, 2018.

Articles on Gaza

Al-Mughrabi, Nidal, and Khaled Hatem. "Israeli Strikes Across Gaza Kill at Least 57, Palestinian Health Officials Say." Reuters, July 16, 2024.

Jahjouh, Mohamed. "Israeli Strike Targets the Hamas Military Commander and Kills at Least 90 in Southern Gaza." Associated Press, July 13, 2024.

Articles on Millionaire Migrants

DiStefano, Joseph N. "$1.4B Bought Green Cards for 2,000." *Philadelphia Inquirer,* September 10, 2023.

Monyak, Suzanne. "Immigrant Investors on Edge as EB-5 Lapse Enters Eighth Month." *Roll Call,* February 16, 2022.

Qi, Liyan. "Chinese Investors Warm to Sweetened U.S. Cash-for-Visa Program." *Wall Street Journal,* August 2, 2023.

Articles on Racial Targeting of Asian Americans

Griffin, Nicole. "Real Estate Agents Struggle with Confusion Over Ban on Chinese Nationals Owning Property in Florida." Spectrum News, June 11, 2024.

Hernández Caraballo, Lillian. "Florida's Chinese Community Calls for Reform, Repeal of Law That Limits Property Ownership." WLRN, September 29, 2023.

Kreighbaum, Andrew. "Florida Blocked from Banning Home Buying by Chinese Citizens." Bloomberg Law, February 2, 2024.

Qin, Amy, and Patricia Mazzei. "When Buying a Home Is Treated as a National Security Threat." *New York Times,* May 6, 2024.

Thanawala, Sudhin. "Georgia Governor Signs Bill into Law Restricting Land Sales to Some Chinese Citizens." Atlanta News First, May 1, 2024.

Venkatraman, Sakshi. "Bill That Set Out to Restrict Chinese Property Ownership Dies in Texas House." NBC News, May 25, 2023.

About the Author

Daisy Hernández is the author of *The Kissing Bug,* winner of the PEN/Jean Stein Book Award and an inaugural title for the National Book Foundation's Science + Literature Program. Her memoir, *A Cup of Water Under My Bed,* won Lambda Literary's Dr. Betty Berzon Emerging Writer Award and was a Publishing Triangle Award finalist. She co-edited the classic feminist anthology *Colonize This!* and is a regular contributor to *Tricycle: The Buddhist Review.* She is an associate professor of creative writing at Northwestern University.

Instagram: @iamdazeher

About the Type

This book was set in Bembo, a typeface based on an old-style Roman face that was used for Cardinal Pietro Bembo's tract *De Aetna* in 1495. Bembo was cut by Francesco Griffo (1450–1518) in the early sixteenth century for Italian Renaissance printer and publisher Aldus Manutius (1449–1515). The Lanston Monotype Company of Philadelphia brought the well-proportioned letterforms of Bembo to the United States in the 1930s.